Under the Hammer

Andrew Davidson followed the 1991 ITV franchise battle as a journalist on the *Sunday Times*. Winner of the Business Writer of the Year Award in 1989, this is his first book. He lives in London and Kent.

ANDREW DAVIDSON

Under the Hammer

The inside story of the 1991 ITV franchise battle

Mandarin

A Mandarin Paperback
UNDER THE HAMMER

First published in Great Britain 1992
by William Heinemann Limited
This edition published 1993
by Mandarin Paperbacks
an imprint of Reed Consumer Books Limited
Michelin House, 81 Fulham Road, London SW3 6RB
and Auckland, Melbourne, Singapore and Toronto

A CIP catalogue record for this title
is available from the British Library
ISBN 0 7493 1404 4

Printed and bound in Great Britain
by Cox and Wyman Limited, Reading, Berks

For Vanessa

'When I was at school I was told the important thing was not winning but taking part. I did not believe it then and I certainly do not believe it now.'

David Frost, founder of LWT and TV-am, bidder in the 1991 ITV franchise round.

Acknowledgements

Few books such as this can attempt to offer the whole truth; they can, however, offer a flavour of what it was like to work through extraordinary times. They call television 'the most powerful communication tool mankind has invented'; it can also be, on the evidence of those I talked to, one of the most exciting, frustrating, malicious, greedy and cynical industries there is. If I have caught a tenth of that, I have won.

Under the Hammer was put together from over 100 interviews with bidders, regulators, civil servants and observers involved in the 1991 ITV franchise round. My thanks, then, to all those who agreed to the long, taped interviews which provided the core of the research: Rudolph Agnew, Simon Albury, Andy Birchall, Christopher Bland, Michael Braham, Patrick Cox, Charles Denton, Richard Dunn, David Elstein, Greg Dyke, David Frost, James Gatward, David Glencross, Michael Grade, Michael Green, Tom Guttridge, Leslie Hill, Mike Hollingsworth, David Keighley, Clive Leach, Roger Laughton, Charles Levison, Gus MacDonald, David McCall, Bob Phillis, David Plowright, Nik Powell, Stewart Prebble, Andrew Quinn, Phil Redmond, Ian Ritchie, Sir George Russell, Lord Thomson, Harry Turner and Nigel Walmsley.

Others who contributed invaluable insight and assistance include: Roy Addison, Bill Brown, Geoff Brownlees, Gerry Buckland, Michael Buckley, Ian Coulter, Barry Cox, Robert Devereux, Claire Enders, Simon Forrest, Jeremy Fox, Gerry Grimstone, Douglas Howell, Peter Ibbotson, Gerard LeFebre, Jane Leighton, Dominic Prince, Philip Reeval, Chris Scobel, Bob Southgate, Ray Snoddy,

Paul Stewart-Lang, Sarah Thane, Will Whitehorn, John Whitney and John Wood. My gratitude also to those who asked to remain unnamed.

As every keen reader of acknowledgements knows, the refuseniks tell their own story. Of those involved in the franchise round only two declined to give full interviews after the event: Lord Hollick and Bruce Gyngell. I had interviewed both before and during the summer of 1991. By 1992 Lord Hollick was feeling bruised by the press interest in his links to the Labour party leadership, and was refusing all interview requests (he did, however, agree to a short interview once the book was close to proof stage). Gyngell simply did not want to rehash the past, but gave his senior executives full permission to talk to me.

More tellingly, no politician or adviser involved in drafting the broadcasting legislation would agree to be interviewed on the subject. Lady Thatcher declined 'due to the enormous demands on her time'. Nigel Lawson said he was 'trying to complete his own book'. David Mellor agreed to the principle of an interview on 'lobby' terms, but cancelled three times. Lord Sterling said that any of the areas in which he had acted in an advisory capacity to the DTI should remain confidential. Lord Griffiths' secretary said he was 'too busy'. Many in the broadcasting industry believe that these architects of the 1991 ITV franchise round are now too embarrassed to discuss it. It is hard not to agree with them.

Special thanks must go to James Conway at the Independent Television Commission (ITC) who patiently dealt with all my queries on dates, legislation and processes. The ITC, like the IBA before it, was not entirely at ease with the idea of an author probing around its franchise decisions. Predictably it was unwilling to allow me to see the minutes of the meetings which decided ITV's future (although certain ITC documents, leaked by disgruntled staff, are in circulation in London). It did, however, put forward its two most senior decision-makers, Sir George Russell and David Glencross, for a frank discussion of what took place within the ITC during that summer of 1991. The two-hour session, interrupted only by the dramatic thunderclaps of a June storm rolling over London, took place in the ITC chairman's eighth-floor office in Knightsbridge. Excerpts from the interview are included in the appendix at the back of the book.

I am also grateful to the ITC for use of its library. Three books in particular, *Broadcasting in the United Kingdom* by Barrie MacDonald (Mansell Publishing 1988), and *Independent Television in Britain* volumes 3 & 4 by Jeremy Potter (Macmillan 1990), were invaluable primers. I recommend them to anyone seeking to make sense of commercial television in the 1990s.

Further afield, much of the groundwork for this book was accomplished while I covered the franchise round for the *Sunday Times*. I would like to thank two of the paper's executives, Tony Bambridge and Roger Eglin, for the insights given.

Some thoughts on the structure and style of this book: anyone expecting a thorough examination of the events in every ITV region will be disappointed. I have deliberately concentrated on the major stations – Thames, LWT, Central, Granada, Yorkshire, TVS and TV-am – and their rivals because the sheer volume of activity nationally, much of it very similar, could not be accommodated into a comprehensible narrative.

Likewise those looking for an answer to the perennial question 'whither broadcasting?' will search in vain. No country in the world has agonised over television like Britain (indeed no country other than Britain could have produced such a strange hybrid of old and new as the 1991 ITV franchise round). I have no overwhelming desire to add to the mountain of speculation. Now here is the 'but': in response to interviewees continually asking me for why's and wherefore's, I *have* included a short essay of initial thoughts on how the ITV franchise round came about, and where it leaves ITV. The joy of it being in the appendix is that weary readers can avoid it.

As far as the style goes, because of the co-operation of nearly all the leading players in the franchise round, I have been able to reconstruct particular events and conversations in detail. The usual health warning applies: most people's memories are selective and, while I have tried to check specific details with all present at a particular event, an author is always vulnerable to collective spin-doctoring. Where a conversation is based on only one source, or where memories have differed, I have indicated as much. In the case of two refuseniks, David Mellor and Bruce Gyngell, I have relied on earlier interviews, both by myself and by colleagues, and on the impressions of those who worked closely with them over the period.

Finally I owe debts of gratitude to my agent, John Pawsey, and my editor, Tom Weldon, for their invaluable help; to two close friends, Rufus Olins and Martin ('how's-it-going') Brierley, for support and wit; and to my daughters, Elena and Rosa, for continually running their sticky fingers over my keyboard. They say writing a book can be like swimming the English Channel: daunting when you start out, inspirational when you finish, and horrendous when you lose sight of both coasts in the middle. I would undoubtedly have drowned but for the support and encouragement of all the above. But more than anyone I must thank Vanessa Nicolson, who swam the distance with me and without whom I would never have had the time, space and inspiration to finish the work.

Contents

The
Players

POLITICIANS

Government
Margaret Thatcher – Prime Minister
Douglas Hurd – Home Secretary
David Mellor – Broadcasting Minister
Nigel Lawson – Chancellor of the Exchequer
Lord Young – Secretary for Trade and Industry
David Waddington – Home Secretary
Timothy Renton – Broadcasting Minister

REGULATORS

Independent Broadcasting Authority
Lady Plowden – former chairman
Lord Thomson – chairman
John Whitney – director

Independent Television Commission
George Russell – chairman
David Glencross – chief executive
Sarah Thane – head of public affairs

TELEVISION LOBBY

Richard Dunn, head of the Independent Television
  Association (ITVA)
Stewart Prebble – founder, Campaign for Quality
  Television (CFQT)

Simon Albury – director, CFQT
Claudia Milne – director, CFQT
Rowan Atkinson – writer/comedian
Terry Jones – writer/comedian
Michael Palin – writer/comedian

ITV

Anglia
David McCall – chief executive

Border
Paul Corley – programme director

Central
Leslie Hill – chairman and chief executive
Andy Allen – programme director
Marshall Stewart – head of public affairs

Granada
Gerry Robinson – chief executive, Granada group, 1991–
Alex Bernstein – chairman, Granada group
Derek Lewis – former chief executive, Granada group
David Plowright – chairman, Granada TV
Andrew Quinn – managing director, Granada TV
Stewart Prebble – director of regional programmes, Granada TV
Jane Leighton – head of corporate relations, Granada TV

HTV
Charles Romaine – chief executive 1991–
Patrick Dromgoole – former chief executive

London Weekend Television
Christopher Bland – chairman
Brian Tesler – deputy chairman
Greg Dyke – chief executive
Barry Cox – director of corporate relations

Scottish TV
Gus MacDonald – chief executive
Bill Brown – chairman

Thames TV
Richard Dunn – chief executive
David Elstein – programme director
Roy Addison – head of corporate relations

TSW
Harry Turner – chief executive
Ivor Stolliday – company secretary
Paul Stewart-Lang – programme director

TV-am
Bruce Gyngell – chief executive
David Frost – director
David Keighley – head of corporate affairs
Jane Ironside-Wood – chief press officer

TVS
Rudolph Agnew – chairman
James Gatward – founder, former chief executive
Lord Boston – former chairman
Tony Brook – managing director
Claire Enders – corporate development director
Gerry Buckland – head of corporate relations
Gerry Grimstone – director, Shroders Bank
Pierre Lescure – chief executive of Canal Plus
Etienne Mallet – chief executive of La Generale d'Images,
    Generale des Eaux's media subsidiary

Tyne Tees
Ian Ritchie – chief executive 1991–
David Reay – former chief executive

Yorkshire
Clive Leach – chief executive
John Fairley – programme director
Allan Hardy – commercial director

OUTSIDE BIDDERS

Carlton TV
Michael Green – chairman, Carlton Communications
Charles Denton – chief executive, Zenith
Nigel Walmsley – chief executive, Carlton TV
Paul Jackson – programme director, Carlton TV
Brian Wenham – director, Carlton TV
Peter Ibbotson – Director of Corporate Affairs, Carlton TV

CPV-TV
Richard Branson – chairman, Virgin
David Frost – TV presenter/chief executive, David Paradine
    Group

Robert Devereux – chief executive, Virgin Communications
John Gau – chief executive, CPV-TV
Charles Levison – managing director, CPV-TV
Will Whitehorn – head of corporate affairs, Virgin
Jeremy Fox – bid consultant

Meridian
Clive Hollick – chief executive, MAI
Roger Laughton – chief executive, Meridian
Simon Albury – director of strategy, Meridian
Michael Palin – director, Meridian
Allan McKeown – chief executive, SelecTV
Michael Buckley – chairman, SelecTV

Mersey TV
Phil Redmond – chief executive, Mersey TV
Alexis Redmond – managing director, Mersey TV
Philip Reeval – head of public affairs

London Independent Broadcasting
Michael Kuhn – senior vice president, Polygram
Nik Powell – chief executive, Palace Pictures
Tim Bevan – chief executive, Working Title
Tom Guttridge – chief executive, Mentorn
Andy Birchall – bid director

Sunrise
Michael Braham – chief executive, Broadcast
  Communications
Etienne de Villiers – chief executive, Walt Disney UK
Chris Stoddard – chief executive
Lis Howell – programme director

Daybreak
Bob Phillis – chief executive, ITN
Conrad Black – chairman, *The Daily Telegraph*
Sir Paul Fox – chairman, Daybreak
Patrick Cox – director, NBC Europe
Mike Hollingsworth – freelance producer
Dick Emery – chief executive designate
John Whitney – adviser
Stewart Purvis – editor-in-chief, ITN

Westcountry
Stephen Redfarn – founder, chief executive

'It is the will of Allah.'
Thames TV worker

Every morning, just after six, Michael Green, multimillionaire businessman and art collector, likes to pad down the stairs of his Mayfair house and gather the papers from outside his front door. Wednesday 16 October, 1991, was no different, except that when he opened the door he got a surprise.

There, just a few yards away, parked directly outside his house, was a man napping quietly at the wheel of a car. Green, still in his pyjamas, his thick hair tousled from sleep, paused. In the same moment the hapless man, a photographer, woke up, fumbling with his camera, startled to see his quarry at so early an hour. In an instant, Green scooped up the newspapers and slammed the door. The man had barely had time to focus.

Today, thought Green, padding back up the stairs to his bedroom, is clearly going to be different. Soon it would be time to walk to his Hanover Square office. Maybe this morning he would leave by the back door.

The first journalists reached TV-am a little later. The station's Camden studios, a low, grey, steel and concrete hangar topped by grimy yellow and blue egg-cups, looked forbidding in the morning drizzle. By 9.30 a.m. the initial knot of photographers and reporters had swelled to a large pack, clustered across the station's front entrance. Inside, past the sunshine-yellow reception desk, up the palm-fringed central stairway and across the open-plan, blue and grey offices, the TV-am board was meeting. No one felt too sunny that morning. Bruce Gyngell, the TV-am boss, a tall, emotional Australian, was tense. David Frost, an old hand at the ITV franchise game, chatted quietly to the other directors.

Two miles away, halfway up London Weekend Television's riverside towerblock, the mood was different. Christopher Bland's thirteenth floor office was packed. Behind his desk stretched a panoramic view of the City. No one was looking. All eyes were fixed on the fax machine installed by the door. Greg Dyke, the LWT chief executive, stood triumphantly by it, waiting. Bland, the LWT chairman, a plump, patrician man, fiddled with his father's signet ring. He rarely wore it, but today, as a lucky omen, he had put it on again. Now he felt edgy. He left the room and started walking up and down the corridor.

The waiting was the worst of it. Waiting for a fax that meant life or death for a company. They had all joked about it: *the fax of life, death by faxecution* . . . They had waited five months for this moment. Now the waiting was almost over. In a matter of minutes the Independent Television Commission, ITV's regulatory body, would announce the winners of the sixteen new licences to broadcast on Britain's biggest commercial TV network. For the forty bidders, it had been an extraordinary game of corporate poker. Most now waited nervously in their offices. Others stayed away. Richard Branson, the Virgin boss, sat at home in Holland Park, waiting for his executives to call him. Rudolph Agnew, the tall, grey-haired chairman of TVS, did likewise, pacing the floor of his Belgravia living room, watching the phone, smoking a Gitane.

Outside Thames TV in London's Euston Road, the journalists could smell blood. Staff entering the drab 1960s block looked ashen. Up on the fourth floor, the atmosphere was worse. Richard Dunn, Thames' chief executive, stood alone at the fax machine outside his office. A slim, silver-haired man, he was renowned throughout the network for two things: his good looks and his cool imperturbability. Now, however, even *his* nerves were showing. He checked his watch. It was 9.40 a.m. He looked again at the fax machine beside him. His secretary and her junior, sitting side by side under the window, busied themselves anxiously, trying not to catch his eye. Thames' head of corporate affairs, Roy Addison, watched closely from the corner of the room.

Suddenly all four tensed at a new, unmistakable sound. With a click and a whirr, a fax had begun to edge warily out of the machine. Line after line was measured out with the same metallic rasp. First the covering sheet. Then the head of the notepaper. The date. The addressee.

'You are either with us or against us.'

Margaret Thatcher

The chauffeur-driven cars carrying the cream of Britain's broadcasting establishment swept down Whitehall one by one. It was a sunny Monday morning in September, 1987. Leaves still clung to the trees in Parliament Square as the twenty or so chairmen, chief executives and managing directors decanted into Downing Street. Each clutched a personal invitation.

The event was Margaret Thatcher's first (and only) 'seminar' on commercial broadcasting. All were excited, some a bit nervous, about the prospect of meeting a Prime Minister already famed as one of the most radical Britain had ever had. No one doubted her combative qualities. She had beaten the Argentinians in the south Atlantic. She had ground down the miners in Britain. Now, in late 1987, only months after she had been returned with a huge 100-seat majority in Parliament, she was taking on the broadcasters.

Few of the guests that September morning were sure what to expect. Ushered through the front door of 12 Downing Street, the Chief Whip's office, they were shown up the stairs into a first-floor reception room. There a strange sight greeted them. Five semi-circular rows of uncomfortable, hard-backed chairs all facing a long desk at the front, with six chairs behind it. To some, it was eerily reminiscent of going back to school.

There was an uneasy camaraderie as the room filled. Representatives of all the major broadcasters were present: John Birt and Michael Grade from the BBC, Jeremy Isaacs, chairman of Channel 4, soon to join the Royal Opera House, Ian Trethowan from Thames, Bill Brown from Scottish TV, David McCall from Anglia TV, David Nicholas, boss of ITN, John Whitney from the Independent Broadcasting Authority, the body which regulated ITV until 1991, Richard Hooper, boss of the newly formed satellite venture Superchannel, and others. All had met before at the various functions, dinners and parties that dominated a working life in broadcasting. Most were comfortable in each other's company.

But they were not alone. They already knew from the guest lists sent out earlier that others had been invited too: representatives from outside the broadcast establishment. In walked Dick Johnson, marketing services director of Proctor & Gamble, the soap giant, Michael Darlow from the Independent Producers Association, David Graham from Diverse Productions, another production independent, and Professor Peacock, the only guest to have walked from the tube station. Sir Jeffrey Sterling, chairman of P&O shipping and a 'special adviser' to the Department of Trade and Industry, was also there, along with Brian Griffiths, head of Thatcher's economic think-tank. There too, chatting to Lord Young, the Trade Secretary, was Michael Green, the young TV facilities millionaire whose attempt to take over Thames two years previously had been unceremoniously thrown out by the IBA.

The room hushed as Thatcher herself, blue suit, pearls and handbag, swept in, the only woman among forty men. She took her seat behind the desk facing the broadcasters. Young, Douglas Hurd, the Home Secretary, and two civil servants joined her. Nigel Lawson, the Chancellor of the Exchequer, bustled in late, sweating, and sat alongside her.

Thatcher glared at him. 'It is always the boy who lives nearest the school who is late,' she snapped, pulling a small red notebook out of her handbag. Lawson, looking cross, said nothing and spread his papers out as Thatcher made the first entry in the notebook. *Good God*, thought many of the cream of British broadcasting, *is she giving Lawson a black mark*? It was an unnerving start to what proved to be a very revealing morning.

The Conservative party had had an uneasy relationship with ITV right from the start. On the night in 1954 when the bill first enacting ITV was passed, Norman Collins, a vociferous lobbyist for Independent Television and a staunch Tory, had received a visit from Winston Churchill. Roused by the sound of breaking glass, he looked out his window to see figures in the street below. One was Churchill. 'You traitor, Collins,' he roared. 'You traitor.' In common with many top Tories, Churchill regarded the start of commercial broadcasting as an outrage.

Margaret Thatcher's attitude was more ambivalent. Like any politician she was conscious of the enormous power wielded by the media – it could determine election results, after all – and she was certainly not the first Prime Minister to take a close personal interest in the industry. Her concern was more its structure and the pivotal role ITV in particular played as Britain's largest advertising medium. In the past, limited competition between the tightly regulated monopolies – the BBC and ITV – had achieved both high programming standards and large audiences. But within ITV there seemed little incentive for efficiency. And the advent of satellite TV, cable and other new technologies meant that huge changes were on the horizon. New broadcasters were demanding free and fair competition. Advertisers were demanding lower prices. The more she looked at commercial television, its well-heeled bosses and their powerful union counterparts, the more it became plain to her: something had to change.

The Prime Minister's antipathy was no surprise to the men who ran ITV, the bosses of the fifteen regional companies. They already knew that on a personal level they had little common ground with her. A lunch given in her honour in 1985 at the ITV Association, the network's organising body, had gone badly. She had complained that ITV was ludicrously overmanned – she cited a visit to Thames for an interview when she had counted sixteen engineers for the one broadcast – and moaned that on the one night when she had time to watch TV, Saturday, there was nothing on worth watching.

'Why don't you have some nice orchestral concerts on or

something?' she berated the bosses. Some found her simplistic approach risible. 'Have you tried watching *Union World* on Channel 4, Prime Minister?' joked Bill Brown, managing director of Scottish TV and one of ITV's longest-serving executives. Brown discovered that senior politicians do not have great senses of humour. Her riposte was, in his own words, 'Ninety seconds of the famous icy, laser stare.'

Thatcher's point was simple. Both advertisers and viewers were now suffering because competition was stifled in ITV. Since its launch in 1956, it had been tightly regulated by authorities worried more about the social and cultural effects of broadcasting than its financial efficiencies. Growing swiftly into a network of regional stations, ITV broadcast a similar mixture of programming to that put out by its rival, the BBC. The difference was that ITV was supported by advertising revenue; the BBC by the state. And each ITV station had a regional monopoly on television advertising.

But even when new stations like TV-am or new channels like BBC2 or Channel 4 were launched, it was more on a complementary than a competitive basis. TV-am, running only in the morning, could never compete head on; BBC2 and Channel 4 – whose airtime was sold by the ITV companies – were bound by their remits to offer something different, and no one else could get on the terrestrially broadcast spectrum. For a believer in the benefits that real competition can bring, ITV looked suspiciously feather-bedded. The only way in, as Michael Green had found out in 1985 when his takeover attempt was blocked, was to win a regional ITV licence at one of the periodic franchise rounds, generally every eight-to-ten years.

These too raised Thatcher's suspicions. The last, at the end of her first year in power, had been a shambolic, controversial affair. Two established stations – Southern and Westward – had lost their franchises and a whole host of other changes had been somewhat arbitrarily implemented by the IBA. No one really knew what the criteria for success and failure were. Bidders were simply grilled by a panel of the great and the good on their programme plans. The reasons behind the decisions were kept secret.

Thatcher herself asked the outgoing IBA chairman Lady

Plowden why Southern had failed. 'I can't possibly tell you that,' replied Plowden. Lord Thomson, who took over as chairman shortly after, acknowledged the process had to change. 'There has got to be a better way,' he told a Royal Television Society conference in Cambridge in 1981. They were words that were to return and haunt him.

By 1987 a sizable lobby was growing against ITV and its regulator. The ad agency empire being built by Charles and Maurice Saatchi was particularly vociferous in its demands for change within broadcasting. Its call for the BBC to take advertising had prompted the government to set up a Home Office committee, headed by the Scottish economist Professor Peacock, to investigate. It had been unenthusiastic. Advertisers like Saatchi then turned their sights on ITV itself.

Their main complaint was that ITV was abusing a commercial broadcasting monopoly. Advertisers bought ads on the basis of how many people watched. But in a monopoly situation – which is what ITV effectively operated in as Channel 4 did not compete for the same type of viewers and the BBC did not compete for ad revenue – the market was turned on its head.

The less people watched, the more the advertisers had to pay to reach their targets. The post-1985 surge in the British economy created an unprecedented ad boom. ITV got richer and richer, while its ratings appeared to get worse and worse. The Government, itself spending ever-increasing amounts on high-profile ad campaigns to back Lord Young's privatisation programme, was only too aware of the effect.

That was not the only complaint. Independent producers, who had mushroomed with the launch of Channel 4 in 1980, found it virtually impossible to get work out of ITV. They argued that the majors wanted to carve everything up for themselves, in particular the 'big five stations' – Thames, Central, London Weekend, Granada and Yorkshire – who controlled most of what appeared on screen. Even the smaller ITV companies accused the IBA of not doing its job properly, allowing too much power to fall into the hands of the bigger companies, who wanted not only to produce most of the programmes on the network, but schedule them as well.

The results of it all were plain to see. Both management and staff in ITV, they argued, were leading a life of luxury: a long round of lunches, dinners, overseas conferences and concentrating on making fine programming. That was the key that underpinned everything, the *raison d'être* for how the network operated. It had to be so, said many in ITV, or you would end up with the sort of television people watched in America. It was no coincidence that the IBA's headquarters were in Knightsbridge, one of the most expensive parts of London. ITV was an expensive, quality act.

Successive governments had bowed to the logic. A special tax on broadcast profits, the Exchequer Levy, gave the ITV stations little incentive to pursue efficiency. Why try and increase profits when most is taken away in tax? The ever-increasing demands of the broadcast unions were simply met. Much better to spend the money, reasoned ITV executives, before it reaches the bottom line. A chance for a final showdown with the broadcasting unions during 1979's winter of discontent, when they blacked out ITV for eleven weeks, was sidestepped, and ended in public and costly humiliation for the companies. The levy was eventually changed in 1986 but the stories of ITV's fat cat lifestyle lived on. At LWT, through a series of bizarre anomalies and overtime arrangements, one videotape engineer was earning £100,000 a year. (The joke went round: 'What's the difference between an oil sheikh and an LWT engineer? The oil sheikh doesn't get London weighting.')

By 1987 even some ITV insiders agreed with the critics. The network was clearly overmanned and inefficient and lacking incentive to undertake radical reform. For the free market theorists driving Thatcher's Government it was too much to take. ITV had to be opened up to competition. The question was how?

The Downing Street seminar was divided up into a number of short formal presentations and an open session. Thatcher chaired it all. Young, Hurd and Lawson nodded frequently, took notes but said little.

First up was Professor Peacock. His Committee's conclusion that the BBC would be better off without advertising was widely rumoured to have angered Thatcher. It was not the sort of thing to worry the irascible Scot. (When later he had been placed next to Thatcher at lunch, he had joked: 'Is this the seat of penitence?')

He was perplexed by the fact that the one recommendation which really intrigued the Prime Minister – that the Government should consider auctioning off the ITV franchises to the highest bidder – had only been an aside to the main thrust of his report.

He now complained that his committee might have recommended something different if they had been briefed properly on the technical advances likely in the next decade. Why sell off the ITV franchises when the possibility of a vast new range of channels will bring in the competition the Government is looking for?

His introduction was followed by six papers on different aspects of broadcasting, from new technology and methods of funding to the role of independent production and public service broadcasting. It was soon clear where Thatcher's sympathies lay. Halfway through the first presentation (new technologies) by Richard Hooper, the lugubrious former British Telecom executive who headed Superchannel, she revealed her hand. Hooper had been complaining that his satellite service had been hamstrung by a dispute with Equity, the actors' union, over repeat fees.

Thatcher, clearly enjoying the friction between some of those present, rose to her feet and addressed the broadcasters. 'You gentlemen are the last bastion of restrictive practices.' There was a sharp intake of breath as she looked around the room. She settled on Jeremy Isaacs. 'Coupled with the Royal Opera House, Mr Isaacs,' she added with the hint of a smile. The opera's musicians were currently out on strike. 'That's the first time I've ever been castigated before I even started a job,' riposted Isaacs. Everyone, including Thatcher, laughed. (She was reluctant to let him have the last word, however. Later over drinks, as Isaacs promised her he would do his best to raise private money for the Royal Opera House, she fixed him with a stare. 'Mr Isaacs, the day you can keep the Opera House *open* is the day you'll have all the money you need.')

Her interruption set the tone for the rest of the morning. She listened intently to the complaints of advertisers and producers, and had little time for the broadcasters, who kept arguing that it was simplistic just to say 'there should be more competition'. More channels meant a fragmented audience. That was not necessarily a cheaper one, they contended. Ian Trethowan, chairman of Thames and a doyen of the broadcasting industry, begged Thatcher not to rush into making wholesale changes.

But Thatcher, it soon became clear, was more interested in the Big Idea – not the fine print. She was particularly sympathetic to Michael Green, the young entrepreneur. He rose at one point and said simply: 'I have spent twenty years building up a £600 million pound business based firmly in the television industry, but I am still an outsider. I had a franchise bid turned down in 1980, a takeover bid blocked in 1985, and an application to run Britain's first direct broadcast by satellite venture passed over in 1986. What do I have to do to become an insider?' There was no reply.

Many of the ITV representatives were uncertain what to make of it all. They knew their cause was not helped by John Whitney's clumsy speech about regulation just before lunch. Misreading the mood of the occasion he put up a tortuous defence of the status quo. He stumbled over the arguments. 'Is that all, Mr Whitney?' Thatcher said at one point. 'No, there is more,' said a hesitant Whitney. Thatcher tapped her desk impatiently.

They moved to Number 10 for lunch. They ate round a large four-sided table, and then left. Thatcher, smiling and courteous, stood by the door shaking each by the hand as they went. *News At Ten* that night showed the bosses, clutching their notes, exiting Number 10 in ones and twos, like so many brow-beaten ministers. More than one was frowning.

Their suspicions that ITV was about to top the Thatcher agenda had been confirmed. They noted, too, the influence of 'outsiders' like Green. Spotting Green and Young together as they left, one ITV boss had nudged another and whispered with a wink: 'Haldeman and Erlichman.' The allusion to President Nixon's notorious, unelected advisers was only in jest, but it captured their antipathy. *If Michael Green felt like an outsider, that is because he was one*, they reasoned. If he wanted a TV franchise he could go through the same laborious process of public meetings and committee scrutiny that they had done. There should be no easy way in.

Seven months later, prime time one April evening, Thames showed *Death On The Rock*. The documentary, by the *This Week* team, questioned how three IRA terrorists had been shot dead by the SAS in Gibraltar. It drew a huge audience. The timing was provocative; the official inquest into the shootings had not even started to reach its conclusions. The documentary argued that the shootings were close to murder. It produced an anonymous witness who claimed to have seen one of the three IRA members, Sean Savage, shot several times while lying wounded on the ground. Few in the broadcasting industry realised quite what an impact that statement would have.

Thatcher was outraged, not just by the programme, but by the IBA's refusal to bow to pressure from Geoffrey Howe, the Foreign Secretary, to postpone it. In an extraordinary departure from normal protocol she even appeared on TV – Channel 4 – to denounce it. The programme, she told colleagues, made her 'deeper than furious'.

'If you ever get trial by television or guilt by association, it is a black day. Freedom dies,' she said later. Lord Thomson, outgoing chairman of the IBA, defended the authority's decision. For many Conservative MPs, it was the final nail in the IBA's coffin.

It was also, by any estimate, a public relations disaster for Thames, ITV's biggest company. Richard Dunn, its chief executive, was caught, unable to satisfy both his programme-makers and the politicians. Dunn and Trethowan, his chairman, promised an internal inquiry. Tory MPs reacted with withering scorn.

A month later, on a bright morning in May, Richard Dunn stepped briskly from his chauffeur-driven Jaguar onto the Pall Mall pavement and strode into the offices of P&O. He had been invited to attend a 'broadcasting breakfast' hosted by Sir Jeffrey Sterling, the shipping boss acting as adviser to Young and Thatcher on broadcasting. He was intrigued as to what he would find.

Dunn, the son of a British insurance man and Icelandic mother, from whom he inherited his steely good looks, was one of the most powerful men in television. With the good looks came a certain sang-froid – a ready source of irritation to other, more harassed ITV bosses. Dunn rarely shouted or lost his temper. He was always charming and reasonable. Perhaps, as colleagues complained, there was a little too much of the patient schoolteacher in his manner, but television was a bitchy industry, after all. If these attributes masked his hard-nosed ambition, he was generally good at concealing it.

Dunn joined Thames in 1978 as personal assistant to Jeremy Isaacs, then the station's programme director. He had already cut his teeth at Associated British Pathe and a small cable television station in Swindon. His rise to the top was rapid. By 1981 he was director of production and on the Thames board. His attempts to cut costs precipitated a series of strikes in 1984, during which he organised a management service. In 1985, when Thames boss Bryan Cowgill was forced to resign after attempting to poach *Dallas* from the BBC without ITV backing, Dunn was his replacement. From p.a. to boss of Britain's biggest ITV company in six years was fast even by television standards. By the summer of 1988 he had already fought off one takeover attempt – from Michael Green – and the Government assault over *Death On The Rock*. To industry insiders, his unflappability marked him out as a survivor.

Like others who had received the same invitation, he was not quite sure what to make of Sir Jeffrey Sterling's attempts to canvass opinion in broadcasting circles. Sterling's qualifications for the task were unclear, except, of course, that he was close to Thatcher and a prominent Tory supporter. Television executives saw him as a ponderous man with little sense of humour. It was Sterling who had told those involved in the initial DBS (direct-broadcast-by-satellite) project, the Club of 21, that they had to buy a British satellite. 'How would you like to be told to buy all your ships from Newcastle?' responded Andrew Quinn, the Granada TV managing director. That project had collapsed. Few found him good company. However, knowing that Sterling would have a key influence on the forthcoming broadcasting White Paper, Dunn, like others in the industry, attended his breakfast without quibble.

He already knew that Thatcher's advisers were having difficulty finding out exactly what she wanted in the way of broadcasting reforms. After the Downing Street seminar, Thatcher herself had set up and chaired a special cabinet committee, involving the most senior members of her government, to examine alternatives to the old ITV franchise system. Civil servants watched with interest.

By the middle years of her premiership Thatcher's original agenda was reaching an end and, they reasoned, she was looking for new dragons to slay. An overhaul of commercial broadcasting, like the reform of the rating system, had now caught her imagination. This, ran the whisper in the Whitehall corridors, was obviously her next big campaign.

The problem was that her instincts took her in two conflicting directions: to deregulate, yet at the same time to restrict what could be shown to whom. Again and again, she told broadcasters she was concerned about the level of sex and violence on television. But at the same time she told her political colleagues she wanted a franchise-awarding system that was 'transparent', clearly objective and without provisos for the sort of programming shown. The market would ensure quality.

She liked Professor Peacock's suggestion that the ITV franchises could be sold off. Those inside the media thought the idea of auctioning television franchises was ludicrous. At Sterling's breakfast that May morning, no one could find a good word for it. They sat in the sumptuous ground-floor dining room of P&O's Pall Mall head office. It took Rupert Murdoch just two, typically terse words to sum up his reaction to the idea: 'bloody ridiculous'.

He cited the experience of other countries, like New Zealand and Australia, which were already looking at similar plans for auctioning their broadcast networks. There, politicians argued the advantages: with entry into the broadcast market limited by both technological and regulatory restrictions, auctions maximised the amount of money you could raise from a scarce national resource. And in their purest form, they provided a clear way of making a decision that might be politically sensitive if made on more subjective grounds. But anyone with experience of broadcasting could see what would happen. There would be disaster as companies overbid for the licences. Everyone chipped in. Only Brian Griffiths, the Welsh economist judged to be one of the most powerful figures in Thatcher's coterie, was quiet. Later, as Dunn was leaving, he saw Griffiths turn to Sterling and say quietly: 'It won't work.' Both looked pensive. '*And that is that,*' thought a cheerful Dunn on the way back to his Euston Road office.

The row over *Death On The Rock* rumbled on all summer. It was nearly a year after the programme was broadcast that an independent inquiry chaired by Lord Windlesham exonerated Thames of any bias. Despite that, many politicians never forgot, or forgave. So, in September 1988, when the ITV bosses elected Dunn as chairman of the ITV Association, their central administrative body at the forefront of negotiations with the government over change, some thought it a very curious move indeed.

Dunn was wrong about the auction. If Griffiths' and Sterling's resolve weakened, others drove it on.

Thatcher's senior colleagues had no such qualms about the idea. Young and Lawson in particular became vehement supporters. Lawson's logic was clear: the Treasury had a dismal track record in trying to pin down ITV profits with a special levy. A cash sum up front, especially if paid on a regular basis, looked an attractive alternative. Fears about the consequences – reckless overbidding and a headlong chase for ratings at the expense of quality programming – were brushed aside. It did not have to be an auction, anyway. A 'competitive tender', in which each interested party put in only one bid, would get round the problem of rival parties driving the price ever upwards.

The one politician who should have been close enough to the

industry to voice its concerns, Tim Renton, the broadcasting minister, a junior minister at the Home Office, was not even on the cabinet committee. His boss, Douglas Hurd, the Home Secretary, backed the competitive tender idea anyway.

If the IBA had a chance of influencing the White Paper, it lost it with the row over *Death On The Rock*. Privately, Thatcher had resolved that the regulator had to go. By October 1988 it was too late. The cabinet committee endorsed a host of radical recommendations for the broadcasting White Paper. Among them, the intention to replace the IBA with a new regulatory body operating with a 'lighter touch', to award ITV franchises by competitive tender, and to remove ITN from ITV ownership.

It was the most radical package of change for British broadcasting since the introduction of commercial television in 1955. Broadcasters were surprised, but vowed to fight it. It would take at least a year before the White Paper became an Act, then months after that to pass through Parliament and become law.

The same morning that Thatcher's Cabinet rubber-stamped the White Paper, another meeting was taking place across London. Oscar Mammi, the Italian Minister of Posts and Telecommunications, was welcomed at the IBA on a visit to investigate Britain's success in encouraging media owners to make quality programmes.

The *Financial Times* reported: 'Mr Mammi, who was entertained by Mr Douglas Hurd, the Home Secretary, at an elegant dinner in Lancaster House on Wednesday evening, said he thought it very strange that Britain was deregulating broadcasting at the very time that he was trying to re-regulate Italian television.'

2

'How about lunch?'
David Mellor

Thirteen months later, on a cold December morning in London's Victoria, Rowan Atkinson, Terry Jones and five TV producers filed into the Home Office to see David Mellor, the newly appointed Minister for Broadcasting. For them, representatives of the programme-makers' pressure group, the Campaign for Quality Television, it was a vital meeting, their first with Mellor. They had breakfasted well at St Ermin's Hotel round the corner to discuss tactics and decided they would not have much time. It was important that they did the talking, and Mellor, a politician with a reputation for smug abrasiveness, did the listening.

A lot had changed since the publication of the White Paper the year before. Three events in particular had given the broadcasting industry cause for thought: George Russell, chairman of Marley Tiles and a businessman admired by Thatcher, had been chosen to head ITV's new regulatory body, the Independent Television Commission – he had already replaced Lord Thomson at the IBA; Douglas Hurd, the Home Secretary, had announced in June that the ITV franchises definitely would be put out to tender; and in October Nigel Lawson had resigned from Thatcher's government. The subsequent reshuffle shunted Hurd and Renton out of the Home Office, and David Waddington, as Home Secretary, and David Mellor in.

For pressure groups like the Campaign For Quality

Television, the arrival of a new broadcasting minister was an opportunity. The campaign had been set up in 1988 by Stewart Prebble, the lanky producer of *World In Action* at Granada TV. Worried about the effect of the forthcoming legislation and the endless stereotyping of 'fat cat' ITV executives, Prebble had voiced his concern to Granada TV's chairman David Plowright, a former *World In Action* producer himself. 'I don't know what you programme-makers are up to,' replied Plowright, 'but if I was you I certainly would not be quiet about it.'

Ringing round friends, Prebble got an impressive list of signatories together for an initial ad in the *Independent*. It ran on 21 September as an open letter to the Prime Minister, warning that the new legislation could lead to a 'narrowing of real choice for the viewers'.

The argument was simple. One of the chief qualities of British commercial television was its range: everything from high-rating soaps and dramas to less popular but critically acclaimed fare like documentaries and regional programming. The new legislation could wipe all that out, transforming the network into a desert of game shows and cheap imports. It was no good saying the BBC could provide it instead. That would make it even more vulnerable to political pressure.

The Campaign was not the only body lobbying the Government – television was an issue in which just about everyone had a right to voice an opinion. The average Briton watches TV for over twenty-five hours a week, equivalent to roughly 60 per cent of the estimated leisure time of the average employed adult. Any government meddles with television at its peril. But by the end of 1989 the Campaign was establishing a voice out of all proportion to its size. That was because it had a secret weapon. It had mobilised the stars on whom TV depends for much of its ratings.

Atkinson, star of *Not The Nine O'Clock News*, and Jones, the *Monty Python* founder, had both played high-profile roles. Atkinson, despite his aversion to personal publicity, had given a good speech at a Campaign fringe meeting at the 1989 Tory party conference in Blackpool. Jones, like his fellow Python Michael Palin, had been hauled in by the Campaign's first full-time director, Simon Albury, a former *What The Papers Say* producer. Albury had spent the year frantically mugging up on American lobbying techniques. An enthusiastic, loquacious man, with thick glasses and frizz of grey hair, he knew that stars ensured publicity, and publicity often brought access to politicians. Mellor had already asked to see some of the better-known supporters of the Campaign.

To many political commentators, the bespectacled, baby-faced MP for Putney had seemed an odd appointment to see through such key legislation. He had left his previous post in the Foreign Office under a cloud. His shouting match with an Israeli commander over the arrest of a Palestinian youth, while visiting the Gaza Strip, had caused headlines worldwide.

He had in the past, however, proved adept at supporting unpopular legislation in the face of well-informed groups – he had served as a junior health minister, after all. He was combative, pugnacious, and his avowed love of opera *and* Chelsea football club gave him a wide range of interests. After Hurd and Renton, both somewhat disdainful old Etonians, Mellor (Swanage Grammar) could be relied upon to find a populist approach, if he got the room to manoeuvre. Thatcher, now coming under pressure over the poll tax and Lawson's resignation, gave him just that. Only two elements of the White Paper were sacrosanct: competitive tendering and the reduction of ITV's stake in ITN. But Mellor was a political pragmatist. To those who asked for too much he had a simple response: 'I'm not going over there just to get handbagged on this one.'

That December morning, in a large Home Office meeting room dotted with sofas and chairs, the Campaign brought along a full team to face Mellor: Albury, Prebble, Atkinson, Jones as well as programme-makers Angela Graham, Paul Hamann and Claudia Milne. They felt confident. They had organised a five-minute promotional film backing the Campaign to go out on BBC1 the night before. That way, as Albury put it, they were 'punching their full weight' for the meeting. Mellor was backed by three civil servants. The Broadcasting Act was imminent, but it still had to be pushed through Parliament, where Tory backbench unease was growing. All knew they still had a lot to play for.

There were also signs that the Government's adherence to free market principles was wavering. George Russell had told a press conference at the IBA in March that if the franchise process became a simple auction to the highest bidder, once contenders passed a quality threshold, he would resign. As if in response, Hurd's statement in June had suggested, for the first time, the important proviso that the highest bidders for franchises could be discounted if there were 'exceptional circumstances'. Just what those circumstances were remained the subject of speculation.

Albury opened first, telling Mellor what the Campaign wanted: effective guarantees that the range and quality of programmes would not be sacrificed in the rush for profits. He mentioned how they could be linked to NAR, the trade term for network advertising revenue. Mellor grinned his gap-toothed smile and interrupted him. 'What do you mean by NAR?' he asked.

Both Albury and Prebble realised that Mellor, a Cambridge-educated barrister with a lawyer's ability to master a brief quickly, knew very well what it meant, but was simply trying to throw them. Albury took a risk. 'Oh, I can't define it. It's whatever Douglas Hurd meant when he used the term in his June speech.'

Mellor cracked and laughed. The ice was broken. 'Let me set my stall out . . .' began Mellor. 'No,' interrupted Albury, who remembered how Timothy Renton had talked them out of time at a previous meeting, 'you listen to us.' And Mellor did just that.

By the end of the hour Mellor had not only suggested dinner for all of them in January, he had also invited himself out to lunch with Rowan Atkinson. Suddenly the programme-makers had an entrée that their bosses – 'those anxious-eyed ITV executives' as one journalist described them – could only dream about. There then began an extraordinary courtship between producers, performers and minister that underscored key changes in the broadcasting legislation.

The next day, 7 December, the Government published the

Broadcasting Bill. It included proposals for a competitive tender for ITV (henceforth to be known as Channel 3); a 25 per cent quota of work to be given to independent producers; the launch of a new channel, Channel 5, in the mid-1990s, and three new national commercial radio stations. The tender was to be a 'blind bid', an annual sum which the bidder promised to pay for the retention of the licence and which had to be linked to a realistic business plan for operating the licence. There were few surprises, as the bill had been well leaked to the press.

Mellor was typically defiant. There should be no 'griping and groaning' about auctioning ITV franchises to the highest bidder, he said. This was a competitive tender, not an auction. 'This is a great leap forward in the direction of wider choice in broadcasting and greater opportunities for broadcasters,' he said. But exact details of how the tender would operate, and what quality assurances bidders would have to give, had been left vague.

For Richard Dunn, charged with heading the ITV lobby, it was an uncomfortable time. There seemed little ITV's senior executives could do. The Government clearly saw them as representatives of the 'vested interests', and was disinclined to give them much time. So he worked closely with Russell, who as a Thatcher appointee carried more weight with the politicians and civil servants supervising the legislation, and watched uneasily as the Campaign For Quality Television took up the running. To help them, he gave the Campaign £5000 to spend with Westminster Strategy, Thames' lobbyists. Prebble and Albury assumed it was a naive attempt to monitor their actions more closely.

Sitting high in his fourth-floor Euston Road office, Dunn had other problems too. Many saw Thames as one of the fattest turkeys in the run-up to Christmas. Despite a programming record of extraordinary quality – in a purple patch in the mid-1970s it had produced documentary series like the 26-part *The World At War* and the 13-part *Hollywood* – it was laden with high costs and riven with ill feeling between workers, executives and shareholders.

Ever since its creation in 1968 out of a shotgun marriage between two contractors, Rediffusion and ABC, devised by the regulatory authorities, Thames had been dogged by long-running disputes over control. In the late 1980s the situation had worsened. Its main shareholders wanted out. Its executives were hopelessly divided on strategy. Its employees were demoralised by round after round of staff cuts. It was not a great way to approach the franchise round.

Nor was Dunn finding it any easier dealing with his fellow ITV bosses. While he took the Government's 'nothing to watch on a Saturday night' jibes as the sort of behaviour that had now become commonplace among senior Tory politicians, getting any consensus from the fifteen different stations that made up ITV was proving impossible. Each had their own axes to grind.

The ITV response to competitive tendering had been to suggest four different methods. Dunn argued lamely that it was not right 'intellectually' for ITV to suggest to the Government exactly how it should be done. The simple truth is that on this, as on virtually everything else, the ITV executives just could not reach agreement.

Some, backed by the Campaign For Quality Television, wanted the money bid for the franchises to be pledged to programming. At a conference on broadcasting at Sussex University on 12 January Mellor rejected this, arguing that this would simply encourage ITV to go back to its old practices.

But he pledged himself to finding some kind of compromise. In a frank conversation with Albury during a coffee-break at the conference, he assured him that was going to 'get it right'. His political career was just starting. There was no way he would allow himself to be tagged 'the man who ruined British broadcasting'. He ended: 'If you need anything, talk to Paul Wright at the Home Office. It is as good as talking to me.'

Albury was suprised. What Mellor had told him was, in effect, how to work as a good lobbyist. Wright was Mellor's key civil servant, who wrote many of his speeches. Access to him established a continuous dialogue with Government. All he had to work out was what to say.

On the train back from the conference Albury sat with David Glencross, a former IBA director of programmes earmarked for the chief executive slot at the new ITC, and David Elstein,

Thames' director of programmes. They agreed on one thing: it was now vital that they got clear agreement from the Government on an 'exceptional circumstances' clause, applicable to all regions, regardless of how many times it might be used. That way, the ITC would be allowed to disregard a higher offer if a low bidder proposed programmes of exceptionally high quality. It was political dynamite, of course, moving the system away from 'transparency' and 'openness' back to the subjective judgements of old. But if the Government was prepared to talk, it was worth trying.

L'Amico is a large, old-fashioned Italian restaurant popular with politicians. Just a brisk walk from the Houses of Parliament, it offers a bar and enough twists and turns to its dining room to separate the most bitter of political rivals. Above all it is discreet. MPs meeting the occasional celebrity there are unlikely to find the paparazzi waiting for them as they leave.

It is one of David Mellor's favourite places to do business. On the night of 24 January, 1990, he was very much at home sparring conversation with a selection of the Campaign For Quality Television's luminaries. All of those at the December Home Office meeting were there, except Atkinson who was filming elsewhere. Michael Palin came in his place. Mellor brought Paul Wright and another civil servant.

The dinner had a serious agenda. The day before Albury had sent Wright a list of topics to be discussed. He had also come with armfuls of research showing how sport, light entertainment and imported programming were the cheapest ways to get big TV audiences. That was set aside as they all assembled for drinks first. Mellor's mood was good. He teased Albury on his fondness for garish, hand-painted ties: 'Simon, you must tell me where you get your ties – so I can avoid it.'

But over dinner it changed. Flanked by both his civil servants, Mellor made it plain that the Campaign's first topic – that the Government should specify a whole slew of extra programme categories for ITV bidders to offer – was a non-starter. So was the third: using the bid money for programming, which he had already rejected.

'But if I was able to move on exceptional circumstances, would you say it was a significant advance?' Mellor played with his wine glass. 'That might help me with the people I have to discuss it with.'

Albury and Prebble thought quickly. What Mellor was asking for was some form of public support that could then be used as a lever with Thatcher and her cabinet colleagues. What he was offering in return was for exceptional circumstances to be firmed up, and made applicable in as many regions as the ITC deemed necessary, regardless of how often it was used elsewhere. They agreed immediately.

By February the Bill had moved into committee stage in the House of Commons. Mellor was putting in an extraordinary performance, responding to questioning with witty ease and attempting to calm fears that diversity on television would not be affected. But he would not allow a range of programme categories to be specified, other than children's and religious programmes, as a prerequisite for bidders. Appearing on BBC2's Newsnight on 6 February, Mellor assured his interviewer, Donald McCormick, that market forces alone would ensure diversity.

The next day Albury rang Paul Wright at the Home Office. He told him the Campaign might have difficulty backing Mellor's proposals while other programme categories were downgraded. 'What other categories are there?' asked Wright. Albury, realising that he did not have the full list in front of him, said they wanted drama, documentaries and arts to be added to children's and religious programming. He forgot education.

On 8 February it was clear the message had got through. Mellor told Standing Committee F at the House of Commons: 'In agreeing to consider the case for specifying children's and religious programmes, I am not implying that other categories which are not listed are in danger of disappearing . . . Important categories such as drama, documentaries, arts and social action will be expected to be shown on a diverse service.'

Albury was pleasantly surprised. Others were more cynical.

When a press cutting showing Mellor and Albury was pinned up at the Campaign's headquarters in Stuckley Street, north London, a wag rose-tinted Albury's glasses with a red felt pen.

'Andrew Ehrenberg of the London Business School — who's always been extremely helpful to the Campaign — once advised me to always put the conclusion at the start.' Albury paused and looked around the room, a private dining suite at the Garrick. 'So first of all I would like to say, in conclusion, thank you David Mellor for saving us from catastrophe.'

Everyone at the dinner laughed. Albury ran through the apologies from those who could not be there. Then he singled out others who had helped the Campaign, performers like Rowan Atkinson, Jeremy Paxman and Esther Rantzen, politicians like George Walden, the Tory MP who ran a campaign of guerrilla journalism against the legislation through the pages of the *Daily Telegraph*, Mark Fisher and Robert McLennan. The speech, delivered on a hot August night as part of a Campaign thank-you to Mellor, mentioned nearly everyone there.

'Now I'd like to turn briefly to David Mellor and Sir John Gielgud,' said Albury. 'In the 1950s John Gielgud went to a party in New York hosted by the American actress Mercedes McCambridge. After an hour or so he went up to McCambridge and said: "I'm terribly sorry, I've got to go to another party given by that ghaaastly woman Mercedes McCambridge." She was stunned and said, "But I'm Mercedes McCambridge." Gielgud replied: "Oh, it's not you my dear — it's the other one."

'Now, Tony Banks and others warned us that there was another David Mellor. And I am very relieved we haven't had to deal with him.'

Mellor, sitting just along from Albury, smiled broadly. The credit he was getting was an endless source of pleasure to him. Certainly the Broadcasting Bill that would go for Royal Assent in November would be a very different document to the White Paper of 1988, but that is the nature of politics. Safeguards had been introduced, compromise reached. These included a greatly strengthened quality threshold, the facility for bids of exceptional quality to triumph over higher financial offers, and the obligation imposed on licence holders to provide certain programming strands.

Commentators were already hailing it as a 'typically British' compromise. Mellor was touched. They believed he had single-handedly fought off Thatcher to get this result. What did they think she was going to do – tear everything apart and start afresh? Yes, after the poll tax fiasco, they probably did. Oh well, he mused. *If he was getting more praise than perhaps he deserved, so what? It made up for all the other times when people had blamed him.* And if the ITV companies thought they were in for an easy ride, they had another thing coming.

3

'When you enjoy what you are doing, you don't stop to use words like success.'

Michael Green

'How nice to see you, Mr Green. You are eating with a Mr Harris? Your host is already here. This way, please.'

The manager of the Savoy Grill weaved swiftly through the tables towards the back of the restaurant. Michael Green followed with an assured step, well used to crossing the thick pile that leads to the best-placed tables.

The restaurant, a wide oblong room just to the left of the hotel's front entrance, had long been established as one of the key power-broking venues in London. Adroitly positioned off the Strand, halfway between the City and the West End, it regularly attracted a handful of the truly powerful, a large clutch of aspirants and scores of fixers and hangers-on – public relations men, City editors, 'communications' specialists.

The table-linen was crisp, the service obsequious. The due deference of the ageing waiting staff was reassuringly nostalgic; rather different from the flip disdain of some of London's trendier watering-holes. It was reliable and did good trade as a place simply to be seen at, hence it was especially popular with bosses from outside London. They bought into the mystique and placed themselves; at the same time they got to gawp at others.

Green, who like any other £500,000-a-year chairman and chief executive was happy to eat there occasionally, did not object to a little recognition himself. The restaurant was full,

27

even though it was a Monday. It was 5 November, 1990, and Green was rather enjoying his role as 'king-in-waiting' of British television.

A lot had changed since his impassioned speech at Margaret Thatcher's broadcasting seminar. The Green soft-shoeing his way across the Savoy was a rather different animal from the rough-edged, media-shy entrepreneur of the mid-1980s. His company, Carlton Communications, was bigger now, and Green was a little greyer, a little wiser. He was hungry but not desperate. He was still prowling ITV looking for his main chance; the difference now was that the prey was coming to him, rather than vice versa. *It was just a question of making the right choice.*

Right from his earliest years Michael Green had known only one business logic: expand. His strength was his numeracy, his faith the bottom line. Friends joked he could read a balance sheet before his bar mitzvah. 'I like the numbers,' he would tell journalists later. 'They mean something to me. They have relevance.'

A slightly built man with boyish features and thick black hair, Green was used to doing things his own way. His was a rags-to-riches story with a twist. His father Cyril, a north London businessman, ran Tern Shirts. His mother was a psychologist. As a teenager, he could not wait to earn money. A month's holiday experience as a shoe shop assistant convinced him that retailing was too slow – he hated waiting for the customer to come to him.

At seventeen, eschewing his mother's aspirations for him to follow a professional career, he dropped out of Haberdashers' Aske's School in the middle of A level Economics to work for a printing company. With just four O levels, he began training as a compositor. By the age of twenty in 1968, he had set up his own company, Trident Industries, with his brother David Green.

Typically, his first move was to buy another company, the Direct Mail Centre, a direct marketing specialist. Before his twenty-first birthday, he was employing 150 people, all older than himself. 'We generated some money, we borrowed some money and we knew what we were doing,' he said later.

His second fortunate move came in 1972. He married an heiress, Janet Wolfson, daughter of one of Britain's richest men, Lord Wolfson, owner of Great Universal Stores. Suddenly he found he could mix freely with some of Britain's most powerful businessmen, many of them prominent figures in north London's Jewish society. Some, like Janet Wolfson's cousin David Young, later Lord Young, the Trade and Industry Secretary, went on to become useful political contacts. Others, like a young advertising executive called Charles Saatchi, became firm friends and a strong influence on Green's ambitions.

Throughout the 1970s Green worked hard to build up a successful printing and photographic business, without attracting much attention. Then in the 1980s he moved into first gear. In 1982, anticipating the growth of television services, he bought a St John's Wood editing suite. A year later he got a stock market listing for the newly named Carlton through the reverse takeover of *Fleet Street Newsletter*, a sharetip sheet he later sold. Then, through Charles Saatchi, he met Mike Luckwell.

Luckwell was co-founder and managing director of the Moving Picture Company, the biggest producer of television commercials in Europe. A brilliant technician, he was a gadget man. 'The reason Moving Picture Company got to number one,' said an ex-colleague, 'was that every time someone brought some new device onto the market, Mike Luckwell bought one, took it apart, figured out how it worked and installed it into his editing suites.'

Saatchi was his biggest client. Realising both Luckwell and Green were looking to expand, Saatchi provided the introduction. In June 1983, Carlton bought the Moving Picture Company. Luckwell became group managing director with 16 per cent of the company; Green held 12 per cent; his brother, David Green, later to become boss of Colefax and Fowler, held slightly less. But Michael Green ran it, plotting the subsequent spree as they bought up video-editing firms, prop hire companies, electronic businesses, riding the boomwave of the 1980s.

They used the same techniques that Saatchi himself was using to build his advertising empire, raising money with new share issues, then allowing the new companies to push the profit potential of the buyer yet higher. The share price kept climbing, fuelling more purchases. Green's ready charm and consummate grasp of the bottom line wowed the City analysts, allaying any fears that he might push it too far. 'Michael took an acquisitions policy invented by Charles Saatchi and polished it,' said one outsider. Raise money, buy businesses, tie in the key staff on earn-out contracts, raise more money . . .

By his mid-thirties, Green had developed a reputation as a ruthless financial engineer. Bosses of new subsidiaries who crossed him were quickly moved sideways, analysts who queried his techniques were shunned. Like Saatchi, Green refused to put a public face to his growing empire. He mistrusted personal publicity, spoke only to trusted financial journalists, and declined the chance to answer the critics and mould his own image. Unlike Saatchi, whose mystery served only to make him more celebrated, Green managed, for the most part, to keep out of the headlines.

So his image was moulded for him: some who had lost out in deals to him depicted him as a cunning and aggressive man who could not be trusted. Many suspected Green enjoyed that kind of testimonial. Like a lot of the entrepreneurs burning up the 1980s, he felt accountable to no one. His success spoke for itself. That was enough.

Then came Thames. Both Green and Luckwell knew that the logical progression to their ambitions was to get a broadcasting franchise. They had bought the back of the shop, now they wanted the front. Carlton's stake in LWT, carefully built up, was one possibility but Green was reluctant to bid against his friend Christopher Bland, recently installed as chairman of LWT. They had met in the 1970s, when both worked in the printing industry. They got on well and Green was wary of Bland's grasp of the internal politics of ITV. Bland had served as deputy chairman of the IBA, and knew his way around the network.

Thames, racked by union problems and poor management, was a more attractive fish. It was certainly more profitable than LWT. All Green had to do was convince the IBA that the takeover was in everyone's best interest.

He had sat in the back seat of John Whitney's Rolls Royce Corniche in the Independent Broadcasting Authority car park in London's Knightsbridge thrashing out the deal. It was the autumn of 1985 and the IBA's rabbit warren of offices opposite Harrods had been evacuated after a security scare. An IRA mainland bombing campaign was in full swing. Any Government-linked building was a target. Whitney, director general of the IBA, had rescheduled his meeting downstairs, rather than cancel it. He had listened carefully as Green outlined his intentions. Green had not specified which station he might take over – he had only wanted to talk 'principles'. Whitney had made it plain that he saw no special difficulties. If it was an agreed takeover, the IBA could certainly look at it.

Green left the meeting confident that he would soon be running his own ITV company. Thames had two large stakeholders, BET and Thorn, who he knew were keen to sell. In October of the same year – after two meetings with Whitney – he pounced.

Within a matter of days, BET and Thorn signed a binding contract to sell Thames to Carlton. Green's company had an opt-out provision if the IBA blocked the deal; BET and Thorn did not. Green was exultant. He had snapped up Britain's biggest commercial broadcaster at the bottom of the market. He was only thirty-eight years old. Then all hell broke loose.

Richard Dunn, Thames' new managing director, three months in the job, was astounded when he heard the news. He made a passionate plea to Lord Thomson, the IBA chairman, to preserve the company's independence. Forget the fact his two main shareholders had gone behind his back, Dunn argued, Carlton simply had no track record in public service broadcasting. Green was simply a money-man who would asset strip the station and squeeze the maximum profit out of it.

He cited the experience of Michael Cox, a former Thames

engineer who had sold his company, Cox Electronics, to Carlton. Within days of the sale Mike Luckwell had arrived at Cox's Feltham headquarters overhauling everything right down to the office decor with barely a word to Cox, nominally the managing director of the new Carlton subsidiary. How could they be trusted to run Thames? The viewers' interests, and those of Thames staff, would be better served by blocking the takeover and allowing Dunn to head a partial flotation, finding new, more suitable owners for Thames.

Thomson came back to Green with a compromise: buy 49 per cent of Thames, become the biggest single shareholder, but allow BET and Thorn between them to retain the majority. Green told Thomson Carlton must have the controlling interest. Thomson consulted the other IBA board members. Six days before the board was due to meet and decide, the IBA put out a terse statement saying it was blocking the sale.

Green hit the roof. *How could they do this?* He received a courtesy call only a minute before the announcement reached City screens. The IBA was still in the process of getting information from Carlton about its intentions.

Green believed the IBA had misled him. How could it object? Carlton after all was a public company, something many ITV stations were not. The IBA had recently made it clear they wanted to see all ITV companies in public, rather than private hands.

He still had his trump card: BET and Thorn's promise to sell. All the IBA could do, if Green held the two shareholders to the commitment, was revoke Thames' licence to broadcast and readvertise the franchise. But would they?

Call their bluff, urged Luckwell. Make BET and Thorn honour their promises to sell, take over the station and then see what the IBA does. Will it take away the franchise, beaming in an alternative service from LWT or TVS? Of course it won't, said Luckwell.

Thomson waited. Green consulted lawyers. He worked the phones in his office furiously, calling in favours. Eventually he got Stuart Young, then chairman of the BBC, to plead Carlton's case with Thomson, but to no avail.

Green was torn. He suspected Luckwell was right, but at Carlton's stage of development, he reasoned, it did not make sense to antagonise the authorities. In the end he decided to back down. Luckwell was furious, and later sold out of Carlton. Green was unperturbed. He had friends he could talk to, others who believed that ITV's cosy cartel was an anachronism in Margaret Thatcher's new Britain. Those close to him knew he would bide his time. Men like Green are not easily deflected.

Green already had an entrée to Government through Lord Young. Soon he had Margaret Thatcher's ear as well, writing briefing papers on television for her and becoming a well-known face in political circles. Few doubted that he played the system well. Other politicians acknowledged his influence on Thatcher. Norman Lamont, newly appointed Financial Secretary, summoned Green to the Treasury in 1989. 'You seem to be the only person supporting the Government's position on broadcasting. Why?' To Green's amusement, Lamont took notes as he explained.

Yet while the lobby over the Broadcasting Bill continued, Green never stopped building his empire. He bought a small stake in Central TV in 1987, with the management's full blessing, and took Zenith, Britain's largest production house, off their hands as well. Then a year later he plunged into the American market to buy Technicolor, the duplication and film processing company. Eight months on he bought UEI, a television engineering specialist. The latter two had cost him more than $1 billion. He had built up Europe's largest television services empire. All he needed to crown it was the licence to broadcast on top.

The purchase of Zenith, which made films and TV programmes, showed how far he was prepared to adapt to achieve his goal. The high-risk, high-overhead element of production was anathema to Green's obsessive financial prudence – he later sold 49 per cent of the company on to Paramount, the American media giant – but he knew that, if he was to be seen to be an acceptable person to run an ITV station, he had to do more than just supply facilities. He had to show an interest in the programmes as well.

At the same time his friends helped him to devise a more sympathetic image. He had always run with a media rat-pack of bright, Jewish high achievers – men like Charles Saatchi, Michael Grade, retail magnate Gerald Ratner, BBC2 boss Alan Yentob. They warned him that his very invisibility as far as the media were concerned aroused distrust.

It was no good saying, Garbo-like, 'I want and will insist on keeping my private life private' (*Financial Times*, May 1989). He wanted to become the most influential man in British television. People had a right to know what he was like.

So gradually he changed. At Lord Young's suggestion, he took on the chairmanship of the Open College. Following Saatchi's lead, he competed at collecting modern art. (Green's friendships were nothing if not competitive.) He turned up at television functions, he started talking about his love of film, his boyhood watching the movies at the Baker Street Classic, his taste for good design. Gradually he developed an image the media could latch on to: the yuppie mogul so common in the fastburn industries of advertising and 'communications'. To television stalwarts it all looked rather sinister. Michael Green, went the whisper, is coming on like an ad-man.

Profiles drooled over his Mapplethorne prints, Arteluce lamps and Corbusier chairs, the art books next to Czech and Speake toiletries in his office bathroom, his professed love of Freud and fishing. He had always been an able and attractive talker, often adopting the camp, knowing tones of his high-flying set (close business colleagues were 'darling' or 'sweet-heart', an affectation he shared with the Saatchis). Now he turned his charm on the media, not because he wanted to, but because he needed to.

Those who knew him well noted how difficult it was for the leopard to change his spots. Overnight he became as obsessive about his image as his bottom line. Journalists would always be referred to cuttings, interviews became bizarre negotiations over what could or could not be written, editors would be threatened with lawsuits.

'What's that?' he would shout in mock horror, pointing at a journalist's tape recorder, 'You know I hate those things.' Then a moment later he would kick his shoes off, pucker his face round a large cigar and pontificate. It was, they joked, just like working for him. So long as you were on the right side of him or he wanted something, he was the most charming man in the world.

Many in the industry concluded that this bizarre contradiction of the urbane sophisticate who actively courted anonymity by endlessly discussing it with the press was a rather devious construction. They may have been right but it was totally in character: it was all about control and ambition.

He knew that simply being a wealthy man (the dividends alone from his Carlton shareholding far outstripped his £500,000 salary) running a wealthy company was not enough to ensure success in the world of commercial television. As Thatcher's original, radical ideas for selling off the franchises became watered down, so Green ensured that he, stage by stage, became a far more acceptable figure. By 1990, sensing the air of compromise now surrounding the legislation, he had modified his position. When Mellor told him he was surprised he never came to see him, Green responded that he had already seen so many ministers and advisers he was exhausted, and anyway he had little problem with the quality safeguards. All he had wanted was that ITV companies should be open to takeover, like any other public company. The outsider had become, almost, the insider.

He still had to tread carefully. The recession had caught up with Carlton with a vengeance at the end of 1989. By autumn 1990, over a billion pounds had been wiped off the value of his company in less than a year. Its share-price had nose-dived, going from 820p the previous December, when he had sold 1.3 million Carlton shares to support his divorce settlement (he later married Carlton's investor relations executive Tessa Buckmaster), to near 350p. After an extraordinary run – Carlton had a record of 47 per cent compound growth every year for five years – the first cracks were appearing in the Green empire.

The end-of-year results offered little succour. The City wanted him to split his chairman and chief executive role; his last experience of power sharing had been a bitter falling out with his former partner Mike Luckwell five years before. Luckwell, a constant source for journalists digging into his past, had dogged him ever since, throwing court cases and patent actions against Carlton.

Most importantly, the wavering of City confidence in Carlton – totally unwarranted, Green reasoned, more the result of Carlton being bracketed with other fast-falling idols – was in danger of affecting his television ambitions. He had waited ten years to get a television franchise. He had prepared assiduously, collecting information on just about every possible rival bidder. *He was in no mood to let the City spoil it all for him now.*

The invitation had arrived out of the blue: would he care to have lunch at the Savoy with John Harris, chairman of the East Midlands Electricity Board, to discuss issues of mutual interest? He was intrigued. He guessed it had something to do with his 20 per cent stake in Central TV, picked up from Ladbroke in 1987.

Green had long wondered what he should do with his interest in Central. The Central management had been keen for him to buy it. Better to have him on your side, they reasoned, than bidding against you. It had been useful. It had given him an entrée into ITV and a feeling for the tortuous politics that governed the network. But he was not a man who liked collecting small stakes – they offered little control, only leverage. He did not, however, want to make the wrong move too soon.

He had considered taking a majority stake in the company earlier in 1990. He had known an agreed bid was possible after a chance meeting in the Caribbean at Christmas. He had been on David Bowie's boat off Mustique on Christmas Eve with his new wife and friends when a vast white motor cruiser, two satellite dishes perched precariously on top, had moored alongside. A large man dressed in a marquee-like white kaftan stood on the bridge, waving imperiously. Soon a message came across. His heart sank but his guests were unanimous: an invitation for drinks with Robert Maxwell was too good to miss.

After he had got over his shock at the *Lady Ghislaine* – the thick white pile carpet, the mahogany-floored discotheque, the incessant piped music – he realised Maxwell wanted to make a business proposition. He had swiftly guided Green to one side, leaving the others to caviar and champagne, and asked him if he wanted to take over Central. He had a 20 per cent stake in the company too. Did Green want to buy it? It was clear to Green, who normally was not inclined to take Captain Bob too seriously, that he was a very keen seller. Nor was he the only one.

Green had toyed with the idea of buying the company for much of early 1990. He reckoned he could have got 80 per cent; only DC Thomson, with 20 per cent, would have been unwilling to sell. The senior management, wary of Maxwell's indecision over what to do with his stake, were keen to have a strong shareholder behind them. But Green hesitated, unsure whether he should commit himself. Perhaps this meeting with the East Midlands Electricity boss would help him decide.

Reaching the table Green found John Harris surrounded by a retinue of advisers: on the one side Ian Coulter, his PR man, on the other John Wood, a director at Allen Brady Marsh, East Midlands' ad agency. Introductions were traded. Green, half in jest, smiled at Wood and asked: 'What are *you* doing here?' Wood, a short, bespectacled man, smiled back and explained that he was engaged as adviser to East Midlands on corporate affairs.

Harris, a tall, perennially cheerful engineer, was flush with the success of the recent privatisation of his company, one of the largest utilities in the Central region. Green picked at his sole and listened as Harris talked about how good the cash-flow from electricity was, how they were looking to spend some of the cash in other areas, and how they had decided to look at television. Would Green like to join them in a bid against Central?

Green was taken aback. He sat thinking for a moment. *Why are they talking to me?* If you are planning to make a franchise bid against an ITV company, the last person you would want to discuss it with is one of their shareholders. It was completely insane. And yet, if they want to discuss it and they are fully aware he is a shareholder who is likely to report it all back to the board, why not? It could only be useful in protecting the value of his investment.

'Why are you putting this to me?' he asked.

'John Whitney suggested it,' said Harris. The thought of his old adversary from the IBA made Green smile, but also made him wary. Whitney, now working for Andrew Lloyd Webber's Really Useful Group, had presumably heard that Green was considering what to do with his stake in Central. If he baled out, he would make an invaluable ally for anyone bidding against Central. Indeed, was there anything to stop him keeping the stake and still bid against Central? This was more insane than he thought.

'You do know I am a director of Central and bound by strict rules from discussing the company's affairs in detail?'

'Yes of course,' said Harris, smiling.

'Well, you would be better off buying into the company,' said Green. He then talked at length of the possibilities involved in a London franchise.

His audience was puzzled. Green, they thought, was being somewhat disingenuous. Everyone knew he either wanted control of Central or out. And Harris would not have organised a Guy Fawkes meeting in so public a venue as the Savoy if he was plotting anything underhand. Perhaps Green wanted them to invest in a London bid?

The difficulty, they found, was working out exactly what Green wanted to do. Either he was very good at keeping his own counsel, or he did not even know himself.

'Michael, we have got to make up our minds what we are doing.' The warning had been given to Green from inside Carlton time and again throughout 1990. By the autumn Green's group managing director, Bob Phillis, a former managing director of Central, had already signalled his concern with his feet.

He had resigned, throwing in his £250,000 salary and telling Green he could not refuse an offer from the ITV bosses to replace Sir David Nicholas as chief executive of ITN. Phillis's friends knew there were other reasons he was leaving: one was his frustration at trying to get Green to fix on exactly what he wanted for Carlton.

By 1990 everyone outside Carlton assumed that Green would bid for Thames' franchise, the London weekday licence. Not only would that have settled old scores, but by then, they reasoned, Green must have more than enough information on how Thames operated to put himself in a strong position.

The new legislation also offered him one crucial advantage: it gave licence holders the option of setting up simply as 'publisher-broadcasters', commissioning most of their programming out of house and avoiding the need to set up their own large programme-making departments. Such a structure had already proved successful with Channel 4.

It was a considerable change from 1980, when the largest companies had to show they could produce nationally networked programming in-house. Consequently stations like Thames and Granada had invested massively in studios, technicians and huge specialist departments producing drama, comedy and current affairs. The payrolls were enormous. Each station employed thousands – one of the reasons they were instinctively hostile to independent producers' demands for more work as the 1980s progressed.

But the new legislation made that hostility pointless. Broadcasters now had to commission a quarter of their output from independents. New bidders like Green planned to commission out much more, keeping overheads down and profits up. Such a structure was better able to ride a recession, they argued, and better able to respond quickly to changing viewer needs. More importantly, it appeared to give them an advantage in the forthcoming auction. Bids had to be linked to the likely profits expected and, according to some at least, such stripped-down stations were likely to be far more profitable.

Green appeared to have all the cards. He had political connections, he had ITV network experience through his stake in Central, he had technical nous through his facilities empire and he had programme-making expertise through his share of Zenith, by then turning out award-winning series like *Inspector Morse* and critically acclaimed films like *The Dead* and *Wish You Were Here*.

Not only that, but the emphasis on commissioning out meant

that nearly all the leading production independents were expected to take stakes in bidding consortia, or sign 'output deals' with either new bidders or incumbents. The courting had already started and Green, as majority stakeholder in Britain's biggest production independent, had a better idea than most of what was going on. He was the one bidder every ITV company dreaded coming up against. Consequently he was spoiled for choice.

Would it be cheaper to buy in before the franchise process? What if his station then lost it against another bidder? And which station should he buy into? So many wanted the cash – Central, TVS, Thames – but his empire's remorseless drive for growth and profit appeared to be faltering. For once in his business life Green appeared paralysed by indecision.

He had certainly made the right preparations for the London weekday licence, holding a series of secret meetings with Christopher Bland and Greg Dyke, chairman and chief executive of London Weekend, on whether the two London stations, traditionally bitter rivals, could work more closely together. He amassed knowledge and prided himself on the fact that there was not a single ITV franchise bid being prepared that he did not know about. But he would not take the plunge himself.

Colleagues tried to explain it. 'The trouble with Michael,' said one, 'is that he is a juggler. He likes to have as many balls in the air as possible at any one time.' Only this time he was in danger of leaving it till it was too late.

The crunch came in November 1990. He had flirted with Central, he had turned down an offer to take over TVS, holder of the lucrative south-east franchise. Then came yet another call from Thames' two major shareholders, BET and Thorn. Was he still interested in buying? Green had kept in close touch with both shareholders throughout the late 1980s. Again and again, talks had broken down over price. By late 1990 BET and Thorn were determined to sell; Thames took a roadshow round Britain to whip up prospective buyers but nearly all were chary of the forthcoming franchise round.

Only Green remained interested. That autumn he met repeatedly with Dunn and Derek Hunt, Thames' finance director. It all seemed settled. Green would take over the BET and Thorn stakes, then make an offer for the rest of the company. When the deadline for offers was up, only one had come in, from Green, valuing the stakes at £2.75 a share. Everything was approved. Thames' management expected the deal to go ahead. But at the last moment it fell through. Thames said that Green got cold feet. Carlton said that Thames had pulled out. Instead, Thorn bought BET out for £2.50 per share in cash, with 50p on top to come, and pledged itself to backing Thames through the franchise process.

That was it. Slowly but surely, Green was being pushed into bidding against an ITV incumbent, rather than buying into one. For a man who liked to control everything, it was an alarming situation. Padding softly round his office in stockinged feet that autumn, he realised his options were being whittled away.

It was a tense time for all would-be bidders. Up and down Britain producers, financiers and consultants were poring over the broadcasting legislation trying to fathom where the advantages lay. Everyone agreed that 'greenfield' bidders should be able to bid more than the incumbent ITV stations, burdened down with staff and studio costs. But other factors now seemed to be skewing the process in ITV's favour.

For one thing, running an ITV station looked a lot less attractive than it had two years previously. The depth of the recession gripping Britain was tearing a large hole out of ITV advertising revenue. As each month went by, and revenue dropped further, the stations once described as 'a licence to print money' looked more like a licence to lose money. And the bombshell in early November of Sky's 'merger' with BSB had upped the ante considerably. The likelihood of a profitable, streamlined satellite TV service emerging, which concentrated on competing with ITV for viewers and revenue, was like a bucket of cold water over many would-be bidders outside the system.

It was also now clear that putting together a bid would not come cheap. The draft invitation to apply for Channel 3 licences released by the shadow ITC on 19 November read like a lengthy exam paper. Gone were the days when bidders could throw something together over a weekend. The raft of programming requirements indicated and the depth of detail demanded, both on the programming and business side, were huge. These, and the introduction of both a clear quality threshold and 'exceptional circumstances', clearly favoured the incumbents. They were already producing the programming strands stipulated, and it was widely acknowledged that they provided the benchmarks for the quality threshold.

Many ITV companies were also stripping down fast, laying off thousands of staff, placing costly studio facilities into separate companies and commissioning an increasing amount of programming from independents. They did not need the ranks of highly paid consultants to tell them of the threat from so-called 'publisher-broadcasters'. Month by month, it was becoming a far more evenly balanced contest than people had expected. For some outsiders, the combination of cost and uncertainty involved in the competitive tender process was just too much.

Speculation as to who would still bid now gripped the network. Green was a virtual certainty, but others? The legislation placed no limit on the stakes that could be held by European companies, while non-EC companies could take up to 49 per cent providing they did not have control. Surely, the pundits argued, there would be some interest from the giant media groups like Time Warner, Sony-CBS, Bertelsmann or Hachette?

British interest was more difficult to predict. Restrictions on cross-media ownership meant that the large press groups like Rupert Murdoch's News International, Lord Rothermere's Associated Newspapers and Conrad Black's Daily Telegraph group could take only 20 per cent of a bid.

Outside the press barons there were few with the inclination and weight to lead a bid, certainly, against any of the major stations. The problem was not expertise but cash; the legislation made it clear that 'quality of money' was as important as quality of programming, and to raise the sort of money required to run a large ITV station for at least ten years you needed some sort of track record.

Yet for all bidders it was crucial to know who you were up against. As in any poker game it could have an important effect on the stakes wagered and the chances of winning. Knowledge of what your potential opponents might be planning became vital.

The ITV incumbents aside, by the winter of 1990 Green had narrowed his major rivals down to two. Both led multimillion-pound companies with media interests in London and the south. One, Richard Branson, was all too easy to track. You just had to follow the journalists. The other was less so. He worried Green. *It was like dealing with a large, slippery fish that you know is out there, but which has no intention of being netted.*

'Clive, I've got a proposition for you.'

Clive Hollick leaned back in his chair as he listened to the call. Behind him the City of London stretched away: St Paul's dome, the Nat West tower, London Bridge. In front of him sat a desk, a table, some chairs and a rather unprepossessing office. You might expect more from a man running a £330 million business. But that was Hollick's style: understated, no frills, nothing fancy. He only kept the view because it's free, joked his enemies.

He was listening to an old friend, Simon Albury, who wanted to put together a TV bid. So did he.

Albury liked to tell friends he had thought of it in the bath. It was February 1990, only a few weeks after Albury had hosted the Campaign For Quality Television's dinner with David Mellor at L'Amico. Lying under the suds one Monday morning at his north London home, mulling over the significance of a strengthened exceptional circumstance clause for quality, he had had an idea. Why not put together his own bid for an ITV franchise?

He reached for the portable phone, which he always kept by him and, in a state of some excitement, phoned Michael Palin, another of the guests at the L'Amico dinner. 'Michael, with the changes we're making in the Bill, it's clear ITV could be a quality service.'

'Yes . . .' replied a vexed Palin.

'So if we can change the Bill, the next thing we should do is get inside and influence the system. We should go for a franchise.'

'But . . .' interjected Palin. Albury cut him short, summarising what he thought would be needed and which ITV stations might be vulnerable to an outside bid. By the end, Palin was interested. But they would need a backer. That was when Albury rang Hollick.

That winter Hollick still had as low a profile outside the City as Green had in 1985. A brilliant banker who had built up MAI into a £330m media, research and money-broking group, he abhored personal publicity. He did not even give interviews off-the-record.

His aversion to the press stemmed partly from his left-wing politics. Despite enjoying the lifestyle of a successful City financier (houses in London's Notting Hill and the New Forest, a flat in Paris), Hollick had been a Labour party member since his grammar school days in Southampton. In 1988 he set up the Institute for Public Policy Research, the left's leading think-tank, and became a close adviser to Neil Kinnock, the Labour party leader. As such, he was always a likely target for Britain's Tory-supporting tabloids. Wags in the City nicknamed him 'the Red Baron', or 'left wing by Lear jet'. He was not bothered, so long as he kept his privacy.

His rise to success had been unusual from the start. A skinny, bearded man with a cautious manner and sharp, pinched features, he left Nottingham University with a degree in sociology, politics and psychology, determined to enter journalism. Instead he found himself sidetracked into Hambros, the blue-blooded merchant bank.

There he had then cut a swathe through the public school boys to become, at twenty-eight, the youngest director in the bank's history. He was acclaimed as one of the brightest minds in banking, yet when Hambros sent him in to rescue the secondary banking casualty Vavasseur in 1974, he never came back. Out of it emerged MAI, a multinational conglomerate specialising in money-broking, market research and posters.

In 1977 he married Sue Woodford, a Granada TV producer who went on to become one of the founding editors of Channel 4. Shortly after, in 1980, MAI joined an unsuccessful bid for the breakfast franchise. Those who worked closely with him realised that Hollick, for all his aversion to publicity, was fascinated with the media. But he was a businessman first and he knew that television was always a good cash-flow enterprise. For MAI, it could provide a central plank for further diversifications into related areas.

Albury had first met Hollick in the mid-sixties at Nottingham University. They had got their first taste of production working together in student theatre. They bought over Cafe La Mama, the New York-based experimental theatre company, to do a series of plays directed by Tom O'Horgan, the underground director who found fame two years later producing *Hair*. They studied sociology together. They became firm friends.

When Hollick went into merchant banking and found he was exceptionally good at it, Albury was one of his escape routes from the staid pinstripe world of the City, a contact point with the world of arts and current affairs. It was Albury who had introduced Hollick to Sue Woodford, when both were working at Granada, and Albury who had been best man at their wedding. He had also introduced Hollick to Palin, another friend, early on.

After the initial phone calls Albury worked hard to pull the bid along. He put Hollick and Palin together in March, over dinner at his house in Kilburn, London. It did not take long for them to make up their minds that they would bid. 'But who should we have as chief executive?' asked Hollick. Albury reached for a BBC Enterprises brochure which he had picked up at a conference in February. Before he could show it to the others, Palin spoke. 'Why don't you ask Roger Laughton?' Laughton, director of co-productions at BBC Enterprises, had produced Palin's *Great Railway Journeys Of The World* series. Albury laughed and flourished the brochure. Inside, he had drawn a circle around Laughton's head.

They agreed he would be first choice. Not only did he have the right track record and expertise, moving from production to management, he also knew Albury and Palin well. Besides producing *Great Railway Journeys Of The World*, he had attended the same school in Sheffield as Palin. He had also lodged with Albury's mother when he had worked for the BBC at Pebble Mill. But they knew it would be difficult to lure him away from the safety of a BBC career path. They would wait.

They finally made their move for Laughton after a conversation with Allan McKeown, boss of SelecTV, a production independent which had enjoyed success putting together comedies like *Birds of a Feather* and *Lovejoy* for the BBC. McKeown was keen to get an equity stake in a franchise bid.

He had had unsuccessful discussions with Schroders and British & Commonwealth with a view to organising his own bid against Tyne Tees in the north-east. When Kip Meek, a consultant at the accountants Cooper & Lybrand Deloitte, suggested that McKeown should talk to MAI he jumped at the chance.

'Who's going to be your chief executive?' he asked Albury. 'We'd like Roger Laughton but we're not sure if we'll get him,' replied a candid Albury. He had already made tentative approaches to others on a short-list they had drawn up, including Michael Grade and Jonathan Shier, Thames' aggressive Australian sales chief. McKeown had recently spent hours across the negotiating table from Laughton at the BBC. 'Try,' he said.

Laughton, a tall, bald man judged to be one of the best commercial minds in the BBC, was sitting in his office when Albury called. 'There's something I'd like to have a talk to you about,' said Albury, ever the fixer.

'Fine,' said Laughton, 'fire away.'

'No, it's probably best if we speak outside the office.'

Days later, over the August Bank Holiday, Laughton was sitting in Albury's north London back garden, listening to Albury outline his objectives. He left with a copy of MAI's annual report under his arm.

That summer Albury decamped to Edinburgh to attend the annual Television Festival. To lighten up proceedings, the organisers had arranged the Franchise Game, a mock auction following the likely guidelines laid down in the forthcoming legislation. Three teams would outline programme plans and bid for a major franchise.

Albury chaired one group, led by McKeown, with Meek and Janet Street Porter on his team. Michael Grade and Patrick Dromgoole, chief executive of HTV, headed the other teams. Albury's team won, outbidding Grade, while Dromgoole was knocked out for overbidding. This is a very good omen indeed, thought Albury.

Newly enthused after Edinburgh, he set up a meeting between Hollick and Laughton in September. The BBC executive got hopelessly lost trying to find MAI's riverside headquarters next to London Bridge. But when he got there he liked what he heard. The BBC roots of both Albury and Palin convinced him he was on home ground; the thrust of the bid would be their commitment to quality. The target: either London or the south-east, both strongholds of BBC viewing. He agreed to meet Hollick again.

For Green, who prided himself on his intelligence network, the whispers of an MAI bid being put together were tantalising. Hollick was always the rival he feared most. He was too much of an unknown quantity – he had the right connections, the right quality of money and he was swiftly drawing to him the right programming expertise. But he was hard to second-guess: he did not move in the same social circles as Green; he was not a regular at television functions or high-profile charity fundraisers.

All they had in common was Hambros, which had acted as advisers for Green in his 1985 Thames bid. Guy Nabarro, the account executive who had worked on the bid, had gone on to be a board director of MAI.

The word was put out to Hambros. How about a meeting? In October 1990 Michael Sorkin, a director of Hambros, rang Green back. Hollick had said yes to a private, confidential discussion about areas of interest in ITV. Green did not have to think long before agreeing to a date. He wondered how far Hollick had got in putting his franchise bid together.

*

The meeting took place on a dark Tuesday night in November. Hollick and Green sat opposite each other at the dining table in Hambros' first-floor hospitality flat in Belgravia, playing a cautious game of verbal poker. Neither wanted to give the other too much information about their plans, but both wanted to find out what the other was doing. Between them their hosts, Michael Sorkin and Antony Beevor, the Hambros directors who had brought them together, eased the conversation along.

They talked around the key subject: what their bid targets were. Green's agenda was simple. He wanted to find out if, as he had guessed, Hollick was a potential bidder against Thames, and warn him off. He could only do that by convincing him that he was so well prepared for a Thames bid that it would be a waste of time opposing him. Hollick, for his part, wanted to assess Green's strength and avoid telling him who he had signed up. He noted Green's concern about what others might be plotting. Hollick, a man with a sharp sense of humour, had heard that this made Green eminently teasable. He had to restrain himself.

The game went on for some hours. Eventually Hollick made it clear that the south-east was his favoured target. Green was not totally convinced. Hollick agreed that if you were going to bid for a London station, it had to be Thames – it was bigger, and looked more vulnerable that LWT. If you are going to win, you might as well win the biggest.

'Obviously we are interested in London and the south,' said Green. He pointed out that an agreement not to bid against each other would give each a far better chance of winning but warned: 'You know we can't do that.' He explained that before the meeting he had taken legal advice that any kind of agreement could be subject to restraint of trade. It would be very dangerous to come to any commercial understanding. Hollick nodded.

But there was nothing to prevent them swapping a few ideas. They discussed the best ways of running ITV stations, and the possibility of putting together a consortium to bid against TV-am for the breakfast TV franchise.

Green was impressed with what he heard. Hollick was no

star-struck entrepreneur sucked in by the glamour of television. He knew how to run a business. He wanted an ITV station because he believed he could run it at a large profit. This was rather different to the man he had heard was flirting with Granada and the Campaign For Quality Television. It made him all the more dangerous as an opponent.

Dinner over, the staff sent out, Sorkin switched on the TV. All were conscious that events more momentous than their own plans were taking place that night. Margaret Thatcher, driving force behind so much of the broadcasting legislation, was on her way out.

A challenge from Michael Heseltine had enforced a Tory leadership contest. Doubts over the poll tax, Europe, the health service and education reforms had created a wide schism among the ranks of Tory MPs. The results of the first ballot of the leadership contest were due that evening. Hollick, the Labour party member, and Green, the one-time Tory acolyte, drew up their chairs.

Thatcher won, but without a large enough majority to prevent a second ballot. With a brusque flurry, she pushed past the BBC reporter on the steps of the British Embassy in Paris, where she was staying, to tell the cameras she would stand again. But her government looked hopelessly crippled.

Both Green and Hollick knew they were witnessing the end of an era. When Green left that night, he hoped he had made himself clear. If Hollick stayed in the south, that would leave just Branson to beat. He had a feeling that would be an easier contest to win. Branson, he knew, had a lot on his plate at the moment. Could one man run an airline and win an ITV station? Green did not think so, but then he and Branson were not exactly two peas in a pod. Just look at how he handled the media.

4

'Richard and I have always cherished a desire to work together.'

David Frost

Richard Branson, entrepreneur, balloonist and all-round good sport, sat awkwardly in his three-tone jumper, squirming slightly under the television lights. A tall, genial man with a soft voice and hesitant public manner, he was trying to remember why he had said 'yes' to doing this interview. Half an hour into a gentle grilling by Mary Goldring, the eminent and clearly well-researched journalist, Branson was feeling the heat.

The reason he was on, he knew, was to boost his airline. He had embarked on a determined lobby to break British Airways' stranglehold on landing and take-off slots at Heathrow airport. Because of limited capacity, only those airlines which had been using Heathrow before 1977 were allowed in. That hamstrung new competition like the six-year-old Virgin Atlantic. Branson was doing what he was best at: raising publicity and pushing Virgin's interests simultaneously.

The problem was today, a Wednesday afternoon in early November, he had to be careful. The man he had entrusted with preparing Virgin's ITV franchise bid, Charles Levison, had begged him on the phone: 'Whatever you do, Richard, don't mention Westinghouse.' The giant American electrical company was close to signing a deal, agreeing to partner Virgin in its bid, but was insisting on total secrecy.

Branson knew that pulling in Westinghouse was the coup Virgin needed. It would be the first significant tranche of

American capital to be committed to the franchise process and would show that Virgin was now a serious player on the international stage. Westinghouse was a huge multinational, with interests in everything from defence to electricals and media. It was also highly sensitive to whom it operated with. Virgin's leftfield image and reputed love of publicity made it a potentially dangerous partner to fall into bed with.

The interview, recorded for Channel 4's *Answering Back* series, was due for transmission the following Sunday. It was halfway through when Goldring, looking resilient in a deep blue suit, started probing Branson's media ambitions. Her tortuous, clipped diction, reminiscent of a pre-war elocution lesson, cloaked a sharply critical mind.

'*Neow* the airline is the first *rarely* successful venture you have had outside music. You have fidgeted and *pleyed* around in a lot of other areas. You have a whole portfolio of what I *theenk* merchant bankers describe as the walking dead, you have had some expensive failures – magazines, films – you have had a bit of an interest in European television. And *neow* there is talk that you are getting interested in one of the new British ITV franchises. There is also talk you might be bidding for Mr Rupert Murdoch's *Today* newspaper. *Neow* which of all these rumours do I take *seeriously*?'

Branson, hands clasped in front of him, laughed nervously and defended his record. He spoke precisely, pausing occasionally for thought, giving a soft 'erm' between phrases, but never floundering. He was back on solid ground by the time he started describing his love of start-ups and aversion to takeovers. Goldring pressed on relentless.

'So what about starting *orf* with a fresh ITV franchise?'

'We might apply for a franchise and if we did win it, we would run it fairly differently from how the current ITV franchises are run.' He described how it would have a small staff and commission most of its programmes out-of-house, like Channel 4. The targets could be any of the major stations. 'We are keeping our powder dry.'

'Back of the envelope *celculations* suggest that it might cost as much as £1 million to prepare a bid, *eeynd* the franchises are going to go at a very high price, the Government's tax take is going to be high, advertising does not *reely* encourage a gamble, so is this the time to have second thoughts about it?'

Branson looked defiant. 'Well, I am not a gambler. Erm . . .'

'You give an extremely good impression of one.'

'Well, I would never go near a casino, I can assure you. I am a great believer in protecting the downside, and for instance with the airline I did a deal with Boeing where we could hand the plane back at the end of the first, second or third year if my vision did not work out. The downside was protected. With our franchise application we are bringing in an American partner who will fund the application. They have the advantage of tying up with Virgin and using our expertise. If it doesn't work out they are willing to suffer the financial consequences of that. Any move we do we protect the downside.'

'So does the law allow a foreign partner?'

'Up to an extent. You can have at least 20 per cent foreign partner,' said Branson, trying to remember the ownership stipulations.

'So who is your foreign partner. Disney?'

'It has not been announced yet but it looks likely to be a company called Westinghouse who are a large cable operation in America.' If there was any recognition that he should not have said it, it did not show.

Some hours later, when the film crew had left the office at his home in London's Holland Park, Branson rang Levison in New York. 'Charles, look, I'm sorry, I mentioned the word Westinghouse.'

Levison groaned. He was experiencing first-hand just how sensitive the Americans were. 'Don't worry. Tell me what you said and I will smooth it over.'

Branson was used to flying by the seat of his pants. It had already made him a fortune; he was, by 1990, one of Britain's richest and best-known entrepreneurs. Along the way he had piled into (and out of) different businesses with the same determined, boyish enthusiasm that typified all his ventures.

His life story was already the stuff of business legend. Born into a family of lawyers in the Home Counties, he walked out of Stowe aged seventeen to launch a national magazine for students. The magazine became a mail-order venture, the mail-order venture became a record company, the record company led to adventures in retailing, publishing, broadcasting and air travel.

Underpinning it all was Branson's ability for ruthless negotiation. Ask him to lend you a fiver, it was said, and he would negotiate you down to £4.50. By the time Virgin started thinking about an ITV bid, it was a billion-pound empire that had already been on and off the Stock Exchange and was always looking for new areas of expansion.

What made Branson special, however, was his mutual love affair with the media, and through them, the great British public. Journalists and punters alike were captivated by the image of the rock-and-roll capitalist – despite his wealth, Branson never wore a tie, never lost his love of adventure and fun. He hated stuffiness. That streak of eccentricity, combined with his approachability, which he admitted was devised simply to gain publicity for his airline, always made good copy. Branson would discuss questions that most multimillionaires spent a lot of money avoiding.

The business press was less certain. Branson would constantly pay lip-service to strategic considerations like synergy – Virgin was all about entertainment, he would tell bemused critics looking for the links between records and planes. Privately, his Virgin colleagues, many of whom had been with him since the beginning in the late 1960s, acknowledged that the empire was not about entertainment at all, but about people. 'Richard backs people. That is how Virgin works.'

There were doubts, which always exasperated Branson, over the strength of Virgin's bottom line. Since Branson's abortive fling with the stock market – he took Virgin public in 1987 and bought it back in 1989 – few in the City were certain just how financially healthy the group was. Branson had put a lot of money into launching Virgin Atlantic against the advice of his closest colleagues. By 1990 he had started bringing Japanese money into the group: media giant Fujisankei paid £150m for

25 per cent of Virgin Music in 1988. Later the leisure chain Siebu Saison took 10 per cent of Virgin's Voyager Travel Holdings.

Few were surprised that Branson had gone to the Japanese for investment. He was a popular figure in Tokyo, and his clear dissatisfaction with the British financial establishment – he hated the short-termism of the City and its inability to understand creative businesses – had started to rebound on him. Many in the City believed Branson was 'flakey': he did not operate 'by the rules', and hence any kind of liaison with him or his business would always be jeopardised by his rapacious desire to shoot off to the press. In short, Virgin was as leaky as a sieve. You dealt with the organisation at your peril.

It may not have been a fair appraisal, but by 1990 Branson had made some powerful enemies. His activities in the airline sector, railing against the dominance of BA, and in particular the political clout of its chairman Lord King, had started to make waves. The seventy-two-year-old BA boss was one of the most powerful figures in British business. Not only was he a director of Daily Telegraph newspapers, but an essential contact for the handful of City editors that moulded British business opinion. He was also one of the biggest clients of Britain's largest advertising agency, Saatchi & Saatchi. Both the Saatchi brothers disliked Branson. These were not people that any businessman would wish to have ranged against them.

Branson had dealt with Michael Green before, too. Both had bid for Britain's first direct broadcast by satellite licence. Virgin was in a consortium of Pearson, Granada, Amstrad and Anglia. Carlton had linked up with Saatchi's and London Weekend. Realising that both were front-runners for the licence, Virgin had attempted to pull Carlton into its group.

Just days before the IBA began questioning the consortia, Green had met up with Branson's brother-in-law, Robert Devereux, who ran Virgin's publishing business. Green's insistence on control meant that a deal was unworkable. Later, when Virgin's consortium had won and launched British Satellite Broadcasting, Green had marked it down as one of his greatest errors, even though the award nearly bankrupted the companies involved.

Typically, Branson had pulled Virgin out of BSB just in time, shrewdly selling its stake on to Alan Bond, the Australian entrepreneur, at £1 million profit. It summed up Virgin's track record in broadcasting: strong on winning licences but remarkable more for what it had pulled out of than what it held on to. By 1990 original stakes in BSB, and radio stations Mercury and Piccadilly, had been sold. Only stakes in Superchannel, another satellite TV operation, and Kiss, the London radio station, remained.

But bidding for an ITV franchise made sense for Branson. The Virgin group had its own studios and facilities arm, Virgin Communications, which already claimed to be the biggest seller of music programming in the world through its Music Box subsidiary. It wanted to expand into drama, light entertainment and youth programming. It needed an assured broadcasting outlet.

It had already come closer than many realised in 1990. Branson had spent weeks early on in the year working on preparations for a secret takeover bid of TVS. He had even lined up Michael Grade to head the station and flown to Paris at Easter to convince TVS's two French shareholders, Canal Plus and Générale des Eaux, to back his bid. Ironically they demurred, saying they were happy with TVS's management. It was a decision they would later regret.

Branson knew the bid would have been welcomed by TVS employees. He had close links with the company. His balloon trip across the Atlantic had been the subject of a TVS documentary and he had made a number of appearances (rather aptly, some would say) on Motormouth, its high-rating children's show. Staff had repeatedly moaned to him about the way the company was managed, in particular the ineptness of some of the senior executives. He had heard the same sort of thing from employees of other companies, but he knew that many ITV stations were being profligately run.

He did not make his move, however, until after a row with the TVS management over its failure to get the ballooning documentary on to the network. Branson was furious, and told colleagues TVS management had behaved appallingly over their promises, for which Peter Williams, the station's head of documentaries, had apologised. If James Gatward, TVS's founder and chief executive, could not run it properly, he would run it himself. Gatward, who knew nothing of the plans, simply thought Branson's ego was piqued.

The company was already in Virgin's sights for the franchise round. A year earlier Branson had appointed Charles Levison, a former entertainment lawyer and record company boss who had worked with him in the 1970s, to draw up plans for an ITV bid. He wrote two briefing papers in November and December of that year identifying the London, TVS and Anglia regions as Virgin's prime targets, with Central and TSW as possibilities.

But in the end the takeover had not fallen into place. It would have cost too much and many in Virgin were opposed to the scheme. Takeovers were not Virgin's style – they usually led to redundancies, which was bad PR – and buying into an ITV station just before a franchise round was madness. Getting the right calibre of management was not easy either.

Branson had three meetings with Grade, chief executive of Channel 4, in the spring of 1990. Grade knew Branson well, and sat on the board of Virgin's Healthcare Foundation. Branson had discussed the possibility of either a takeover of TVS or a greenfield bid for an ITV franchise. Would Grade like to head them up?

At the final meeting, over breakfast in Branson's Holland Park mansion, Grade had said no. 'It didn't feel right,' he told friends afterwards. Branson told colleagues Grade's salary demands, made through his lawyers, were too high. They had asked for a £250,000 signing-on fee and £250,000-a-year salary minimum. Branson had decided he could do without superstar executives.

With TVS off the agenda, Levison and Robert Devereux set about scouring the world for suitable partners to help Virgin tackle the franchise round. The meetings read like a *Who's Who* of media moguldom: Havas and Hachette in France, Berlusconi in Italy, Bertelsmann in Germany, Fuji in Japan, ABC, NBC, CBS and the Tribune group in America. Just in case anyone might be missing, they press-released their intention to bid as well.

56

By the autumn they were beginning to get somewhere. Levison had lined up a prospective chief executive, Jeremy Fox, a British producer who had recently returned from America, and a prospective partner, Westinghouse.

The company, best known for its electronics interests, had a fast-growing broadcasting arm. It already ran five TV stations, a larger number of radio outfits and successful programme syndication business, but it had done nothing outside of North America.

A joint venture with Virgin to bid for one or more ITV licences looked an attractive proposition. Levison had proposed a 51–49 per cent split, leaving Virgin with the majority stake but allowing Westinghouse the maximum investment possible (the ITC guidelines on ownership stipulated that non-EC companies should not have control). Bid costs were estimated at around £2 million, total investment in the new company at around £30 million each. Everything looked on course for a satisfactory conclusion – then came the Goldring interview.

That November in New York Levison was finding Westinghouse tough work. They had been in talks off and on for the best part of a year. In that time the Americans had made it clear how uneasy they were dealing with Virgin and how little they knew about the Virgin management. They had insisted on total secrecy, not easy in a world as promiscuous and gossipy as television, but Virgin had kept their word. No hint of the talks had leaked out yet. They were days away from signing heads of agreement on the new company. Then the anxiety would be over.

All this was nothing new to Levison. He was a confident man by nature. A square-jawed, self-assured lawyer, he had developed a reputation within Virgin as a Mr Fix-it who had handled a few of Virgin's trickier start-ups. He had also negotiated Branson out of some of his nastier situations.

He and Branson went back a long way. It was widely believed that Levison had drafted the contract that made Branson his first million – the one that Mike Oldfield, a scruffy nineteen-year-old with an unpromising tape of instrumental music, had eagerly signed in 1972. The tape became Tubular Bells, one of the biggest-selling records of the 1970s. The contract, which Branson had adapted from Levison's draft, locked Oldfield into a ten-album, 5 per cent royalty deal with Virgin – slim pickings for the musician when most new artists could expect 8–10 per cent. Branson also acted as his manager. Oldfield, who still made millions out of the deal, spent most of the late 1970s and early 1980s trying to get out of it.

Levison went on to help Branson sell Virgin's artists round the world. His experience was vital. He had done stints on both sides of the Atlantic, starting at solicitors Harbottle and Lewis, before working in New York and the Bahamas for Chris Blackwell's Island record label. He was as happy partying with machete-wielding reggae stars like Peter Tosh, as he was discussing contracts and salaries in multinational boardrooms. He worked for others, but kept coming back to Virgin.

The morning after the warning call from Branson, Levison entered Westinghouse Broadcasting's Sixth Avenue offices still in good heart. At least they could be warned about the programme. He wished he had not nagged Branson about keeping Westinghouse secret. His anxiety over it all had probably contributed to the slip-up.

Levison put it straight to the Westinghouse team. Branson was going to mention Westinghouse's involvement in talks with Virgin at the weekend. It would be in the papers – as they knew, anything Branson does is news. He was sorry, but it was one of those things. Their reaction was that it was a shame, but not important. Levison flew back to London confident he had rescued the deal.

Levison had not taken Westinghouse's demand for secrecy lightly. Branson and Devereux aside, few at Virgin realised just who he was talking to in New York. The first Jeremy Fox heard of the talks was when he idly turned on his TV that Sunday and caught Branson mid-broadcast. He was astonished. He was Virgin's prospective chief executive and he knew nothing about the deal. Anyway, Westinghouse was a bizarre partner for an organisation like Virgin.

Fox knew America well. The forty-year-old son of Sir Paul Fox, former boss of Yorkshire TV and the BBC, he had run a small production company in Los Angeles, Mac III, backed by Scottish TV. He had returned to Britain that summer looking to head up a possible franchise bid. Levison, who had tracked him since the beginning of the year, snapped him up on a three-month consultancy agreement with a view to him heading the Virgin bid. By November, Fox had already started to put an executive team together for bids in either the TVS or Thames regions.

He knew the Virgin way of doing things. He had worked with the company before. In 1986 he had helped assemble programming proposals for Virgin and Granada when the British Satellite Broadcasting consortium was being put together. He liked the way Virgin put faith in individuals and dispensed with clear lines of command. He also knew that Branson and Devereux valued him highly. Many at Virgin believed his programming presentations were a key reason for BSB's success in getting the licence.

He also had good contacts among production independents. Before going to America, he had sold his own production company, Action Time, to Michael Green in 1987 in an earn-out deal that had locked him into the firm for a limited period afterwards. It was well known he had fallen out with Carlton over the earn-out payments, though he never blamed Green personally, just his over-zealous finance department.

He often told the story of how he had met Green at the lifts in Carlton's offices one day, and joked: 'I'm going to sue you if you don't get those payments right.' Green laughed uneasily, saying: 'I don't think that is a good idea, do you?' Fox agreed. As he saw it, it was a staff problem. Green's obsession with the bottom line often led some of the Carlton team to overstep the mark. They were just trying to impress the boss.

It was another world from Virgin. But for all Green's idiosyncrasies, he got things done. That November, Fox was not even sure Virgin would get the money together for an ITV bid, let alone get the application in. Branson was too busy running his airline to take a personal interest and had now told Levison to report to Devereux. For all their dancing round speaking to prospective partners there was precious little to show for it. If Westinghouse was Virgin's best bet, it could have problems.

The day after the interview was broadcast, Fox met Levison in Virgin Broadcasting's newly painted offices behind Notting Hill. Fox ribbed him: 'Westinghouse build nuclear reactors, don't they Charles? Weren't they involved with Three Mile Island?' Levison's face fell. Fox was even more surprised. It was as if no one at Virgin had realised.

By Christmas Fox's relations with the Virgin team were beginning to become strained. Levison knew Fox's salary demands to head up a Virgin-run ITV station were not acceptable to Branson. The Virgin boss would not pay £200,000 salary packages, even if TV executives in America earned over $500,000. Fox was also sceptical about Virgin's chances of pulling off the Westinghouse deal.

Fox returned to Los Angeles over Christmas to think things over. He had offers from other prospective ITV bidders – maybe now was the time to cut his losses and break with Virgin. He came back in January to do another week's work in Notting Hill before jetting to America again. There, by chance, he bumped into Westinghouse production chief Dirk Zimmerman, who seemed unenthusiastic about a Virgin deal. Realising a lot of the Virgin entourage were in town to welcome Branson after another of his ballooning escapades, this time across the Pacific, he organised a meeting with Devereux. Enough was enough, he thought.

They met for lunch at the Four Seasons hotel in Beverley Hills: Fox, Devereux, Devereux's wife Vanessa and Branson's other sister Lindi. It was not hard to spot the tourists, thought Fox. They were the only ones eating outside. Sipping Perrier, they small-talked about Las Vegas, where the Devereux had just visited. Fox loved the place. Devereux hated it. Eventually Fox turned the conversation to the ITV plans.

'Look, Robert, it's not working out, is it?' He was surprised by Devereux's cool reaction. 'No, I suppose it isn't.'

'We're never going to sort out who is doing what on this bid and I'm not even sure you are going to do it at all,' said Fox.

'OK then,' said Devereux.

'Well,' continued Fox, 'why don't we just forget it?'

'Fine,' said Devereux. Fox was taken aback. There was no argument. Devereux, who had long before decided that Fox was too expensive, was clearly happy to see him go.

The next day Fox's lawyer contacted Virgin to request a cheque for Fox's services. Virgin paid generously and in full. When Fox talked to Levison he thought he sounded rather confused about it all.

Back in London Devereux was still sure Westinghouse could be hauled in. He was not the only one interested in their response. He had already had an approach from Central, who were keen to take a 20 per cent stake in a Virgin bid against TVS, but had asked Devereux to keep their involvement secret. Devereux knew he was on dangerous ground with the ITV company as they did not want Michael Green, who sat on the Central board and was also likely to bid against TVS, to find out until the last moment. The whole process was in danger of becoming hopelessly Machiavellian.

By late January Westinghouse had indicated to Levison that it might have a problem with the deal. Unbeknown to Levison, as he had jetted out of New York for London in November, a fax had winged its way in the opposite direction. It was a copy of the report in *The Times* of Branson's Goldring interview. Three sentences had been marked out for Westinghouse's senior management to read: 'Westinghouse is to fund the application for the franchise. "If it doesn't work out they are willing to suffer the financial consequences," Mr Branson said. "I am not a gambler." ' The unfortunate juxtaposition of quote and (inaccurate) precis had infuriated the Americans.

Devereux sat in his west London office trying to sort through the mess with Kevin Betts, Central's finance director, who was handling the secret talks with Virgin. Fox had joked about Westinghouse: 'It thinks it is indecisive, but it is not sure.' They determined to find out once and for all. Betts, a bluff Northerner who had been holding his own talks with the American multinational, rang Dirk Zimmerman on Devereux's phone. 'We've got the heads of agreement drawn up, Dirk. Are you ready to sign?' Zimmerman's reply left him exasperated. *Maybe*.

The talks between Virgin and Central spluttered on, but Devereux and Levison knew they now faced not one but two major problems. They had no main partner and no chief executive. Then Levison made a suggestion.

The Rib Room of the Carlton Tower hotel off London's Sloane Street is rarely full on a Sunday night. However, on the last Sunday that January, anyone venturing in for a meal might have got a surprise. Around one table, set for four, all the other tables had been cleared.

The restaurant's customers later that evening, a sprinkling of winter tourists and well-heeled locals, would have been hard-pushed to put names to three of the faces seated around the table so discreetly segregated from the rest. The fourth, belonging to a medium-height, sandy-haired man who puffed incessantly on huge cigars and was clearly a regular, was somewhat easier to place. After thirty years of broadcasting in Britain and America, David Frost needed no introduction.

The others – Charles Levison, Robert Devereux and Frost's business partner and old friend Michael Rosenberg – were all listening as Frost, one of the media's great raconteurs, spoke animatedly. Round and around the cigar hand waved as he illustrated his stories; time and again he leaned forward, chin out, eyes wide to emphasise a point, in almost a parody of the manner he had made so familiar in all those years of broadcasting.

Levison and Devereux were entranced. There was little about television that Frost did not know. More importantly, few had a track record like his in putting together successful ITV franchise applications: he had co-founded LWT in 1968 and TV-am in 1980. He had already spent the best part of a year preparing his bid for 1991.

There was no doubt, thought Devereux, that working with Frost would be fun, if nothing else. He had seen it all. The son of a Methodist minister, Frost had been catapulted to fame in 1962 as the fresh-faced presenter of the satirical TV show *That Was*

The Week That Was. He had been a household name ever since. His big-name interviews – prime ministers, presidents, royalty – attracted large audiences on both sides of the Atlantic. He was the master of just about any television format. He was also an old hand at ITV politics.

Of course, both LWT and TV-am had been beset by problems early on. In each case Frost had been hard pushed to meet the initial promises, and rows, resignations and rating collapses had followed. But Frosty, as he was known, was always a great survivor, helped by his immense charm and all-round niceness.

Even those who fell out with him acknowledged his endurability. One anecdote summed it up. When TV-am's all-star team of founding presenters split up, leaving only Frost behind, he sent a pot plant to Anna Ford by way of consolation. Furious, she hurled it against her garden wall, shattering the pot. She told friends that weeks later she found the plant had taken root where it fell – typical, she thought.

Frost hated being disliked. He always tried hard to please – a result, said some, of his Methodist upbringing. He was still a director of TV-am and presented their high profile Sunday morning show. But everyone knew that Frosty was always hungry for more.

With Rosenberg as a co-director, he ran his own group of companies from a small suite of offices high above a mews in London's Camden. The David Paradine group (so-called after his Christian names) produced corporate videos, training programmes and Frost's jaunts into jocular down-market entertainment – shows like *Through The Keyhole*, where contestants have to identify celebrities by the contents of their houses, and the *Spectacular World of Guinness Records*, which chronicled brave and bizarre attempts at world records. (Frost always had an eye for the main chance: he shrewdly bought the television rights to the world's biggest-selling copyright book in 1973.)

But his main strength was that he knew everyone. While TV-am may have been kept outside the main coterie of ITV bosses, Frost, aided by a near-photographic memory for names and faces, was an assiduous socialiser. Thirty years at the top – his *Who's Who* entry is three times the length of most others –

gave him an address book second to none. He numbered James Hanson, Evelyn de Rothschild, James Goldsmith and Paul Hamlyn, four of Britain's richest tycoons, as his personal friends. Most of the great and the good had passed through his shows and he kept in touch. Raising cash to make an ITV bid was unlikely to trouble him.

Levison had known for months that Frost was planning to bid. He had sat near Frost at a small dinner party given by Terence Donovan, the photographer, in his Notting Hill home the previous summer. Virgin had already made public its intention to bid. Frost had quizzed Levison on Virgin's plans and at the end of the evening said: 'We ought to get together to discuss this ITV thing.'

The next month Frost's office rang Levison to suggest breakfast at the Carlton Tower, just a short walk from Frost's Belgravia home. He agreed, keen to find out what Frost was up to. It was a guarded affair. Virgin had already started talks with Westinghouse, which Levison knew he had to keep secret. But he was intrigued to hear that Frost had already raised money in America and was now looking for British partners. They agreed to meet again.

By the end of November, breakfast with Frosty had become a monthly event in Levison's diary. Both had found out that they were keen on the same ITV regions, London and the south, and shared similar ideas on who the key production companies were to have on board. It was a civilised way of keeping tabs on the opposition. But Virgin did not need Frost. In the end they agreed to part, acknowledging that they would have to compete.

By the end of January they were back together again. Virgin, still hoping to clinch the Westinghouse talks, were focusing on a bid against TVS, believing that Carlton would be too tough to beat in the battle for the London weekday licence held by Thames. Then Levison got a call from Charles Armitage, joint managing director of Noel Gay Television, the production independent which made *Red Dwarf* and *Juke Box Jury* for the BBC.

Armitage, like Levison, had spent his early years in the music business. He came to the point quickly. There was another strong bid being put together for London weekday besides Carlton. They had already approached Noel Gay for a deal. 'If you got together with them, Charles, you could beat Carlton. You should talk to them. Are you interested?' Levison said yes.

Minutes later the phone rang again. It was Frost. 'I'm the mystery man Charles was referring to,' he said. They agreed to meet for breakfast again, this time at the Halcyon Hotel. As Levison listened to Frost outlining how far he had got, he realised the Frost bid now had to be taken very seriously.

As Levison had suspected, Frost had sorted out his financing early on, raising cash from Herb Siegal, the multimillionaire head of BHC, America's ninth-largest broadcasting organisation, and forming a joint venture with Charterhouse Bank the summer before. Victor Blank, Charterhouse chairman and a well-known city figure, was another of Frost's legion of personal friends. But Frost had a further ace up his sleeve. He had signed John Gau, ex-deputy chief executive of BSB, to head the bid.

Gau was quite a catch for Frost. One of the few executives to escape the BSB debacle with his reputation relatively untarnished, he had just the right pedigree to reassure the authorities. Eighteen years at the BBC, during which he rose to become head of current affairs, ten years running his own company John Gau Productions, which had an exemplary track record in producing factual programmes, one-time head of the Independent Producers Association and a former chairman of the Royal Television Society – few doubted he had the experience or wherewithal to run a major ITV station. When Michael Grade had been appointed chief executive of Channel 4, he had remarked that the only other man with the know-how to do it was Gau. (Ironically, he was never in the running as he sat on Channel 4's board.)

When BSB announced its merger with Rupert Murdoch's Sky in November 1990, and Sky's management took over, Gau had been the one senior BSB executive they had wanted to stay on. He was not interested. He went back to the JGP offices in Putney and waited for the phone to ring. He knew that with the

ITV franchise bids only six months away he would not be short of offers.

Virgin had put out feelers to Gau in January when Fox had walked. By then it was too late. But Levison did not know who he had signed up with. The prospect of joining up with Frost began to look very attractive indeed. But he had to meet Devereux before a decision could be made. Inevitably Frost suggested the Carlton Tower. (Aside from liking the food, Frost had a sentimental attachment to the hotel; he had rehearsed his successful breakfast television bid there eleven years before.)

Devereux and Levison were late that evening. Devereux, unused to Sunday night business meetings, had mistimed the drive in from the country. Frost was unperturbed, exhorting them to try the fried potato skins, his favourite, and ordering the wine. For three hours they talked. By 11.30 they had the basis for a deal. They would draw up heads of agreement for a joint venture the next week. There would be room for Central, with a 20 per cent stake, and Westinghouse, if it changed its mind. It looked a good mix.

Only one thing bothered Devereux: Frost's insistence that they prepare bids for not two but *three* regions – Thames, TVS and Anglia. Multiple bidding was allowed, he argued, you simply had to specify your preferences if you won. The bulk of the work for each region – projecting the finances, suggesting the programming contribution to the network – was the same. So why not? *It seemed like a lot of work*, thought Devereux.

Michael Green knew about it the moment Victor Blank started trying to raise money for the venture in the City. No franchise targets were specified, but he had heard the gossip among the production independents that Frost had approached: a bid against LWT, which Frost had co-founded, was out, but a bid against Thames, as well as at least one other, was in. Few deals had been done yet, though. Green took comfort from the fact that if they were going to bid for more than one licence, they were leaving it very late indeed.

Their clear intention to bid against Thames, however, was a blow. That January many had believed, correctly, that Virgin was focusing increasingly on the TVS area. Green had met with Devereux twice the previous autumn to discuss the possibility of bidding together. Ironically it had not been his suggestion, but that of a banker, Ian Richardson at Crédit Suisse, hoping to earn some commission by bringing them together. Both Devereux and Green knew there was little likelihood of a joint venture, but there was always the possibility of gleaning information.

It was *déjà vu* for both of them. Sitting in Green's office off Hanover Square they joked about Carlton's mistake in not linking up with Virgin over DBS, and agreed there could be a basis for working together this time around.

Another meeting was fixed up. It petered out when they both acknowledged that arguments over control were always going to make any joint venture an unrealistic proposition. Green, as always, wanted a clear majority stake; Virgin wanted at least 50 per cent to make it a worthwhile investment. Much as he liked Green on a personal level, Devereux thought he was too autocratic. He had long decided he would not want to put Virgin money into a Carlton venture unless some degree of control came with it. Green for his part knew all too well the misgivings of his friends the Saatchis and others in the City about Virgin. But there was never any harm in talking.

By January Green's own plans were falling into place too. After much nagging to make up his mind, he had finally committed Carlton to preparing two bids, first for Thames, then for TVS. At a noon meeting in his office on the first Tuesday of December, he had told Charles Denton, the lanky, greying boss of Zenith, of his decision.

Denton, a former Central programme director and a widely respected figure in the industry, was disappointed; he had hoped Green would concentrate on London alone. As he saw it, Thames was an exhausted company and if Carlton got the bid right, it would easily win the licence. TVS, he thought, was a tougher nut to crack. Its past financial incompetence and rich advertising area would attract powerful rivals, and its local programming, likely to be a crucial factor in the franchise round, was of a very high standard.

He knew, however, that once Green had made up his mind, it was best not to argue. He agreed to supervise the preparation of the London bid. Green had taken on Brian Wenham, the former BBC2 controller, to organise the bid against TVS. The more he thought about it, the more Denton assumed it was a diversion. Bidding against TVS ensured that powerful rivals like Hollick and Branson would think twice before coming in and bidding against Carlton for the London weekday licence as well. With Carlton up against them, they would want to concentrate on getting their first choice application exactly right.

Green's next problem was who would run Carlton TV if it was successful in winning an application. Denton had assumed that Michael Grade, best man at Green's recent wedding and a good friend of the Carlton boss, had already agreed to head the bid. But at a meeting with Green in December, Grade, his lawyer as ever at his side, had thrashed out a pay package reputed in the industry to be worth £500,000 a year plus a £1 million signing-on fee, and then turned the job down.

His decision not to join Carlton surprised many. The move had been widely speculated upon in the press. Grade informed colleagues that his first loyalty was to Channel 4. Friends told a different story. Grade had canvassed a number of his closest advisers, among them Bill Cotton, the former managing director of BBC TV, as to whether he should take it. They had said 'don't do it'. It was known that Bob Phillis, who was leaving his job as managing director of Carlton that month, had resented Green's inability to fully delegate authority. The same would happen to Grade. They were better off remaining friends.

Grade had a suggestion, though. Perhaps he should look for someone outside the television establishment, and if so, what about Nigel Walmsley, chief executive of Capital Radio? Walmsley, whose wife Jane ran her own independent production company, was well known on the London media circuit, and widely admired for the way he had built Capital into Britain's biggest commercial radio station. The son of a Manchester schoolteacher, he had worked in the civil service, and the Post Office, rising to be director of marketing, before joining Capital. For Green, he had exactly the right mix of creativity and management skills.

Walmsley was easily hooked. After an hour-long meeting in Green's office, where he confessed he had been too busy running Capital to take much notice of the ITV auction, he said yes. Then Walmsley had to break the news to Capital's chairman, Sir Richard Attenborough. Ironically Attenborough was also chairman of Channel 4, and was just congratulating himself on keeping Michael Grade out of Green's clutches.

At Zenith's head office off Baker Street, Denton and his team began the New Year working round the clock to prepare Carlton's London bid. On 3 January they assembled at the Portman Hotel for a one-day meeting to discuss strategy. There was, Denton realised, even more work to do than he had thought. The exact wording of the 'invitation to apply for channel 3 licences' had yet to be announced by the Independent Television Commission, but it was likely to be a 100-page document. The sheer weight of number-crunching necessary was awesome. And they would have to do it twice.

If only Michael had stopped fluffing around over what he wanted to do a lot earlier, he thought, *there would not be this mad panic now.* Green, however, was adamant: it had to be two applications. He wanted London but, like everyone else in the industry, he thought TVS was a sitting duck. After all, it appeared to be imploding of its own accord.

5

'You are living high on the hog, James.'

Rudolph Agnew to James Gatward

The first Rudolph Agnew heard of TVS was a phone call from Schroder's Gerry Grimstone that December. Agnew, hair swept back, Gitane in hand, was in his sitting room in Belgravia one evening when the call came through. They knew each other well – theirs was a friendship forged under fire. Grimstone had helped Agnew through one of the City's bitterest takeover battles, fighting off Minorco's bid for Consolidated Gold Fields, the giant mining group. Grimstone, a former civil servant who had pioneered some of the government's early privatisations before jumping ship for Schroder's bank, was judged one of the City's most effective wheeler-dealers. He came to the point quickly.

He was acting for a company called TVS. It had a split board which needed either a new chairman or chief executive, two directors had just resigned, its French shareholders wanted to do something about it, and Schroder's had been given the task of finding someone suitable. Its founder and current chief James Gatward was out of control. Was he interested in the chairman's job?

Agnew was startled. He was a mining man; he knew next to nothing about TV, less about Gatward. And he already had a good bunch of directorships under his belt – this one hardly looked an attractive addition. But he and Grimstone went back a long way, and Grimstone was nothing if not persuasive. After twenty minutes, he agreed to meet the French shareholders the next week.

Five days later Agnew met Etienne Mallet, director of Compagnie Générale des Eaux, the French media conglomerate which owned 10 per cent of TVS, in a conference room next to Grimstone's office at Schroder's headquarters in Cheapside. Mallet said little, leaving it to Grimstone to outline the difficulties TVS was in.

He ran through the scenario in detail. The ITV company itself was well run. The problem was MTM, an American production company which TVS had bought three years earlier. It had slid into the red. The French shareholders had lost faith in the promises made by Gatward about its performance, therefore unless there was a change they would have to consider their position. It was never said, but the implication was that they would withdraw their support from the company.

In addition, Gatward was running it all like a personal fiefdom, spending large sums on frequent first-class trips to Hollywood and terrorising his executives. Such behaviour could happen at any company, but because it was an ITV company it made it worse. The franchise application had to be completed in less than six months and Gatward had hardly got it organised. Disaster loomed. As far as Schroder's were concerned, their first loyalty lay with the shareholders and the non-executive directors. Something had to be done.

Agnew's eyes widened as he listened to it all. Grimstone was not one to exaggerate. He saw the French investors' dilemma. Two TVS directors – John Elton, who Agnew knew as a former Consgold director, and Baroness Sharples, chairman of the local charitable trust that TVS had set up – had resigned because of Gatward's behaviour; with them, the French had lost their two main independent supporters on the board. The executive directors, as is often the case in boardroom battles, were sitting on the fence.

In short, both the board and the company were in danger of falling apart. The French shareholders' only hope was that a new chairman might bring Gatward to heel. Lord Boston, the current chairman and a close friend of Gatward's, was prepared to resign. There was little doubt that Gatward would try and put his own man in. They wanted to have a more suitable candidate ready. The key word, as Agnew later discovered, was 'suitable'.

TVS had spelt trouble for ITV right from day one. Founded in 1980 by Gatward, a director/producer best known for his work on series like *The Troubleshooters* and *Elephant Boy*, it had been one of a number of strong consortia to bid against Southern TV in that year's franchise round. But no one thought it stood much chance. The *Investor's Chronicle* described Gatward as an 'also-ran'. Southern, after all, had done nothing wrong and had a good programme service.

Gatward, a short, ambitious man, had first raised the idea with friends on the 6.45 to Tunbridge Wells. A bunch of them, all in TV and commuting from the south, liked to hang out in the bar on the train, unwinding over a couple of Scotches. The idea of a bid against Southern had moved gradually from fantasy to reality. The £50,000 Gatward needed to put it together had been raised by a friend, Stephan Redfarn, a merchant banker who worked in the corporate finance department of Ansbachers. With a mix of enthusiasm, persuasiveness and charm Gatward pulled together an ambitious young team. All they needed to win, they reckoned, was a little luck to go their way.

On the day the franchise result was announced a group of them – Gatward, Terry Boston (a former broadcaster and Labour Lord), Bob Southgate (ex-ITN and Thames), Martin Jackson (ex-*Daily Mail*) and Tony Brook (formerly the IBA's director of internal finance) – were sitting in the Bunch of Grapes in Knightsbridge waiting for the IBA's decision.

The franchise process required that the senior executives be on call for interview. When the authority sent for Gatward and Boston the others knew they had a chance, but were not hopeful. The best they thought they might get was a 'forced marriage' with either Southern or another consortium headed by Charterhouse Bank. That sort of thing had happened in the last franchise round; it was more than likely to happen again, they reasoned.

They had moved on to a Chinese restaurant when Gatward

and Boston returned. Gatward was grinning from ear to ear. 'It's amazing,' he said. 'We've got the fucking lot!'

Southern were flabbergasted. Lady Plowden, the IBA's chairman, told David Wilson, Southern's chairman, that his company had not failed, but was a 'victim of the system'. TVS's programme plans and its shareholding structure were simply more attractive. Personalities were also a factor. Like Lew Grade of ATV and Peter Cadbury of Westward, another loser in 1980, Wilson, an aggressive, ebullient manager, was seen as a buccaneering survivor from ITV's entrepreneurial era, less suited to the more stable 1980s. Gatward's team-spirited approach had won the day.

The tremors that followed the decision ran from Knightsbridge to Whitehall. Politicians, civil servants, broadcasters, journalists: everyone wanted to know one thing – why? Wilson's response was withering. 'We cannot believe,' he wrote, 'that a decision of such importance affecting the lives and futures of hundreds of people can have been taken purely on assumptions that a new group of people looked as though they might provide a better service, as against a company whose regional performance is acknowledged across the network as second to none . . . This can be no proper way to conduct affairs of this importance – it surely defies every concept of natural justice.'

It was a tough legacy for TVS to inherit, but Gatward was nothing if not confident. The station may have had a lot riding on its success – certainly as far as the IBA was concerned – but no one could deny that Gatward had grafted a talented team together to launch TVS. Boston had been a minister of state at the Home Office, Brook knew the IBA inside out. Michael Blakstad, a former BBC producer and director, was programme controller; Anna Home, senior BBC children's producer, was designated head of children's programmes (a fact that is believed to have swayed Plowden, who had a special interest in education). As other broadcasters acknowledged, it was a quality act. Gatward, a producer with a good track record himself, had only one problem: getting them all to perform together.

The first sign that all might not be as promised came even before TVS started broadcasting. From the start, those involved had decided that if it won, TVS would be different. There would be less hierarchy, more involvement of the programme-makers in the day-to-day running of the business. In a symbolic gesture, the core founding group of fourteen would all drive the same cars and have the same perks. There would be less 'us and them'. But when the company cars arrived, Gatward got a Daimler Sovereign, the other executives got a Rover. *It wasn't supposed to be like this*, they argued. Clearly, as one of them pointed out sombrely, some are going to be more equal than others at TVS.

The company forged ahead, building studios in Southampton and Maidstone, and (like all ITV companies) opting for some well-appointed offices in central London as well. Yet one by one the senior executives drifted away. By the end of 1984, Gatward had lost Blakstad and Southgate. As the disgruntled executives found other jobs round the network so the rumours about Gatward's behaviour spread.

Anyone who had met him knew already of his charm and conviction. Soon he was tagged with a different reputation – that of being a difficult man to work with, and for. The more successful the company became, the more insecure he appeared.

Many put it down to his background. TVS started on the cusp of the Thatcher revolution. The great and good still controlled British broadcasting. While many of his peers were still predominantly middle class, Oxbridge educated, Gatward (Walthamstow and South West Essex technical college) was rather different. His application for a place on a BBC training course had been turned down because he was not a graduate. That hurt. So he worked his way up outside the system, directing in Canada, working for production independents in Britain. Those who worked with him then described him as a 'driven spirit'.

By the time he had run TVS for a few years, he was still in his forties, married to an equally ambitious actress, Isobel Black, and already paying himself one of the biggest salaries in ITV. He listed yachting and farming as his recreations in *Who's Who*. To his colleagues he seemed perpetually anxious that someone else was going to take it all away. He demanded the utmost loyalty from his executives, but rarely took them into his confidence. Often he appeared convinced that they were plotting against him. By the end of the 1980s, of course, they were.

Above all Gatward was ambitious. As money poured into the affluent south-east in the mid-1980s, TVS grew in size and profitability. Chock-a-block full of wealthy upper and middle class viewers, the 'ABC1s' most sought after by advertisers, its ad revenue spiralled. It was not that it attracted a particularly high proportion of viewers – in fact most preferred the BBC in the south-east. But that did not matter. In the twist that was antagonising advertisers all over Britain, the fewer viewers a station had, the more that had to be spent to reach a fixed number of consumers. TVS profits surged forward, jumping from £4.5 million in 1983 to £26m in 1988. The question for Gatward was: what should TVS do with all that money?

It could not spend it within ITV. The established system of network arrangements, whereby the Big Five – Thames, LWT, Central, Granada and Yorkshire – made most of the programming that was seen nationwide at prime-time, specifically excluded ambitious upstarts like TVS. Any ITV company outside the Big Five that wanted to sell programming the other way had to persuade the big companies to let them in. This, of course, was never in their interests.

To Gatward, the system, which went back to ITV's launch in 1955, was an obvious stitch-up. By the mid-1980s TVS had outstripped Yorkshire in share of network ad revenue and was catching up fast with Granada. He went on the offensive, complaining to the newspapers and the trade press, lobbying the Home Office, and making himself thoroughly unpopular with his fellow ITV bosses.

They pointed out that TVS's programme-making record was poor anyway. In 1986, in a mid-term review of performance, the IBA had judged the company still had 'some way to go before reaching its full potential and fulfilling the high expectations which accompanies the award of its contract'. Clearly the bureaucrats in Knightsbridge were getting edgy, thought Gatward. In the end he just decided to go his own way.

Like other ITV bosses, he had been casting envious eyes overseas for some time. There was a worldwide market for English-language programming. As Gatward told his board: to succeed long-term, TVS had to expand beyond its ITV franchise, and if you were thinking of expanding, America had to be the target. But you could not just make American-style programming in Britain. To be a force in America, you had to produce over there.

Gatward had worked in North America in the early 1960s, before he had joined the BBC. He liked the American way of doing business. And by 1988 he had a company in mind to buy: MTM. The studio, named after its founder Mary Tyler Moore, had already co-produced two joint ventures with TVS. It had an admirable programme-making history of its own, with *Hill Street Blues*, *Lou Grant*, *Bob Newhart* and *St Elsewhere* to its credit. The only problem was its price: with the American media market booming, it would cost a lot – $320m. But it was already turning over close to $200m in revenue and nearly $50m in profit. And Wall Street had recently valued it at $500m. Gatward never flinched.

The TVS board waved it through, even though the company's attempts at diversification had previously been fairly disastrous. (There was the corporate video subsidiary, Blackrod, which was sold to the Chrysalis group with losses of £500,000; the Bristol-based satellite-dish manufacturer, Alba, sold prior to the launch of Sky TV with losses of £480,000; the £5.7 million stake in Superchannel which went nowhere.) But this was on a different scale. Gatward was at his most persuasive.

He did everything correctly. A team from Peat Marwick, the top accountant, spent three months in Hollywood going through the books. Another team from Merril Lynch separately valued MTM's film library ($310m). He brought in two new investors, Canal Plus, the French media company, and Générale des Eaux, a massive French utility with media interests, to stump up extra cash and Chemical Bank, one of America's biggest banks, to underwrite the deal. He tied in the local management to run it, paying the founders partly in TVS shares.

Gatward returned to England to soak up the praise. It was the biggest takeover in British television history, a ground-breaking deal which established TVS as a transatlantic player on a programme-making scale far greater than any of its rivals. He split up the company, making TVS TV a subsidiary of TVS Entertainment, now a multinational media company. It meant that TVS was no longer dependent on its ITV franchise for success, making it a much better investment. Its share price looked strong. Gatward looked unassailable. He took on a corporate PR man and a corporate development director. TVS was going places. Then the American programme market collapsed.

The company had budgeted a massive $90m of profit in its first year of TVS ownership. Gatward knew things were going wrong when its sales director started down-rating its likely domestic syndication revenue from $90m to $60m in 1988. Gatward went over to Hollywood in August and sacked the sales director. Things went from bad to worse. By September 1989 Gatward was issuing a profits warning to the City, cutting its predicted profits by a third from £35 million to £11.25 million. In five minutes TVS shares lost a third of their value on the London Stock Exchange.

MTM was locked into a horrendous loss-making spiral. All of its shows were made on a deficit finance basis, pre-sold to one of the major US network companies for only a proportion of the total production costs. The balance was then recovered through foreign sales and syndication deals to the 1300 regional TV stations dotted round America. The cycle takes five years. But when the syndication fees started to dry up, the losses slowly worked their way through the system. More and more money had to be borrowed.

In December 1989 Gatward flew over to take charge himself, pushing out MTM co-founder and chief executive Arthur Price, a popular Hollywood figure. Price waived his $4 million compensation for loss of contract. He just wanted to be 'out of there'. The MTM board notes recorded that Gatward 'graciously accepted the position of chairman of MTM'. Gatward, now doing two jobs, increased his own salary commensurately.

All this time his relationship with the press, the City and his fellow ITV bosses had been deteriorating sharply. He spurned the ITVA line and ran his own lobby against Thatcher's broadcasting legislation, despite the fact that he had been instrumental in encouraging the Home Office to look more closely at the ITV system.

A series of national press ads, featuring a stripping housewife, warned viewers what to expect if TV was totally deregulated. They caused a furore. Timothy Renton, the broadcasting minister, castigated Gatward personally on television over the ads. Those kind of programmes would never be shown here, he argued. On the same programme Andrew Neil, editor of the *Sunday Times* and later executive chairman of Murdoch's Sky Channel, backed Renton up.

Meetings with City analysts became stormy affairs. They had watched aghast as TVS's share price plummeted – many had recommended the stock to favoured clients. Gatward, increasingly on the defensive, was rattled. He knew that people thought he had a lavish lifestyle – the houses in the New Forest and Provence, the monthly Concorde trips to America, the cars, the box at the opera – but hell, he reasoned, he had a transatlantic business to sort out. He was running a major American TV studio. His family could not stay in a motel when he was there.

He knew where a lot of the rumours came from. A lot of the other bosses were just jealous. *Private Eye*, which had already nicknamed him 'wee Jimmy', joined the hunt, questioning the price of the MTM deal, the executive salaries (MTM co-founder Mel Blumenthal was earning $770,000, Price slightly less), and Gatward's own perks.

When Gatward doubled his own salary to £250,000 it went to town. 'Doubtless some irate investors will want to know why, in the face of massive losses, Jimmy has awarded himself a 100 per cent-plus pay rise. They might also like to ask why he has a five-year rolling contract. Only a cynic would suggest that the pay hike would double the cost of his removal.'

The criticism culminated in January 1990 in a long profile by

Eye journalist Dominic Prince in a dummy issue of the soon-to-be-launched *Independent on Sunday*. Gatward sued, making legal history. It was the first time any publication had been sued before it had even appeared.

Gatward spent more and more time on Concorde. By 1990 he was dividing each month, two weeks in Los Angeles, two weeks in London. He told the TVS board he could not hire a replacement for Price. No high-calibre executive wanted to take on a job which entailed slimming down a company, rather than growing it. He had to do it himself.

A slew of MTM's established writers were dropped. The company had made its name with one-hour series. Now Gatward pushed it into writing more half-hour series. Commissions from the major networks dwindled. New series after new series was cancelled after just one run.

Gatward decided he had to bring new money in. He toured all the major American studios with the offer of a stake. He wanted $160m for 50 per cent, valuing the company at the same price he had bought it for in the boom years. There were no takers. MTM continued to haemorrhage cash out of the TVS bottom line and costs in both companies continued to spiral. An internal report in 1990 concluded that travel and entertainment costs for the British TV arm alone were eating up close to £600,000, including £25,000 on 'flat' (Gatward's apartment in Piccadilly) and £13,000 on 'suits'.

Throughout it all Gatward received full backing from Boston, his chairman. The French investors, who between them held 20 per cent of TVS, appeared to be in shock. For a long while they did nothing. Both their representatives on the TVS board, Pierre Lescure, chief executive of Canal Plus, and Etienne Mallet, chief executive of La Générale d'Images, Générale des Eaux's media subsidiary, were former journalists and spoke uneven English. The joke inside TVS was that they did not understand half of what was going on.

It was not until the summer of 1990 that Gatward had his first private meeting with Michael Green. The Carlton boss had suggested it, just a get-to-know-you session, nothing else. They had met socially before – Green had become quite a feature on the broadcasting social circuit now. No one was ever quite sure about him, of course, mused Gatward, but that might be no bad thing. It was partly because a lot of ITV bosses thought he was still close to Thatcher. What did they know? They weren't sure about him either.

TVS's flat at the Albany in Piccadilly, one of London's most exclusive addresses – no pets, no children – was the perfect venue. Both Gatward and Green were too well known to ship up at each other's offices. Never mind journalists finding out, their own staff were bad enough. Takeover fever would break out. Gatward did not want a Thames-style rebellion from his staff just because they thought, misguidedly, that Green was moving in. So a discreet breakfast was set up. They met and talked over coffee. Nothing came of it.

The next time Gatward saw Green was in the autumn of 1990. Gatward had rung Carlton's Hanover Square headquarters to suggest another meeting. Ironically Green was in Los Angeles at the time. But he always checked his office calls when away on business. Intrigued to hear Gatward's name on the list, he had rung him straight back. It was 2 a.m. Los Angeles time.

Gatward had come to the point quickly: was he interested in buying an 80 per cent stake in TVS TV, the subsidiary that ran the ITV franchise? Green paused. When they had met at the Albany Green had suggested that Carlton might be interested in a controlling stake, say 51 per cent. He was just testing the ground but Gatward rejected any link-up out of hand. Green had made it plain that, if that was the case, he was likely to bid against TVS in the franchise round. Gatward had shrugged.

Now he was waiting for a response. Green was non- committal. 'Let's talk about it when I get back.' Green rarely said no to a meeting, especially with a potential rival in the franchise game. He put the phone down wondering what Gatward was up to.

When they met it became clear: Gatward wanted shot of TVS TV so he could concentrate on MTM, and he needed the money to pay down the debt incurred on buying the American studio. Green wanted an ITV station, and the Government had sanctioned takeovers up until the franchise bid period. It seemed obvious.

What Gatward did not tell Green was that once he had persuaded Carlton to buy 80 per cent of TVS TV, he would then have used the rest of his company to bid against Thames for the even more lucrative London weekday region. To Gatward, it was an ingenious plan, snatching victory from the jaws of defeat. Everyone believed Thames was vulnerable. Equally most knew that Green was preparing his own bid against Thames. But with Government restrictions on how many ITV companies you could control – only one major and one minor, any more and you were restricted to 20 per cent stakes – Green would be out of the running if he bought TVS's British subsidiary. Like many of Gatward's plans, no one at TVS knew anything about it.

Throughout September and October Gatward and his finance director Richard Adams held meetings with Green and two of his Carlton co-directors. To Green, the figures looked worrying. At the third meeting he said: 'Before we go any further I have to know if your shareholders are with you on this.'

Green met with Lescure and Mallet; they were keen but there was one obstacle – what would be left for the French if Carlton took four-fifths of TVS TV? Just 20 per cent of a company with MTM as its main asset and 4 per cent of an ITV station which had no guarantee of retaining its franchise. And the ITV station was the only part of the TVS empire that had ever been consistently profitable. The talks broke down, just as the press was getting the first whiff of an imminent deal. The French went gunning for Gatward instead.

Gatward had known the French were getting uneasy when, earlier in the year, they had suddenly turned up in his Buckingham Gate office suggesting he get a new chairman. Lescure and Mallet clearly felt embarrassed about making the point. Both were short, well-dressed men. Lescure had been a famous journalist before running Canal Plus. He was a well-known face in France, not least because he lived with Catherine Deneuve, the actress. For all his celebrity he regularly deferred to Mallet, whose company owned a large stake in Canal Plus.

Gatward, characteristically, had always presumed that neither knew much about running a TV business in a long-term, competitive marketplace. Canal Plus, he reasoned, had made buckets of cash because there was so little else worth watching in France and, of course, its regular showings of pornographic movies always helped the ratings. As for Générale des Eaux, it was just another of life's cash-rich utilities, always looking for something to diversify into. Water was clearly a good business to be in.

But he understood why both men were edgy. The TVS share price had fallen from close to £3 when they had come in to below £1. He guessed they wanted to put their own man in on top of him. How had Arnold Weinstock, the famous GEC boss, put it? Once a chief executive shows signs of behaving like Napoleon, a good chairman should shoot him. No thank you, thought Gatward. He listened politely and said he would think about it. He promptly signed Terry Boston on to a new five-year contract.

Lescure and Mallet, under pressure from their boards in France, started turning up at TVS with their own advisers and finance men. They signed on Salomon Brothers, the American merchant bank, who through its contacts with Green tried to resurrect the Carlton deal. Again it fell through. Salomon Brothers left the scene. Then TVS's financial adviser, Schroder's, decided to take action of its own.

The next time the French turned up to face Gatward they were better prepared. In Boston's fifth-floor office in London's Buckingham Gate, only hours before a main board meeting on 15 November, they declared that they had changed their mind. 'Boston should stay but you must go,' said Mallet.

'Why?' said Gatward sharply. Because we don't agree with you over the performance of MTM, argued the French. Gatward held his ground, but guessed the French would never have taken this course of action without advice. Half an hour later, when the full board was assembled, Gatward made a short speech. 'In view of what has occurred prior to this board meeting I want to know where I stand. I will withdraw and you can discuss the company's strategy.'

He waited downstairs in his office, opposite Boston's, for an hour. When he was summoned upstairs, it was to be told the board was backing him with a unanimous vote of confidence. The French could not persuade the large block of executive directors on the board to vote against Gatward. Reluctantly, for the sake of unity, they had voted with the majority. But something had to be done about MTM. It had to be sold.

Gatward opened talks with Disney, the American media giant, about buying the MTM network programming and the studio lot, conveniently close to Disney's own in Los Angeles. TVS would keep the programme library.

At a second board meeting towards the end of November Gatward put forward four strategy options for the company. One was for the French to put in more money. Two of the non-executive directors, Pam Sharples and John Elton, resigned, saying Gatward was making a hash of everything, particularly his handling of the French.

Gatward pleaded innocence, pointing out that he had been to Paris only the week before to talk it over with Lescure and Mallet's bosses. He had expected Elton to go anyway; he had been feuding with the Beaulieu-based businessman for months.

But his relations with both the French and Schroder's had reached rock bottom. He suspected that Schroder's were helping the French lobby his own executive team: Tony Brook, the managing director, Clive Jones, deputy programming director, and Alan Boyd, programming director, were all now receiving regular visits from Schroder's director Gerry Grimstone. By a quirk of fate TVS's London offices were split in two, half at 84 Buckingham Gate, the other half at 60 Buckingham Gate. Gatward sat in 84 all December, wondering what his executives in 60 were up to.

That was when Grimstone took the French aside and suggested Rudolph Agnew.

Agnew liked a fight. His handling of Consgold's defence in 1988 gripped the City. Agnew was pitted against Minorco's Sir Michael Edwardes, the diminutive former British Leyland boss.

Agnew pulled out all the stops: he took every opportunity to personalise the battle; he hired Kroll, the corporate private investigators, to dig into the personal affairs of the Minorco directors; he disparaged Edwardes at press conferences. All the time he held a wavering board together behind him.

Edwardes was shaken by the vitriol. 'I've been involved in three major public company battles,' he said later. 'BTR for Dunlop, STC for ICL, and Minorco for Consgold. The other two were conducted in a rather more civilised way.'

No one doubted that behind Agnew's almost languid drawl and patrician charm lay a ruthless streak as wide as his ready smile. It came with the background. His father ran an ore mine for Consgold in western Australia, his grandfather was chairman of the group in the 1930s. Raised in Ireland and educated at Downside, the Roman Catholic boarding school, Agnew spent four years with the Irish Hussars before following the family line.

It was a tough, compassionless world. Consgold ran the most profitable gold mines in South Africa, relying on cheap migrant workers and a political system that ensured black labour costs were kept low. Agnew worked his way up from trainee to chief executive, spending time in South Africa along the way. He became chief executive in 1978, at the age of forty-four. Throughout he defended the company's record against the anti-apartheid protestors who would habitually turn up at its AGMs. Later, sensing a change in the political wind, Agnew forged new links with the anti-apartheid movement to help prevent the Minorco takeover.

Consgold was eventually sold to Hanson for £3.5 billion and Agnew was paid off. By 1990 he cut a rather glamorous figure in the City. His track record as an unorthodox corporate warrior had already brought him several lucrative directorships; at board meetings he would chain-smoke Gitanes, sipping Diet Coke – his doctor had told him he had to give up either the drink or the cigarettes. He chose the drink. In Grimstone's eyes, when it came to dealing with difficult boards and pig-headed executives, Agnew was top of the list. When Agnew agreed, in secret, to allow his name to be put forward to the TVS board, Grimstone was delighted.

On Friday 21 December TVS held another board meeting. It was a cold, grey day. Outside the Buckingham Gate offices secretaries and civil servants bustled round Victoria, finishing off their last-minute Christmas shopping. Inside, Gatward's head was on the block.

The meeting was scheduled to start at 9 a.m. Ostensibly it was to update the board on how negotiations were going with Disney. Again the French turned up early, this time in Richard Adams' office. Adams, the boyish-looking finance director, was leading the negotiations with Disney. They quizzed him as to how it was going, then told him they wanted Gatward out. Adams said they should speak to Gatward himself.

He phoned him. 'I think you should come down, James.' When Gatward came in they came straight to the point. 'We think you should go,' said Mallet. 'Fine,' said Gatward. 'I have a contract, I hope it will be honoured. We can discuss it upstairs at the board meeting.' He knew the French had still to carry the board with them. And a board that had given him a vote of confidence only a month ago would find it hard to push him out now.

Upstairs in the boardroom Lescure and Mallet played their final card. If Gatward did not go, they would. Gatward had half expected it, but was still stunned. As far as he was concerned TVS was a company with a trading difficulty, certainly, but it still had an excellent chance of winning back its TV franchise. If two major shareholders withdrew at this stage, however, it was a different matter. And what would they get for their stake?

The debate raged all day. Gatward talked them through one option after another. The French seemed uncertain as to what they should commit themselves to if they got their way. They were adamant on one thing: Gatward must be off the board. Schroder's and Kleinwort Benson, TVS's brokers, who were also attending, put their weight behind the French. 'If you don't step down, we're going too,' said Grimstone.

Boston then revealed what the French already knew: that he would go as well. Gatward was caught off guard. He thought the French had told him earlier that Boston, the man who had stood by him since the beginning, was staying. He shrugged it off. They could never make up their minds. Boston looked completely at sea. 'Do I have to clear my office immediately?' he asked pitifully. 'You are not going to change the locks or anything are you?'

At 6 p.m. they called an adjournment, so the non-executive directors could consider a new chairman. It was agreed they needed someone with powerful City connections. Gatward put forward a proposal of his own, Robert Clark, the former Hill Samuel chief executive, and one-time chairman of the National Film Finance Corporation. He was vetoed.

The boardroom was on the sixth floor. Gatward went back to his office on the fifth. An hour later Guy Libby, the deputy chairman, and Kenneth Fleet, the former City journalist and another non-executive director, sought him out with a deal. He could no longer head the holding company, but he could stay as executive chairman of TVS TV, concentrate on retaining the franchise and work with the new chairman.

Gatward asked for time. He rang his wife Isabel. He talked to Boston. 'Why should I take this, Terry? Haven't I had my head bashed enough?' Boston pointed out that the franchise was what he started with and he should do it for the workers.

Gatward went back upstairs with his answer. *'Fine I will do it, but I want my autonomy, the same salary package, the same contract and compensation for loss of office.'* He had them in a corner. Most had backed him when Sharples and Elton had said 'there has to be a change, or we go'. They had gone. The directors that were left agreed to his demands.

They then discussed the new chairman. It was the first Gatward had heard of Rudolph Agnew.

Grimstone rang Agnew at nine o'clock that night. The board had adjourned again before voting on the chairmanship. Could he come round and talk? It was only a three-minute drive.

The lights were still burning bright in 84 Buckingham Gate when he arrived. He was ushered into Boston's fifth-floor office where Grimstone introduced him to Libby and Fleet. They offered him the job of chairman. Agnew thought briefly and replied: 'If this is what you really want, I'll take it on.'

They went over the problems again and checked how much time Agnew could devote to the company. They also asked if he would wait and meet Gatward, and give him 'a fair trial'.

The board reconvened. Agnew, left alone in Boston's office, put his feet up and snoozed. At 10.30 they were out. Gatward came in with Grimstone and Fleet. Rising from the soft leather armchair in the corner of Boston's office, Agnew stuck out a hand. 'Nice to meet you,' he said, in his habitual drawl. He lit up a Gitane. No one had told him Gatward was a fervent anti-smoker.

Gatward returned a pinched smile. It was the end of one particular phase, they agreed, now they should put their shoulders to the wheel and get on with the next one. Gatward painstakingly ran through the details of the deal he had struck upstairs. Agnew smiled and nodded. He pointed out that it was the responsibility of the chairman to hire and fire the chief executive. Only later did he realise the importance of what Gatward had been saying: he had in effect been laying down the demarcation lines. *He ran TVS TV*, not Agnew.

It must have been, Agnew reasoned, his way of coping with the humiliation. He could tell the critics he was still running the core of the business. He was like a man who had been pushed off the cliff, but kept scrabbling at fingerholds. He never gave up.

Agnew started at TVS on 3 January, taking over Boston's office on the fifth floor of 84 Buckingham Gate. Within days he was in culture shock. Television, he swiftly realised, was a world away from his old background. The sheer number of detailed executive contracts astonished him: timed contracts, retention contracts, win contracts; basically anything an executive could negotiate. In the world of multinational mining, senior executives had short, simple contracts to protect them if they were fired – that was all.

Gatward, in the office opposite, swiftly made it plain that he wanted a free hand. Within a month he had presented Agnew with his plans for restructuring the senior executive team at the

TV arm. Brook, the managing director, and Boyd, the programming director, had to go. There was no point in them staying now he could give his full attention to the station. He had already told the ITC of his intention at a lunch with David Glencross, the regulatory body's chief executive, on 16 January.

Agnew was perplexed. He knew that half the board mistrusted Gatward. Now here he was proposing that the next two down the line should be got rid of. Doing that would just create a dictatorship within the TV company and make Gatward still less accountable.

He stalled for time, saying he would have to ask advice on it. He told Gatward to consider very carefully if that was really what he wanted to do.

Later Gatward came back and said he wanted to discuss his remuneration. 'I thought that had been sorted out?' said Agnew.

'Yes, but I think I should get some sort of consideration for working on the franchise application,' replied Gatward.

'A win bonus?' said Agnew.

'And something if we lose as well,' said Gatward. 'It's a lot of extra work.'

Agnew was amazed. He was further astonished when he asked how much. Gatward wanted over a million pounds for winning and over half a million for losing. In the few weeks he had been chairman he had already heard a lot of Gatward's reputation as a high liver, but he had put it down to jealousy and exaggeration.

Now he was not so sure. Here was a man who was already earning £250,000, effectively £50,000–£100,000 more than his peers, and who had recently been demoted, yet he was still asking for more. There was no acknowledgement as to what a cripplingly bad investment MTM had been. Momentarily Agnew was stumped for words.

Finally he said: 'It would appear to me that you view your salary as an attendance fee, James.' Gatward shrugged. Agnew concluded they were clearly not speaking the same language. Worse than that, he decided Gatward's judgement was warped.

Gatward, for his part, did not believe his demands were unreasonable. Other ITV bosses had already negotiated lucrative 'golden handcuffs' in the form of win bonuses and share options to keep them loyal. But he sensed the growing antagonism. He knew Agnew wanted to bring Elton and Sharples back onto the TVS Entertainment board, and had already commissioned a report from SPA, the management consultancy, into the structure of the TVS group.

He was also convinced that Schroder's was still working to get him out. Another director had passed on a remark allegedly made by Grimstone to Agnew: that he was sorry Brook did not have the backbone to see Gatward off.

On Wednesday 23 January Gatward flew back to America to sort out MTM. He had promised the board he would find a chief executive to run it, until then he had temporary governance of it. On the Friday Agnew started planning TVS's annual report, meeting with Fleet, Gerry Buckland, the corporate relations director Gatward had hired post-MTM, and Claire Enders, the group development controller he had also hired, a tall, fast-talking American.

'What's it to be?' quipped Enders. 'Another year of euphemisms for disaster? Or another glowing tribute from the chairman on the exemplary efforts of the chief executive?' Agnew quizzed her on her views about the company. Gatward later heard that Enders had been savagely critical of his management and the structure of the group. Agnew had listened attentively.

The next week Agnew made up his mind. Gatward's priorities were all wrong. He did not seem to realise the depth of the problems caused by MTM's losses and unless there was a solution to MTM they were not going to get their licence back.

As Agnew saw it, the priority had to be getting extra cash in; to get that it had to attract another major investor to back the franchise bid. That would be impossible if Gatward remained. Now was the time to act.

So while Gatward was away Agnew methodically contacted each director, either in person or by phone. He started with those he knew would back him – Lescure and Mallet – leaving those he thought still loyal to Gatward, like Fleet and Libby, till last. The approach was simple. 'I intend to ask James Gatward to leave. Of course, as we are dealing with a fellow director, you have as much say in this matter as I do. But that is my intention, subject to your views.'

The majority said, if that is what you want to do, do it. Agnew knew a newly appointed chairman giving a positive lead is rarely blocked. He said he would put Brook in Gatward's place. Only two directors demurred.

At 3 p.m. on Monday 11 February Gatward, back from America, had another meeting with Agnew to discuss his salary. When he crossed the corridor from his office he had no idea what awaited him. Agnew ushered him to the large leather sofa in the corner opposite the chairman's desk, then sat himself in the soft armchair adjacent to it. He looked Gatward in the eye.

'I'm afraid, James, that the board has lost confidence in you. I am going to have to ask you to leave.'

Gatward did not flinch. 'Why?'

Agnew's patience snapped. 'Because you are living high on the hog, James!'

Gatward's eyes widened. 'What do you mean?'

'You are greedy!'

'I'm sorry, I don't understand,' said Gatward.

'Well, your salary package, for a start . . .'

'But that had nothing to do with me, you know that was settled by the non-executives. Your man was part of that,' said Gatward, referring to Elton.

'But you accepted it, didn't you?'

'Is that a sin? To accept a salary that is offered to me? You know I'm working with the pensions manager to try and bring it down.'

'It's far too late. Look at the corporate structure: companies for production, for broadcasting . . . It is all costs.'

Gatward remembered hearing about Enders' criticisms. 'Did your informant tell you why we have two companies there? Of course you wouldn't know. You weren't there when we did it! It was to keep the unions in the production base so if there was ever another broadcasting union strike like 1979 we could keep bringing the programmes out. I'm not going to sit here and listen to this bullshit. If everyone wants me out . . .'

'If you go quietly,' said Agnew, 'we can sort something out. The point is the majority of the board believe you are inadequate, and the total body are supportive of you going. At that point in human affairs, you're gone.'

Gatward looked in shock. 'OK,' he said quickly. 'I'd better go and take advice.' He left the building and walked swiftly to his lawyers. Agnew lit up another Gitane. He thought Gatward handled himself rather well in the circumstances. Now all he had to do was get on with winning the licence. Him and a few hundred others . . .

'If Greg Dyke had just phoned and
offered us all a million pounds
to go away, we would have gone.'

Tom Guttridge

Nik Powell, leather jacket zipped up tight and mobile phone in
hand, loped swiftly down the busy Soho street, dodging the
strollers and dawdlers. Even on a cold December morning the
pavements were crowded: office workers out for a sandwich,
edit suite runners with their spools of film, businessmen in twos
and threes walking to lunch. Powell, a tall, moody man with
distinctive dark hair and moustache, was deep in thought.

It was only a short walk from his office round the corner to
Mentorn's, part of a nondescript block opposite the Celebrity
dry cleaner in Wardour Street. But there was enough time to
work out what he wanted to say. He had only met Tom
Guttridge, Mentorn's boss, a couple of times before, but Dick,
his brother, knew him well and spoke highly of him. And
Mentorn's reputation as a successful producer of arts and
entertainment programming was growing.

He had not told Guttridge what he wanted when he had
phoned earlier. He had just asked if he could pop round for a
chat and discuss a proposition. Guttridge's curiosity was roused.
Powell, a co-founder of Virgin and now boss of Palace, one of
Britain's biggest independent film companies, was virtually a
celebrity in Soho's tightly knit world of producers and facilities
chiefs. All he had to do was reel Guttridge in.

He turned through two sets of doors and gave his name to
Mentorn's receptionist. He noted the refurbished steel and grey

foyer, the designer sofa carved out of the boot of an old car. It exuded confidence. Guttridge, who everyone said ran a tight ship, was clearly doing well for himself.

Upstairs, of course, it was different; drab offices with desks and files crammed close together. He was shown to Mentorn's second-floor meeting room overlooking Wardour Street. A table with eight chairs filled the room, TV and video in one corner, awards and cover shots of Anneka Rice on the wall. He studied the pictures of Rice, star of a new Mentorn production. Guttridge entered, saying hello, and asking him what was up.

'This has got to be totally off-the-record,' said Powell quietly. Guttridge, a cautious, calculating man with steel-rimmed glasses and curly black hair, nodded. Powell continued: 'We are putting together a consortium to bid for an ITV station. So far there are three of us: Polygram, Palace and Working Title. We have an agreement. We want you to join us, equal partners.'

Guttridge sat surprised, thinking. He was flattered. One or two potential bidders had already sounded him out as a potential programme supplier for a future ITV station, but this was different. This was an actual stake in a potential broadcaster.

Powell produced a sheaf of papers, the agreement between Palace, Polygram and Working Title. They detailed how the costs and ownership of the new venture would be split three ways. 'What's the budget?' asked Guttridge. Close to a million pounds, replied Powell.

Guttridge weighed up the pros and cons. It would be priceless PR for Mentorn, giving it a political clout far above that of a simple programme-maker. It might even give him the upper hand in on-going contract negotiations with his ITV customers. He just was not sure. He tried to work out how much good PR you could buy for a company for a quarter of a million pounds.

Powell was on his mobile, talking to someone at Palace. The call finished, he returned to Guttridge and discussed his proposition. The venture would not necessarily harm Guttridge's relations with his ITV customers, said Powell. No decisions had been made yet on which region they would bid for, but it would be one of the large six. He explained why he thought Mentorn and Palace were a good mix. Again, they were interrupted as Powell's phone rang. Guttridge agreed to think the proposition over. He would meet the other partners later.

As Powell left, Guttridge noted he was still taking calls on the phone. A meeting with Powell may last an hour, he thought, but in that time you probably only get to talk to him for about ten minutes.

It had started with the launch of Channel 4. The policy of commissioning most of its programming out-of-house had blown like a breath of fresh air through the television market.

Suddenly little production companies had popped up all over London's West End, close to Channel 4's Charlotte Street head office. Some, as industry folklore would have it, were no bigger than 'a man, a telephone, a fax machine and an office in Soho'. Many failed to last longer than the first commission, but others leapt in to fill the gap.

The first wave were a breed apart from the television establishment. Self-styled as lean, mean and fast on their feet, the men and women who ran them were usually émigrés from the much loathed bureaucracy of major broadcasting organisations. They structured their companies differently. They put creativity first, and hired staff and facilities only when they needed them. Existence was hand to mouth but a good one.

They worked hard and played hard, paying themselves well when they could and filling the bars and restaurants of Soho in their leather jackets and baggy blue trousers, their mobile phones always close at hand. They blended seamlessly into the better-rewarded worlds of advertising and commercials. Profitability was low but, they assured themselves, vigour and vision were at an all-time high. Many inevitably went to the wall.

Those that survived developed a harder edge. They questioned Channel 4's predominance. For all the freedom it had given them, its method of commissioning never allowed them to consolidate their success. It would rarely award long-term commissions and it always paid on a cost-plus basis, a set margin above the cost of production.

This never accounted for the value of the programme to the

broadcaster in terms of ratings, and usually entailed the signing away of all rights. The result was that no production company ever got the chance to build up a programme library – a consistent source of income for the larger broadcasters. Without consistent income, no independent could achieve a large enough capital base to gain security. The cynical said this suited Channel 4 fine: while the production market was fragmented into hundred of tiny companies desperate for work at almost any price, costs were kept low.

While Channel 4 was the dominant source of commissions, there was little the independents could do. They had no muscle. There were too many companies and not enough work coming out of the obvious alternative sources, the BBC and ITV, which had their own studios and staff to keep busy.

So they lobbied, and first in Professor Peacock, chairman of the committee reporting on the financing of the BBC in 1986, and then in Margaret Thatcher, the Prime Minister, they found sympathetic listeners. They showed how commissioning out could bring costs down and make the television industry more efficient. It was not, after all, that different from councils putting their services out to tender. But broadcasters would never do it while they had a vested interest in using their own staff.

Thatcher's agreement to impose a 25 per cent quota on the BBC and ITV – a quarter of all the programmes made outside news had to be commissioned from independents – was a major victory for the Independent Programme Producers Association (IPPA). Combined with the franchise auction and the decision to launch a fifth, terrestrially broadcast channel, it opened up a host of opportunities for independents. It also left a number on the fringes worrying that they might miss the boat.

Nik Powell was one of them. He had come a long way since his Virgin days. A childhood friend of Richard Branson, he had been a 40 per cent stakeholder in the original Virgin empire, providing the pragmatic managerial skills to temper Branson's wilder enthusiasms. Powell's methodical mind earned him the reputation of Virgin's 'axeman'. If staff had to be laid off or costs cut, he organised it. If messes had to be cleared up, he did it. He was always arguing with Branson but they were close. Branson said it was like being a married couple, 'knowing you could shout at each other and it would not matter'.

Eventually, however, the two had split for good in 1981. Powell had had enough of Branson's boundless optimism, always trying to expand the company out of trouble. The final straw had been the £900,000 purchase of Heaven and the Roof Garden, two central London nightclubs, at a time when Powell was pressing for cutbacks. Over lunch in the Roof Garden he negotiated his way out, taking a million pounds, the Scala cinema and Virgin's video editing suites with him. At just over thirty, Powell was one of the richest young men in London.

Using the Scala cinema and the video interests as a base he went on to set up Palace Pictures. As if driven by a desire to emulate his former partner, he expanded it Virgin-style from a video store, to a video label, then a theatrical operation distributing art-house films like *Diva* and *Evil Dead*. By 1984 Palace had moved into production with Neil Jordan's second film, *Company of Wolves*. It went on to produce another fifteen feature films throughout the 1980s, including *Mona Lisa* and *Scandal*, at a time when British film production was dwindling away to an all-time low. To many in the tiny British film world, Powell was a hero.

But the critical acclaim masked the cracks in the Palace organisation. An internal report commissioned in 1989 showed it was involved in too many peripheral activities, so Powell started stripping down the company. But its real weakness was that it was not fully involved enough in TV production, an area experiencing rapid growth. Its only major production deal, with the Power Station channel of BSB, was falling apart because of the satellite station's losses. With the ITV franchise round imminent, Palace's commitment to the more glamorous but financially hazardous world of film meant that it was in danger of being left behind.

Methodical to the last, Powell commissioned another report from a consultant to investigate Palace's strategy alternatives for TV. In a terse twenty-page report, the consultant, John Howkins, had recommended that Palace coordinate its own bid for an ITV station. Thus, if successful, it would gain a measure of control which it could use to expand its TV production arm.

But it needed a major partner, preferably a multinational, to stump up cash and engender confidence in the bid. Powell immediately thought of Polygram, the $3 billion music giant that he had frequently done deals with in the past.

He had put the proposition to Michael Kuhn, boss of Polygram's video, film and TV arm, during the MIPCOM programme sales event in Cannes during the autumn of 1990. Sitting in an empty exhibitor's stand he had summarised for Kuhn how an outsider's bid for ITV fitted in with the spirit of Thatcher's broadcasting legislation, offering more efficient and imaginative programme-making and, through a competitive bid, a better return for the taxpayer.

The advantage was it could be a 'cheap and cheerful bid', based round independents and staffed by young, enthusiastic programme-makers unsullied by years at the helm in ITV. Kuhn, who had known Powell since his Virgin Music days, was hooked. Polygram was feeling bullish, having just bought Island and A&M, two smaller music companies, and Kuhn was looking for investment opportunities in media. It had already taken a stake in Working Title, a film company which had recently moved into TV drama production. They would be natural partners in the bid. Now all that was needed was a major TV production independent to complete the team.

Powell had immediately thought of Guttridge, his brother's friend. A former BBC news trainee, he was reputed to be one of the toughest and most inventive managers in independent production. He also had just the programming expertise that Palace and Working Title were lacking.

Since launching Mentorn in 1984 Guttridge had built it into a successful producer of entertainment and arts programming. Its first major success, *01 for London*, had been a fast-moving magazine programme, developed in conjunction with the listings weekly *Time Out*, which offered a what's-on guide to the capital. It was still running after five years, and Guttridge had smartly spun regional variants out to Central and Anglia, using locally shot inserts to add to his London material. Now he had another hit on his hands with *Challenge Anneka*, a vehicle for presenter Anneka Rice, on primetime BBC1.

That kind of track record commanded respect. Although still tiny compared to companies like Thames and Central, which had £300 million-plus turnovers, Mentorn (turnover close to £15 million) was growing fast and was consistently profitable. The problem was whether Guttridge, who many said was a difficult man to work with, could be persuaded to join them.

Guttridge knew he had to be careful. The next five years was likely to see a huge shakeout in the production market as larger companies started to swallow up the small. Already investment from larger holding companies such as Carlton, Virgin, The Guardian, Aegis and CLT, the Luxembourg-based media owner, was providing certain independents with a secure base for expansion. Others, like Mentorn, were relying on income from diversified interests. He could not afford to make the wrong decision. The prospect of the franchise round offered all of them the chance of cementing long-term relationships with broadcasters.

Not only would it increase demand for independently produced programming – because a number of the bidders planned to commission out most of their programming requirements – it also gave larger independents extraordinary leverage to negotiate exclusivity and output deals. All bidders needed to secure some supply of independently produced programmes, and all, if they could, wanted to corner the market in their region. That enabled them to lock out rival bidders.

The difficulty for the independents was which deal to accept. The deals negotiated could ensure a company's future for the best part of the decade – if it backed the right horse. But no independents wanted to commit themselves too soon, in case better offers came along. And each knew that the biggest gamble of all was equity participation in a bid: the financial upside was a stake in a profitable broadcaster for years to come. The downside was the limit it put on possible output with other bidders. It was a tough one to call.

Guttridge thought about it over Christmas. It all hung, as he saw it, on whom they bid against. Mentorn already produced series for Anglia, Central and Thames. Any suspicion that he was involved in a bid against them would lead to Mentorn's programmes being taken off-air and the contracts given to a competitor – he had no doubt about that. Even if he was involved in a winning consortium, he still had to get Mentorn through 1992 before the new stations started. *And if they lost?* He would end up with nothing.

Yet maybe he could turn it to Mentorn's advantage. A lot of stations would want to ensure that he was not involved in bids against them. The more he thought about it, the more he liked it. It was just a question of playing it right. By the New Year he had decided to tell Powell: yes.

Powell called the first strategy meeting for the bid on 28 December at Arthur Andersen's, the accountant he had taken on to advise on the bid. The Andersen offices were just off central London's Aldwych. Powell and Tony Kelly, the newly appointed chief executive at Palace, were there, as well as Andy Birchall, the former BSB film boss whom Powell had roped in to coordinate the bid. Andersen fielded three executives: Rob Matthews, head of its media division, Bernie Siegal and Simon Edwards.

Birchall had left BSB in early November when it had become clear that the merger with Sky was more like a takeover. A tall, soft-spoken vegetarian, who neither smoke nor drank, he had spent his early years as a journalist before becoming development manager for Pearson's cable TV interests, and later founding the cable TV movie channel Premiere. But he was best known in the London film world as the man who had spent hundreds of millions of pounds of BSB's money in a cripplingly expensive bidding war with Sky for Hollywood movies. Along the way he had also initiated a BSB film investment fund that had backed twelve British movies, including David Puttnam's *Memphis Belle*.

Post-BSB, he did not have to kick his heels for long. Asked by a small consultancy, Goodall Alexander O'Hare, to front and co-write a report on the forthcoming competitive tender – 'Channel 3 Franchises – A Practical Guide For Interested

Parties' – he had found himself sitting in Powell's Wardour Mews office trying to sell the research. After about an hour's conversation Powell had not only bought it but made an offer for the author as well.

The deal Birchall thrashed out with Powell installed him as 'project consultant'. After the wrangling and bitter recrimination that had followed the collapse of BSB, he was wary of being drawn into another large TV organisation. But this bid looked different. It was, as Powell described it, the 'independent's bid', offering something radically different to the old ITV way of running a station. Birchall was enthusiastic.

The mood at the meeting was buoyant. To kick off, Powell suggested they should set out the initial shape of a business plan. Just whom they might bid for, and the sort of programming they might offer, could wait till they had done more research. They all nodded.

The conventional way of writing a plan, noted Birchall, was to start with a list of objectives, even a grand vision, then work down to specifics. That was not Powell's style.

'Right,' he said, 'I want to settle the salaries of everyone now.' He began from the bottom up. The meeting quickly got bogged down as they spatted over how little a doorman could be paid. But they all conceded Powell's point. The staffing of the new station, if they won, was crucial, as the one advantage an outside bidder should have is the ability to operate the business on considerably lower staffing levels than any incumbent. It was important they got those numbers correct from the start.

The problem was none of them had run an ITV station before. They based their projections on the Power Station, the eighteen-hour daily rock and pop channel that Kelly had worked on, and which Palace had supplied with some sixty hours a week of programming.

No mention was made of the approach to Guttridge. It was only later that Birchall discovered he had been asked to join. It was a shrewd move, he thought, not so much because of the quality of Mentorn's programmes but the sheer quantity. Guttridge knew how to turn round a lot of programmes on a short time-scale. That would be an invaluable asset.

100

On 9 January, just days after Guttridge had finally said yes, the consortium decided to go public. At a hastily arranged 6 p.m. press conference in the Groucho Club, the members-only haunt of media and advertising executives, Powell, Kuhn, Bevan and Guttridge announced their intention to bid. The press pack consisted of one sheet of paper on the bid and ten plugging the companies and executives involved.

'This consortium represents the major independent bid for a TV franchise, and looks set to provide a wide variety of the highest quality original programming for the nineties,' read the release.

Most in the industry were sceptical, however. Birchall was already getting sympathetic calls from friends who could not believe he was trying to hold such a disparate and self-interested bunch together.

Those in ITV who had first-hand experience of Powell, Guttridge and Tim Bevan, boss of Working Title, were dismissive of his chances. They were all too egocentric to work together as a team, they said. *They may have been legends in Soho; to anyone else in the industry they were just 'baby monsters'.*

As soon as the announcement was made Guttridge contacted his major clients, Anglia, Central and Thames. His message was simple. Mentorn was bidding but meant them no ill will – provided, of course, it continued to have the relationship it had had in the past. Then he waited.

Anglia was the first to respond. It already knew it was facing a bid being put together by Patrick Cargill, chairman of East Anglian Radio, with backing from CLT. It also suspected, correctly, that Cargill had sounded out Guttridge early on about becoming a supplier for his bid. Anglia asked Guttridge what he wanted in return for an exclusivity deal. He spelt out his terms.

He wanted *Wide Angle*, the weekly arts programme Mentorn produced for the station, to move from a thirty-six-weeks-a-year run to a forty weeks-a-year run, and another series under development, *Up The Junction*, a live music show, to be confirmed. Anglia gave him a three-year contract for both.

Thames followed. It made a two-year offer covering *01 For*

London and a development deal, which guaranteed Mentorn money to develop a number of mutually agreed projects each year. Nearly all Mentorn's contracts until now had been one year long at most. This franchise business, Guttridge concluded, clearly has some attractive spin-offs.

Next he received a letter from Central's programme director Andy Allan. It said that Central was writing to all its independent suppliers asking them to confirm that they were happy working with the station. It hoped to use the responses in the bid.

Guttridge smiled. He decided he would not reply and see what happened next.

Birchall was already finding the coordination of the bid tough going. Meetings were split between Andersen's base in the West End and Polygram's head office in Berkeley Square. But getting everyone together in one place on a regular basis was proving unrealistic.

Kuhn was running a major division of a huge multinational, Powell was running several companies at once under the Palace umbrella, Guttridge was making programmes all over England, and Bevan was off producing feature films. So Birchall spent most of the time on the hoof, moving from one office to another, portable computer under one arm and piles of notes under the other.

It was a haphazard way to organise any project, let alone one as complex and demanding as the competitive tender being organised by the Independent Television Commission. But it was in keeping with the can-do attitude of most successful independents: you did not need a swanky office and expensive teams of people to get something off the ground. Just the right frame of mind. It also suited Birchall, who had always said he was not a natural 'team player'.

By February he had narrowed the consortium's potential targets down to three: Central, LWT and TVS. Granada and Yorkshire had been discounted as too far away, and Thames was never a runner because they all knew of Guttridge's close links to the station.

But they could not agree on which should be top priority. Birchall and Powell lobbied for Central. Birchall cited the research he had done for his Channel 3 Franchise report. That showed that Central was one of the most vulnerable major stations: it had more studio space than it needed, it was overstaffed and its programmes did not perform well on the network in comparison with other franchises.

On top of that, Birchall argued, the creative strengths of the consortium were better matched to deposing Central than they were to either TVS or LWT. Central was one of the main drama producers on the network. Drama was the one programming strand Palace and Working Title were strong on.

But whenever the subject of Central was raised Guttridge always argued against it. He wanted to go against TVS. The others were not sympathetic. They pointed out that none of them had any local knowledge of the region, and it would take an awful lot of research to put together a bid. Besides that, TVS was a mess when it came to the possible competition: they knew MAI were interested but the gossip on Branson and Green was that they were still undecided. All that interest meant that the cost of acquiring TVS was likely to be high. What they needed was a region where the only competition was the incumbent.

Birchall kept sifting through all the options. One of the advantages of having publicised their intention to bid so early was that others were now approaching them. It was not long before he got a call from Mark O'Hare, with whom he had worked on the Channel 3 report, who was now advising John Harris at the East Midland Electricity Board.

Harris had not got much further than he had at his initial lunch with Green the year before. As he had promised, he was keeping Green informed on the progress of his bid against Central (he told him he hoped to bring in Rolls Royce and Boots, both Nottingham-based, as investors). He had also managed to sign up a string of expensive consultants. But he was having great difficulty in adding programme expertise to his team.

O'Hare fixed up a meeting at the West End offices of Allen Brady Marsh, East Midlands' ad agency. Birchall was as surprised as Green when he found out that Harris had entrusted the coordination of the East Midlands bid to John Wood, the ABM director. But he was not going to let that prejudice him. East Midlands' financial clout was not to be sniffed at.

Birchall, Kuhn, Wood and O'Hare sat for the best part of an hour trading good intentions. It was, thought Birchall, the usual round-the-mulberry-bush job. Are you interested in coming in with East Midlands and bidding against Central? Yes, we are. Is there any possibility that we could work together? Very much so. Can you give us an answer now? We'll come back when we've thought about it.

Wood made it plain that, as Birchall had thought, East Midlands needed established producers to give their bid legitimacy. But why does it want to bid, asked Birchall? It was mainly a matter of image, said Wood. It was time to move East Midlands out of its moribund status as a regional electricity company. Birchall was sceptical. It hardly seemed a good reason for making a franchise bid. Even so, he left the meeting optimistic. East Midlands might make very suitable partners indeed.

The next Guttridge heard from Central was a phone call from Rod Hemmings, the station's director of legal and business affairs.

'You haven't replied to Andy's letter,' said Hemmings.

'Well?' said Guttridge.

'Do you have a problem?' asked Hemmings.

Guttridge pointed out that Central had been talking about renewing Mentorn's contract for *First Night*, its weekly what's-on slot, for some time, but nothing had been fixed yet.

'Come and see me,' said Hemmings.

'When?' said Guttridge.

Birchall was still pushing hard for the partners to make a decision when the Independent Television Commission finally announced the formal 'invitations to apply for a Channel 3 licence' in mid-February. It was a vast document, reading like some huge tax form endlessly referring the reader backwards and forwards to other sections. Analysing the requirements in the small print, Birchall was surprised. It was clear that the sheer volume of research that had to be done to back a bid gave the ITV incumbents a head start. They already knew cost figures like the price paid for network programmes and the cost of running ITV's administration. Outsiders did not. As bids had to be linked to a business plan showing you could afford what you were tendering, an inside track on such costs was essential.

For the first time, some of the partners became disheartened. Kuhn, a blunt man, told journalists that he thought the bidding process had become 'a compromise, a muddle and an old boys' network'. In short, 'a fix'. But they would bid anyway.

Other worries were also gnawing away at their planning. Powell's Palace empire was entering free-fall, as its film production failed to come up with another box-office success to match 1989's *Scandal*. Despite Powell's appointment of Tony Kelly as chief executive to sort out the day-to-day finances of the group, its banks were getting nervous.

If that was not enough, the continuing regulatory indecision over the status of independent producers was giving Guttridge second thoughts. Neither the government nor the ITC had made any ruling as to how much of a ITV stake an independent producer could have and still remain 'independent'. Guttridge, so adept at using his involvement in the bid to Mentorn's advantage, suddenly began to contemplate the downside. With quotas to be fulfilled, the independent tag was crucial to the work he was trying to get for Mentorn. Palace and Working Title might be able to survive on a stake in a station and work outside television, but Mentorn could not.

The view of the government, and of the council of the Independent Programme Producers Association, was that no independent should own any part of a broadcaster. If it did, it would gain an unfair advantage in competing for the commissions in the network. Nor should a broadcaster be able to have a stake in an independent.

Guttridge, who saw investment from a broadcaster as a natural option for Mentorn in the future, spent much of January and February trying to change his fellow independents' minds. He argued that, as the government had decreed that programming in the new look ITV would be commissioned by a central scheduler, the idea of anyone gaining such an advantage was ridiculous.

He had a powerful ally in Michael Green, who did not want to reduce his 51 per cent stake in Zenith, should Carlton win a franchise. Green sent Denton, the Zenith boss, to join Guttridge in lobbying the IPPA council and the Office of Fair Trading, which wanted to oversee any new network arrangements.

They argued for a 20 per cent ceiling to investment both ways. They got 15 per cent. With IPPA behind them, the government waved it through.

By March Birchall flew off to the biannual ITV sales conference in Monte Carlo confident that the bid was finally coming together. He had been invited to take part in a rostrum debate between greenfield bidders and ITV incumbents chaired by David Frost.

At the airport he discovered the organisers had only managed to unearth one other new bidder willing to take part, Alan Wright, a former Granada producer who was putting together a bid against Ulster. As a result, they had decided to mix the panel, putting Birchall and Wright next to Greg Dyke, LWT's bouncy, bristly chief executive, and Harry Turner, the cigar-smoking TSW boss known as one of the funniest speakers on the network. Birchall approached the debate with some apprehension.

Dyke and Turner, however, were all courtesy, even though Dyke was convinced, correctly, that Birchall had LWT in his sights. He told him that no decision had been made yet. Dyke, a large grin splitting his bearded face, then made a great show of handing Birchall a piece of white paper and saying to the audience: 'I am now going to ask Mr Birchall to sign this paper pledging that his consortium is not going to bid for LWT's franchise.' Birchall declined. Everyone laughed.

Back in London the final decision had still to be made. East Midlands was waiting for a response, and a final tranche of research – up until now concentrated on the TVS region – had to be brought together. The full bid team of twenty-five, partners, consultants and accountants, met in Polygram's head office to discuss the options. Repeatedly, they tried to second-guess both Green and Branson, talking themselves round in circles.

Eventually all but Powell, Kuhn, Bevan, Guttridge and Birchall left the room. The final decision had to be made. Powell and Birchall were still keen to join with East Midlands and take on Central. Guttridge argued that it would be a huge task. The region was split into three, with separate local news areas, and had a strong local programming record. Even with East Midlands' support, they simply did not have the resources.

In his opinion, LWT should now be the target. It had poor local programming, and Mentorn had long experience of making London-based programming for Thames. His own background was current affairs, he had a lot of staff at Mentorn who had worked in local journalism in London – it made far more sense to pitch themselves against LWT.

There was a pause. It had by now become a standing joke with the other partners that Guttridge's well-structured arguments were often guided by more than just strategic logic. The sport was to tease out whom he most recently signed a new contract with. This time he simply told them.

'Well, I'm out if you're going for Central because I've got a new contract there, and I can't ignore the income Mentorn will gain from it.'

A collective sigh was released. They discovered later that not only had Guttridge negotiated a lengthy extension to Mentorn's contract for *First Night* but he had also been given a highly lucrative development deal, which virtually guaranteed a constant stream of commissions for his new Birmingham subsidiary, Mentorn Midlands. In their eyes, Guttridge had been bought off.

But as Guttridge saw it, he had little choice. If his company was to thrive, he had to get access to the network through a major ITV station. With Thames likely to face stiff competition for the London weekday licence, it made sense to move closer to Central. A bid against LWT or TVS protected his options. His partners could always have gone ahead without him.

Reluctantly they accepted the inevitable. The argument

swung to and fro between TVS and LWT. Eventually they decided it had to be LWT. The amount of work and the money that would have to be risked was about the same in either case; the rewards were considerably greater if they won LWT. It had some of the highest advertising revenues per viewer and was a smaller area to cover geographically, an important consideration when budgeting for local news coverage.

The decision taken, they adjourned. Guttridge looked relieved. The truth was he never really believed the 'independent's bid' would be successful anyway. But he and Greg Dyke, the LWT boss, went back a long way. Dyke was now one of the most powerful men in television. Wouldn't it be nice, he thought, just to put the wind up him for a bit.

7

'I didn't get on with him when I was working there because he was barking. It's hard to work for someone who barks. But as a bloke, he's nice. I like him.'

Greg Dyke on Bruce Gyngell

Finally clear of the usual Friday evening jam, the chauffeur-driven Mercedes moved smoothly out into the fast lane and cruised at an even seventy mph. The motorway was still thick with cars, many piled high with family and food, refugees from the congested city centre. All were heading for the open fields and crowded pubs of Oxfordshire, Gloucestershire and the west.

Greg Dyke, jacket off, tie loosened and top button undone, stretched out in the back of the car with a pile of papers in his lap. It was the first Friday of April. He was en route to a secret meeting in Minster Lovell. It would be another hour before he got there – at last he had time to think.

He had heard the rumours about Powell and Guttridge deciding to bid against LWT. He remembered Guttridge from York University twenty years before – he, Jeremy Fox and Guttridge had all been there together. He had been older than the other two, a mature student; he had not liked Guttridge much then either. What he needed was more information on how strong a consortium he had, and what they were planning. If he could just take some time off to work on them. He would worry about that on Monday. This weekend he had a bigger fish to fry.

He looked back at the sprawling suburbia of outer London slipping away. Lights were already twinkling in the early gloom.

The first workers home would be slumping into their chairs in front of the TV. Ickenham, Uxbridge, Hillingdon, Hayes – the west London he grew up in. He had left that some way behind now.

Journalists called him 'Reg', the TV executive with the common touch. A short, bearded, ebullient man, the son of an insurance salesman, he was ITV's brightest star. Popular programming was his forte. In his early years as a producer, when people brought him 'high-falutin'' ideas, he worked on a simple principle. 'But what would it mean to my mother?' Widowed and retired, she was, he told colleagues, 'part of a network of women who knows what the public wants'. The principle rarely failed. When she sang the praises of the first *Blind Date* shows, Dyke told friends that LWT had a hit on its hands.

Everyone knew what made him tick. He had rehearsed it often enough with journalists who had come to chart his remarkable rise. Sacked from a trainee managership at Marks & Spencer, unemployed after a going-nowhere stint on provincial papers, he had sat on Wandsworth Common on his thirtieth birthday asking himself: 'Whatever happened to me?' Then LWT had given him his first break in television, the job of researcher on the London Programme. Fourteen years later he was one of the most powerful men in the industry. He would never let an opportunity slip. (Typical Dyke, joked his colleagues. The story-line smacks of one of those mini-series he used to like so much.)

Dyke said it was just luck, but he had a knack, just when television needed it. He rose from researcher to producer, inventing the lively *Six O'Clock Show* for LWT, an audience-puller to grab high ratings at the start of a Friday evening. It was full of fun stories, the sort he used to enjoy so much as a kid watching Cliff Michelmore's *Tonight* in the 1960s.

Recommended to Jonathan and Timothy Aitken, the cousins struggling to rescue TV-am after its disastrous launch, he was poached on a salary of £40,000 a year plus £20,000 on top if he could push 200,000 viewers over the million mark. And there was another £20,000 for every million on top of that. Dyke, appointed editor in chief, set to work with a vengeance.

His remedy for the station was drastic but effective. He had noticed the ratings surged at half-term. So he pumped up the material aimed at children. The original TV-am founders' Mission To Explain went out the window, replaced by Dyke's Mission To Entertain. Out also went Famous Five luminaries like Anna Ford, Michael Parkinson and Peter Jay; in their stead came Anne Diamond, Nick Owen and Roland Rat, a glove puppet with a neat line in streetwise patter. Audiences soared to 1.5 million within a year, but a financial cloud still hung over the station. When Kerry Packer, a major shareholder, installed Bruce Gyngell as chief executive, Dyke left shortly afterwards.

Getting another job in ITV was not easy. The populist approach had caused considerable embarrassment to the IBA, which knew standards were being compromised but wanted the station to survive. Branded Roland Rat's Dad by the tabloids (it was jibe which would haunt him forever), he was mistrusted by much of the broadcasting establishment. He was already known as a blunt speaker. In the highly political world of commercial broadcasting this was not an asset.

So Dyke went outside the establishment, taking a job with James Gatward as director of programmes at TVS for three years. But he never lost his profile or his ability to get up rival executives' noses. He swiftly developed his own idea about how the network should be run. He slammed ITV bulwarks like *Crossroads* and *Emmerdale Farm* as 'boring' Northern comedies, incensing stations like Central and Yorkshire. But Dyke's point was simple: the ITV schedule was full of programming that reflected individual stations' interest rather than the viewers'.

Not only that, it reflected a patronising view of 'real life'. Britain had moved on from the days when the working class would keep the television permanently stuck on ITV. The network had to change with them – it was simply too downmarket and old-fashioned for the new ITV viewer emerging from Margaret Thatcher's Britain. The advent of satellite television and increased viewer choice was going to blow it all apart. The old guard of Oxbridge-educated ITV bosses, with their Royal Television Society dinners and endless self-acclamation, could not see that. Dyke, a bristly, bustling ball of energy, was the perfect arbiter of the change in tastes.

But excluded from the Big Five stations who called the shots on the network, there was little he could do about it. Moves to the BBC and America were rumoured, but nothing came of them. Then, in 1987, he was offered the £110,000 post of programming director back at LWT, replacing John Birt. He leapt at it.

The early months were difficult for Dyke. The politics of the ITV system were anathema to him. For years the programme schedule for the prime time network had been thrashed out behind closed doors by the Big Five in a bizarre hybrid of conspiracy and consensus. Which station would make what, how much they would pay each other, what they would allow the smaller stations to make – it was a continuous rough-and-tumble that often made it impossible to schedule effectively against the BBC. Getting your way called for tact, diplomacy and not a little deviousness. Dyke was like a bull in a china shop.

To keep him out of trouble, Dyke, a passionate football fan (Brentford and Manchester United) and keen player (five-a-side every Friday lunchtime), was put in charge of organising sports coverage for the network. Within a year he was trying to break up the Football League, putting together a £32 million offer to ten clubs to form a Super League. When that failed he snatched coverage from the BBC with a huge £44 million bid. He also announced plans to drop darts, bowls and wrestling, a Saturday afternoon staple, from the schedule because they were too down-market.

In the process he rebuilt LWT's weekend schedule too. When Westminster politicians complained about 'nothing-to-watch-on-a-Saturday-night', he knew it was LWT many were pointing the finger at. He kept the stars, signing big-name presenters like Michael Aspel, Cilla Black and Jeremy Beadle to expensive long-term deals, but on top of that invested in costly drama series like *London's Burning*. Gradually he pushed LWT up-market, without losing the popular audience.

When Brian Tesler, LWT's managing director, announced his intention to retire in 1989, Dyke was the surprise package on the short-list of replacements. Most thought he was too rough-edged to get it. But failing to find a businessman for the slot, Christopher Bland, the LWT chairman, plumped for Dyke and packed him off to Harvard for a three-month management course. The inexorable rise of Greg Dyke was almost complete.

Right from the start it was a strange marriage: Dyke, forty-two, a hairy, exuberant, football-crazy west Londoner; Bland, fifty-one, a smooth, patrician, printing boss, Oxford pentathlete and former Olympic fencer. They were chalk and cheese but it worked, partly because they complemented each other so well. Bland knew both the City and broadcasting's regulatory world backwards – he was a former deputy chairman of the IBA (1972–80) and director of the Northern Ireland Finance Corporation – but had little experience of programme-making. Dyke, a newcomer to business and a hopeless diplomat, knew what people wanted to watch and how he thought a TV company should be run. They argued constantly, each practising their own brand of plain-speaking (Rubbish! Bollocks! Right?), but Dyke never forgot what he owed Bland. Those who worked with them described it as almost like a father-and-son relationship.

Bland had already started LWT's franchise preparations before Dyke took the reins. LWT chairman since 1984, Bland had watched the progress of Thatcher's broadcasting legislation with foreboding. He had met both Griffiths and Stirling and been frightened at how little they understood about the television industry. No one had thought through the implications of the tendering process, either for the Government or the companies.

LWT, the butt of so many of the jokes about the network's luxury lifestyle, was a sitting duck. After a tempestuous start between 1968 and 1971, when a ratings collapse and poor management had threatened to scuttle the service, the company had improved to such an extent – *World of Sport, South Bank Show, Weekend World* – that it cruised through the 1980 franchise round. But the economic boom in London and the south during the mid-1980s encouraged it to pick up more staff and costs as cash rolled in. By the late 1980s its overheads were so high it could not hope to win in a competitive tender. So Bland, whose experience included seven years as a management consultant, thought up a scheme for a radical overhaul of the company.

The first Dyke heard about it was in 1989 when Bland asked both him and Tesler: 'Why don't we buy out this company?' The idea was simple. The management would buy LWT, replacing equity with debt, shrink the company and reorganise it, leaving it looking 'rough, tough and determined to win', as Dyke put it. There was only one problem: with just two years to go until the next licensing round, no one in the City would lend them the money to do it.

So Bland devised the next best thing: a complex but innovative capital reconstruction which paid shareholders back large tranches of cash raised by the sale of various assets, bound the senior executives to the company with 'golden handcuff' share options, and shrunk LWT to a leaner outfit. Large-scale redundancies were announced and separate profit centres were created under the main holding company umbrella. The City and the rest of ITV were dumbfounded.

Underpinning it all was the belief that if the company had to fight for its licence in a competitive tender, it would have to be able to match the costs of a new start-up, which was what it would be facing. As he explained it to his board, the last thing you needed as an incumbent for a bid was a cash mountain; TV was a cash-generative business and the bid was not a one-off lump sum, but an amount you had to pay every year. The cash only boosted the share price, and led to heavier dividend payments. Why not take on debt instead, which was cheaper to service than equity? The difference between the cost of servicing equity and servicing debt you would have to bid with.

Bravely, the board backed the scheme. Elsewhere the move was met with blank incomprehension. To replace equity with debt at a time when ITV was entering the worst revenue recession in its history appeared to be a kamikaze move. Worse still, the golden handcuffs – a complex arrangement under which fifty key executives had to buy into options which guaranteed them a top whack of £43 million worth of shares if

114

the LWT share price hit 278p by autumn 1993 – led many to question the merits of the move. LWT battened down the hatches.

High on the thirteenth and fourteenth floors of LWT's windswept South Bank headquarters, Bland and Dyke plotted the franchise bid strategy. On 2 February 1990, shortly after Dyke had returned from Harvard, LWT's bid team met for the first time. Bland, Dyke and Tesler, now deputy chairman, were joined by Peter McNally, LWT's finance director, and three other finance men, Tony Cohen, Tony Kay and Neil Canetty-Clarke, who worked on the capital reconstruction with Bland. The latter three were responsible for the day-to-day work on the bid.

Like the bid planning of many ITV companies, it was a sophisticated, high-security operation. A special library was created to file news cuttings, brokers' circulars and ITC missives, and a 'running day file' was opened, logging meetings, internal discussions, even telephone calls. Everything was kept behind locked doors; rooms were swept for electronic surveillance on a regular basis. Other directors and managers were roped in only on a 'need-to-know' basis. A premium was placed on 'intelligence'. Barry Cox, the director of corporate affairs and a former controller of features and current affairs, was put in charge of getting information about both rivals and regulators. Bland knew from his experience at the IBA how important the personal prejudices of the Independent Television Commission members would be. As the draft board paper from that day summed up: 'If a rival puts in a top bid only slightly higher than ours, ITC enthusiasm for LWT's programming may prove decisive in prompting the Commission to invoke exceptional circumstances in our favour. It is therefore vital that our bid is produced with our ITC market firmly in mind. We should know as much as possible about the perceptions, preferences and prejudices of the relevant members of the ITC. This information will be invaluable in designing and presenting our programming proposals.'

Right from the first meeting it had been decided that 'multiple bidding' – bidding for more than one licence – was an option worth exploring. Three franchises outside LWT were identified as 'ones where LWT should expect to clear the quality hurdle primarily on its current strengths'. They were Thames, TVS and TV-am. But everyone knew that Dyke was itching to have a run at TV-am.

Long after they decided to do it, Dyke argued that it was a decision taken for purely business reasons. Bland had been one of the first to spot the strangest quirk of the competitive tender process: that being a highly profitable public company was not always an advantage. If TV-am wanted to retain anything like its existing profits (around £24 million pre-tax on £81 million turnover in 1990), it would have to bid low. It was also one of the least likely stations to get 'exceptional circumstances'. This made it highly vulnerable.

But others in the industry reckoned it was also a grudge match. If nothing else, Dyke was keen to shake off the 'Roland Rat's Dad' tag once and for all. One way to do that was to bury TV-am and show he could create an even better breakfast station. (Bland too, reckoned some, had his own motivation. It was he who, while still at the IBA, had first pushed through the idea of a breakfast TV franchise in 1979. And later he had married Viscountess Enfield, one of the original TV-am directors and a friend of ousted founder Peter Jay.)

Now, less than two months before the bids had to be in, both men were close to achieving their aim. Dyke had put together a powerful consortium and a fresh-looking programme package for a new breakfast station. All he and his partners needed to do was work out how much to bid. A secret meeting in Oxfordshire had been fixed to decide just that.

It was all coming together nicely, thought Dyke, as his Mercedes turned down the drive to the conference centre that April evening. Only one thing bothered him: Gyngell's in-activity. Bruce may be nutty, he reasoned, but he is not an idiot. He had come so far in the seven years he had run TV-am. *He must have something up his sleeve.*

It was a chance meeting at the Dorchester in London on 23 November 1983 that first took Bruce Gyngell to TV-am.

116

Gyngell, a tall, distinguished-looking Australian who had managed ATV for Lew Grade in the 1970s, and Kerry Packer, one of his consultancy clients, were just checking out when Jonathan Aitken walked through the hotel's swing doors. Aitken, a Tory MP and TV-am backer who had taken on the chairmanship of the new station, knew Packer well.

'What are you doing now, Jonathan?' asked Packer. Aitken told the Australian millionaire about his interest in TV-am.

'You can have 10 per cent of it if you want to,' he joked.

'How much will that cost me?' asked Packer.

'A million quid.'

'Oh, I'll be in that, then,' said Packer, with a casualness that surprised even Aitken. Packer followed Gyngell to the waiting car. Later, on the way to Heathrow, he told him: 'I've just bought 10 per cent of that new breakfast TV station TV-am. Did you catch any of it while we were here?'

Gyngell, who had run Channel 9 in Australia and worked in Hollywood, had seen enough breakfast TV around the world to realise TV-am was way off the mark. He contorted his tanned features as he let Packer know the truth. 'It's dreadful,' he summed up. 'It's absolutely dreadful.'

'Oh well,' said Packer airily, 'it's only a million quid, that's not bad. It must have a huge potential audience. It's bound to be an enormous success eventually.'

Gyngell thought no more of it until, back in Australia, just weeks after the deal was done, Packer received a telegram from Aitken. It read: 'Company in serious financial difficulties. Please can you give your proxy to the chairman.'

Packer's expletives turned the air blue. He showed it to Gyngell. 'Fuck me, Bruce, the ink isn't even dry on the bloody cheque yet and it looks like we've done the money.' Gyngell looked suitably sympathetic. Packer's eyes narrowed.

'I'll do you a deal, Bruce. If you go over to London every six months to represent me on the board you can pocket the director's fees and I'll pay for your travel round the world first class.'

Gyngell said, 'Fine.'

He went over to London on 8 February for his first board

meeting, arriving in Camden at 10.25 a.m. sharp. The sculpted eggcups on top of the squat, Terry Farrell-designed headquarters were already looking a little grimy. Aitken warned the other board members: 'Packer's hatchet man is coming.'

The directors were wary but thought they had little to worry about. Many of the feuding founders – Jay, Ford, Parkinson and Kee – had left. The station, now under Greg Dyke's stewardship, was already showing a large increase in ratings. It was just a case of clinging on and waiting for advertisers to follow viewers.

After introductions, the board moved on to the main business. Gyngell was amazed at the polite formality with which the financial crisis was being handled. Eventually he could take it no longer. The company secretary was describing how TV-am's budget was on target.

'Hang on,' said Gyngell, 'how can you be on target? You are losing £580,000 a month. How can everyone be so calm? The place is a disaster. When I look at the cash-flow, it is obvious you are not going to be here in twenty-two days. I have heard of a stiff upper lip but this is absurd.'

The other directors protested. Gyngell shook his head and continued. 'British law is no different to Australian law. When you continue to trade knowing you cannot meet your bills it is called fraud. In Australia you go to jail for it.'

'You don't understand, Bruce . . .'

'Don't patronise me,' said Gyngell. He demanded an auditor's report and asked for a board meeting the following Sunday night. The response was consternation. How could they have a board meeting on a Sunday? They were all in the country.

'Look,' said Gyngell, 'the company may not be here on Monday if we don't.'

The auditors confirmed the worst. The ratings might be recovering but the station would need a further £4.4 million to survive. Packer agreed to put in another £1.3 million in a refinancing package, taking his stake up to 27 per cent. Gyngell, telling Packer he had little faith in the people running the company, said he would stay in London for six months to watch developments.

It was not long before he decided that the only way he would persuade anyone to listen to him was to run the company himself. The IBA said it would not block his appointment as managing director, so long as he promised to stay in the country for two years. Gyngell, not knowing if he would stay that long, set to work.

He overlapped with Dyke by two weeks. The two swiftly fell out over programming costs. As Gyngell told interviewers later, Dyke thought TV-am's difficulties were just an advertising problem. Gyngell wanted to cut costs to get closer to breakeven. When he cancelled coverage of the Olympic Games, Dyke and his deputy Clive Jones, who later moved to TVS, walked out.

Gyngell then completed Dyke's overhaul of the station. But whereas Dyke had flown on his wits – his imagination pouring forth gems like *Follow Diana Dors On a Diet* – Gyngell worked to a system. He argued that the priorities were all wrong. Out of eighty people working on programming only six were on news; most were making film pieces totally unsuitable for the format. The BBC was producing an up-market but accessible news-based breakfast service, which appealed mainly to the affluent south-east. He wanted to target different viewers, so the service must be streamlined to appeal to a less well-off, less southern-biased audience.

But, right from the start, he added an idiosyncratic element. Depressed at the dourness of the British character, he decided that viewers needed cheerfulness and enthusiasm first thing in the morning. He equated it with the British people's peculiar relationship with the weather. On a rainy day, everyone looked glum, nobody said hello. But when the weather was fine, people greeted you with a smile. So he decided that TV-am would be 'eternal summer'.

Studios were redecorated in pastel pinks and yellows, masseurs were hired to ensure presenters started work in the right frame of mind, younger, more enthusiastic (and cheaper) staff were taken on. Everyone was ordered to wear lighter, summery colours. Gyngell himself sported an array of pink shirts. He told people that was why he was nicknamed 'The Pink Panther' (he had also worked on the cartoon series of the same name in Hollywood). The truth was many of his staff were too stunned to call him anything.

At the same time he began to speak freely about his adherence to alternative medicines. An early interest in acupuncture and macrobiotic diets had led to experiments with Actualisation and Insight, forms of encounter therapy. Gyngell began discussing concepts like harnessing the 'collective consciousness' of the staff. British broadcasters watched with eyebrows raised – many thought Gyngell must have a screw loose. But on screen it all worked. TV-am gobbled up the ratings. Gyngell, who had expected to return to Australia where his wife and children lived, fell in love with a researcher, remarried and stayed.

For all its success, however, TV-am was never fully integrated within the ITV system. It had very different interests, after all: it was a popular national service among a federation of regional baronies. That sense of difference increased as Gyngell's eccentricities became more manifest. Other ITV bosses never really trusted him; to them, he was not just a crank, he was an Australian crank, the only foreigner to run an ITV licence. That explained his drive for profit above quality. For those who had been brought up with the traditions of public service broadcasting, TV-am was cheap and tacky, the sort of service you would expect to find abroad. But as they were soon to discover, times were changing.

Gyngell, of course, had his uses. It was he who first took on the unions head-to-head, while the rest of the network was pussyfooting. It started in November 1987 when he returned from a trip to America to find TV-am facing industrial action. The technical union, the ACTT, had announced a twenty-four hour strike over his plans to introduce remote-control studios. His senior management were preparing to shut the station for the day. 'No way,' said Gyngell. He rang friends in America, asking them to send copies of old series like *Batman* and *Happy Days*, and promptly locked the strikers out.

Gyngell and a management team put out a scratch service for four months. Political commentators compared it to Wapping, Rupert Murdoch's hard-headed stand against restrictive practices in the print industry. By the end of the four-month period Gyngell had sacked all 229 strikers, installed the new technology he wanted and emerged with a vastly more profitable company. Ironically, the hotch-potch of old repeats and shakily directed studio pieces that passed for an interim service had pushed ratings even higher.

The strike took its toll on Gyngell's health. He suffered a heart attack and while he made a complete recovery he never quite got over the shock that it had happened to him. He was, after all, the fittest of television executives – jogging, macrobiotics, meditation. He took a break from TV-am to learn a new discipline, kinaesthesiology, and returned refreshed. His stand against the strikers had also won him influential friends. Among the letters of admiration was one from Margaret Thatcher, Prime Minister.

It was not long before Gyngell was bending her ear about the broadcasting legislation. He, like everyone else in ITV, was not enthusiastic about the prospect of a competitive tender. He had sent David Keighley, his head of corporate affairs, to Australia in 1987 to compile a report for the IBA on the Australian Government's scheme for selling off broadcasting licences. By 1988 he had started actively lobbying against any system of highest-bid wins. In a speech to the Birmingham Press Club in August 1988 he warned that the danger of a tender was that companies would overbid, and go bankrupt, as the Australian government were already finding out. But he also knew the impending legislation was a chance for other sorts of change that might be more beneficial for TV-am. In particular, he was looking for any chance to expand it out of its morning-only slot.

Gyngell had his first meeting with Thatcher in autumn 1988 as the Broadcasting White Paper was being thrashed out by Cabinet committee. The two got on well, cementing his reputation as her favourite broadcaster. He did more than simply voice his concern about how a competitive tender operated; he also lobbied hard for the ITV map to be redrawn. In particular, he wanted TV-am to be given a chance to bid for the new fifth channel proposed by the White Paper, and not just restricted to a 20 per cent stake in it. Nowhere in the world, he pointed out, does a broadcaster have a licence just for the breakfast hours. It did not make sense. Nor, he pointed out, did an ITV map with fifteen separate regions. Here was her chance to remodel British broadcasting so that it would be a force on the international stage. She listened politely, but nothing came of it.

Gyngell had, however, become friendly with Brian Griffiths, who was coordinating the government's thinking on broadcasting reforms. In 1988 Griffiths, a born-again Christian, invited Gyngell to chair a pet charity of his, Cities in Schools. Gyngell accepted, and from then on its board met monthly in TV-am's Camden offices. He now had regular access to a key player in the Downing Street hierarchy as well as the ear of the Prime Minister. With Griffiths he began to rehearse a variant on the competitive tender that he called 'win-win'. Bidders would submit programming plans with a cash bid. The authorities would choose the winner on quality, and then give that bidder the chance to match the highest cash sum offered. If that bidder did not think it was feasible, the offer went down the line.

Griffiths was intrigued and arranged another meeting for Gyngell with Thatcher in October 1989. Gyngell had already put the scheme past Richard Dunn and the ITVA, and got their backing. Scheduled to see Thatcher for thirty minutes, he sat with her for over an hour in front of the fire in her private office talking it through. By the end of it, she appeared enthusiastic. She had assured him that maintaining the quality of programming was of the utmost importance. Gyngell left thinking he had persuaded her. He learnt later that the Treasury had overruled it.

By the beginning of 1990 he had other things on his mind, anyway. An acrimonious bust-up with Anne Diamond had led to the former star presenter suing TV-am for breach of contract. Worse still, Gyngell discovered that Mike Hollingsworth, Diamond's boyfriend and a former TV-am producer, had filed a new company at Companies House. It was called Good Morning Britain.

Hollingsworth only did it to wind up Gyngell. When TV-am ran a series of press ads after the Berlin Wall came down, saying it was the first TV company to broadcast from the Wall, Hollingsworth wrote to the Advertising Standards Authority to complain. Far from being the first, he argued, TV-am was one of the last. He should know, because it was Anne Diamond who had been there for the station as part of her Sunday morning slot. Everyone else had been covering it since Thursday night. He signed the complaint Mike Hollingsworth, Good Morning Britain.

He knew the impact it would have on Gyngell. *Good Morning Britain* was the title of TV-am's main morning programme. Gyngell had never thought to file it as a company name, and was furious. He took legal advice and was told that while the company was dormant there was little point in challenging ownership of the name. But the message from Hollingsworth was clear: if Gyngell was expecting a clear run at the breakfast licence, he was very much mistaken. 'I just wanted to rattle the bars of his cage,' he told friends later.

It was a typical Hollingsworth move; he had been dogging Gyngell for years. A skinny, good-looking man with a flop of blond hair and shark-like smile, he had nurtured a dislike of Gyngell since he had been sacked by him in 1985. Living with, and later marrying, Gyngell's star presenter enabled him to turn the screw.

Hollingsworth had joined TV-am in the summer of 1984, after helping to launch BBC1's breakfast service. He had always claimed he was approached first by the Aitken cousins, who wanted him to tone down some of Gyngell's wilder ideas. They then swore him to secrecy, saying they would get Gyngell to talk to him, but he must not let on that they had made the first approach.

Days later he got a call from Gyngell, who introduced himself, and asked for Hollingsworth's birthdate, saying he would ring back. Hours later he did. 'Michael, I want you to know, good news. We are compatible.'

Hollingsworth joined in June 1984 as TV-am's director of programmes. Within months relations with the technical unions at the station reached an all-time low. Hollingsworth was determined to tackle overmanning and was convinced that, as part of their tactics to destabilise his position, certain union members were leaking stories to the press about his relationship with Diamond, whom he had worked with before. Hollingsworth, already married, was livid.

The rumours of his affair with Diamond had been around for over a year. They had previously worked together at ATV, and had both been earmarked for the BBC breakfast service before whispers of the relationship led nervous BBC bosses to put Diamond on *Nationwide* instead. Their resurfacing in print came at a sensitive time for both of them.

Hollingsworth had been conducting negotiations with ITN, trying to persuade its boss David Nicholas that he should provide a news service for TV-am. Nicholas was reluctant, unless there were clear divisions between the TV-am and ITN output. Hollingsworth sensed he was still smarting from the failure of ITN's bid to get the breakfast licence in 1980. Similar negotiations for an ITN news service on TV-am had collapsed just after the award. It is almost as if everyone wants the station to fail, thought Hollingsworth at the time.

It was not long before he joined the crowd. His relations with Gyngell, never good, were deteriorating. Ratings were on the up and, as he saw it, Gyngell did not like having anyone else in the way to take the credit. Colleagues at TV-am told another side to the story, that Hollingsworth was becoming increasingly difficult to work with, seeing conspiracies behind every innocent action. Eventually Gyngell sent him away on a two-week holiday to Seville. When he returned, TV-am's security guards refused to readmit him.

Hollingsworth never forgave Gyngell. He started a letter campaign, writing to the IBA, trying to persuade it to remove TV-am's franchise because it was not fulfilling its founders' initial promises. The IBA's director of programmes at the time, David Glencross, dismissed it all as 'sour grapes'. Even after he had moved into a senior position at Music Box, Hollingsworth was convinced that Gyngell was still plotting against him. He saw Gyngell's appointment of a new corporate affairs chief, David Keighley, as the start of a personal campaign against him.

Gyngell was in a difficult position. Diamond was now living

with Hollingsworth and he could not afford to alienate his star presenter. Matters took another twist when Diamond announced she was pregnant, and intended to have the child without getting married. Gyngell was angry; he was no puritan, indeed he freely admitted to his own philandering past, but he was first and foremost a businessman. TV-am did continual tracking studies of its presenters' popularity, and Diamond's had plummetted on the announcement.

After a three-month break she returned to work as Britain's most famous unmarried mum. Her life, however, had been made hell by the tabloids. Hollingsworth had attempted to fight off newspaper interest with constant legal action, which only goaded the papers into worse intrusions. When Diamond had a second child, in 1989, she and Hollingsworth went to Australia for the birth. Gyngell gave her six months off on full pay.

On their return, Hollingsworth started putting together a team of editorial people to discuss alternatives to the TV-am style of breakfast television. In his Camden Parkway office, just a two-minute walk round the corner from TV-am, a core group of eight former TV-am and Breakfast Time managers met monthly to swap ideas.

They also followed the progress of the broadcasting legislation. By late 1989 it was clear to Hollingsworth and the others that bidders would need more than just editorial integrity to win. An introduction to Crédit Lyonnais, the huge French bank already involved in investment in Hollywood, gave them the financial know-how they were looking for.

The bank's first point was that, unless Hollingsworth wanted to do it himself, they would need a chief executive to draw up a business plan and head the bid. Hollingsworth first approached Graham Dowson, a former Rank boss who had been involved in Southern TV, and was now running a consultancy. Dowson refused. He then approached Julian Mounter, a former Thames executive now running TVNZ in New Zealand. Mounter, who had been Hollingsworth's predecessor at Music Box, also refused but suggested he contact Patrick Cox, a former Sky TV boss now handling the European interests of NBC, the American broadcaster. Hollingsworth ploughed on.

He saw Cox in NBC's London offices in Hammersmith. He had to play it carefully – ironically he was also talking to NBC's rival ABC about possible backing. Cox, a squat, dark-haired man, was initially unenthusiastic. 'You must be joking,' he said. 'TV-am is the one franchise which is as safe as houses.' It was not only the most profitable TV station in Britain, its boss was also a mate of Maggie's. Hollingsworth must be mad.

It was the same response that Hollingsworth had from everyone he visited. But by now he was determined to talk him round. He explained how the quality provisions being introduced would count against TV-am and how the station had few friends at the new Independent Television Commission, which was staffed mainly by ex-IBA members. Unofficial conversations with them had confirmed to Hollingsworth what the industry believed anyway: they felt TV-am had made fools of them. It was a TV station at the edge of a precipice, just waiting to be pushed off.

Cox was impressed. He was already looking for investment opportunities for NBC in Britain. He thought the proposed fifth channel might be one; he realised breakfast TV, in which the American networks had obvious expertise, was another. He said he would talk to his bosses in America about taking a stake. Meanwhile Hollingsworth should talk to Yorkshire TV. Both knew Yorkshire's managing director Clive Leach well. Yorkshire ran a joint production company with NBC and funded a development vehicle that Hollingsworth ran, Venture Broadcasting.

Hollingsworth discussed the breakfast bid with Leach at Yorkshire's London office in Bedford Row. Leach agreed to finance Hollingsworth through Venture for an initial research period, but he wanted Yorkshire's name kept out of it. Leach was petrified that Gyngell would retaliate by bankrolling a bid against Yorkshire.

By the time NBC had said yes to Hollingsworth, its interest had filtered out to the press; Hollingsworth was already trading information with journalists and was making little effort to cover his tracks. Gyngell, perturbed that Hollingsworth was whipping up powerful support, sent a consultant over to see

David Mellor,
broadcasting minister:
a politician with a
reputation for smug
abrasiveness.

Thames' Richard Dunn,
famed for his cool
good looks, led
the ITV lobby.

James Gatward,
TVS founder:
one of the casualties
of the franchise battle.

Rudolph Agnew,
the tough mining boss
brought into TVS to
confront Gatward.

Roger Laughton,
Clive Hollick, Simon
Albury: the men behind
MAI's Meridian bid
against TVS.

Mersey TV's
Phil Redmond
meets the cast
on the Brookside set.

David Frost and
Richard Branson
on St Paul's steps,
May 15.

TSW's Harry Turner and 'Gus': a big cigar and a big bid on May 15.

The ITC members (George Russell centre) who decided ITV's future.

LWT's Christopher Bland and Greg Dyke
hear the good news, October 16.

Yorkshire's Clive Leach poses with the famous fax.

Central's Leslie Hill hams it up for the cameras.

Michael Green, coaxed down from his office,
celebrates with Nigel Walmsley and Paul Jackson.

Overleaf
Bruce Gyngell, TV-am boss,
with Margaret Thatcher's letter,
Claridges, October 17.

NBC in New York to check the rumours. Dissatisfied with the result, he then went himself. He was cordially greeted by J. B. Holsten III, head of NBC International, who noted what he had to say, and then pointed out it was an NBC Europe affair, not something that New York would bother with. When Gyngell had left, he sent a full note of what had been said back to Cox's office in London.

Cox and Hollingsworth were astounded when they read the contents of the note. Predictably enough, Gyngell had tried to persuade NBC that Hollingsworth was unlikely to win any sort of licence, and that TV-am was watertight anyway. He had even hinted at the possibility of a deal between NBC and TV-am itself. That was no surprise; but what followed was. He had then discussed how much the station was likely to bid to retain the franchise. Cox and Hollingsworth could not believe it. But there the figures were: around £18 million, £20-odd million at the top. It must be a trick, they thought. *Even Bruce can't be that confident.*

'I would like to thank both Bruce and David Frost for doing such a marvellous job in lobbying the Government, and ensuring that genuine quality is in the bid.'

Sarah Thane, the IBA's controller of public affairs, paused and looked around. In front of her, the roomful of TV-am executives and IBA regional officers nodded in agreement. It was March 1990, the occasion of TV-am's annual breakfast for IBA officers in its first-floor management suite. Thane was coming to the end of a short, impromptu speech of thanks. She pointed out that there was still a lot to play for – the broadcasting legislation was going through Parliament as she spoke – but stressed how important TV-am's contribution had been to the issue of quality.

Such thanks, she thought, were no more than politeness demanded. For Gyngell, as with every other little signal he was searching for, it added up to something more.

By 1990 Gyngell had decided that quality was going to be the key factor in regaining the breakfast licence. All the signs pointed that way: his conversations with Griffiths and

Thatcher, the changes to the legislation now going through Parliament, the noises coming out of the Home Office and the IBA — soon to become the ITC — about specific programming strands. He was convinced TV-am was already a quality service, although he was conscious that the British view of quality did not necessarily equate with popularity.

He was also coming to believe that any attempt to restructure the company so it could match the overheads of a greenfield bid would be suicidal. Although he never acknowledged it in public, he knew TV-am had a reputation for 'lightweight' news coverage. But it was still offering a genuine alternative to the ITN and BBC — which is what the IBA had wanted — and hence justified the expense of running its own national news team, rather than just buying news in from a larger organisation. To strip back any further would have been playing into the hands of his enemies.

Anyway, he had an inside track on how the legislation would be interpreted. No other ITV boss had spent as long with Thatcher, or knew her thinking as well as he. The regulators who oversaw the competitive tender could not fail to acknowledge TV-am's achievements.

8

'No one has ever accused Mr Black of being ambiguous.'

Dan Colson, Conrad Black's lawyer

It was Bob Wright, NBC's chief executive, who thought of it. 'Talk to Conrad Black,' he told Cox in the NBC Europe office, 'he wants to work with us.'

Wright had met Black, the Canadian multimillionaire owner of the Daily Telegraph group, in London the year before and agreed that the two companies should find ways of working together. There was no hurry. Something would come up. Now they had the perfect vehicle.

It was early autumn when Cox was swiftly ushered up to Black's fifth-floor inner sanctum at the *Telegraph*'s Docklands headquarters. Black's office, all thick leather sofas and war prints, resembled a gentleman's club. Outside the steel stump of the Canary Wharf Tower was beginning to rise.

Black liked doing deals. He had picked up ownership of the *Telegraph* for £30 million in 1985, in a purchase described as 'the steal of the century'. After cutting jobs, moving offices and introducing new print agreements, he had turned it into one of the most profitable newspaper groups in Britain. Now he was looking to repeat the process, although he acknowledged he would never find another *Telegraph*. But he was eyeing stakes in newspaper companies overseas and related interests in Britain, hoping to spend some of the *Telegraph*'s £38 million-plus profits. Control of the paper restricted him to a 20 per cent stake in a broadcaster under the cross-media ownership rules, but the synergy was obvious, especially if that broadcaster needed news-gathering expertise.

The difficulty was persuading him. A number of television hopefuls had already been across his floor, but few so far had emerged with anything. As Black kept pointing out, he did not get where he was by taking risks.

Cox had already talked to Black about the possibility of investing in BSB, the satellite TV venture that was running on to the rocks. NBC had been considering an involvement in the project for some months. Black had too. They moved cautiously round the subject again, without agreeing anything, then moved on to the breakfast bid. Black, a great bear of a man, was enthusiastic. He freely admitted he knew nothing about broadcasting; but he was keen to learn. Making small investments in such projects were a way of gaining experience. At the end of the meeting he told Cox to come back with a formal presentation. He pointed to Stephen Grabiner, the *Telegraph*'s young marketing director, and the only other executive present at the meeting. 'He will handle it for us.'

Cox and Hollingsworth spent an hour presenting to Grabiner later the same month. They looked at projections of income, why TV-am was vulnerable and the sort of service that could replace it. Hollingsworth did not favour a too radical departure from the TV-am style, which already pulled in high audiences, simply a firmer concentration on 'editorial integrity'. Grabiner was impressed. Another meeting with Black was fixed.

Back in the inner sanctum, Cox and Hollingsworth worked through their arguments. Black said little, just nodding from time to time. Eventually Black smiled and asked who else was involved. Hollingsworth told him who they had approached, and how they hoped to pin down Reuters for a stake. Black looked thoughtful. 'Have you spoken to Michael Green?' No, said Hollingsworth. They had presumed Green would be too preoccupied with fighting Thames. Black raised his eyebrows. 'Give him a call.' I wonder, thought Hollingsworth as he left, what Black and Green have got going together.

'Hello, Mike.' Hollingsworth turned and his face fell. He had been sitting in a small West End restaurant in December with an old friend, Tim Marshall, an executive at Walt Disney's European office in London's Soho Square. Two men had loomed behind him. It was Charles Denton, the Zenith boss, with Brian Wenham in tow. They were taking the table next to Hollingsworth.

After greetings had been exchanged, Hollingsworth turned back to Marshall. Their conversation had to end. He was not sure how much Denton knew about the breakfast bid. He was inclined to be cautious.

Hollingsworth had told Marshall that the breakfast bid would make a good fit for Disney. The American entertainment giant was hoping to build up its presence in Europe to support its £240 million investment in the EuroDisney theme park. And its huge library of children's pprogramming had to be of interest to any breakfast contractor. TV-am's child viewing figures had proved such an attractive draw that the IBA had had to impose limits on the amount of toy advertising that could be shown for fear of swamping the morning ad breaks.

Yet Marshall's response to the arguments was cool. Hollingsworth presumed that was for their neighbours' benefit. They changed the conversation. It was only the next day, when Hollingsworth rang to ask him again, that he realised something else was going on. Marshall was making it plain it was an area he could not talk about freely. *That meant only one thing: someone else was putting together a breakfast bid and Disney was already in.*

Dyke and Bland had finally decided to go for TV-am over the summer of 1990. Most at LWT had no idea what was going on. An ex-LWT producer, Hugh Pile, was recruited to manage the bid, code-named Apollo. Pile, who had only left LWT two years earlier to go on a London Business School course, was given his own office on the nineteenth floor. Most thought he was working on LWT's licence renewal. It was only when others started to be seen round the senior executive offices that staff began putting two and two together.

Dyke had suggested bringing Walt Disney in. Not only would it offer financial credibility, as one of the world's biggest media companies, it was also the world leader in children's programming. Dyke had seen the effect of Disney films on his own children – he thought that ability to latch on to young viewers was one of the greatest marketing ploys of all time. And he knew it worked for a British audience. *Disney Club*, a Sunday morning magazine series for kids made by Disney and Scottish TV, was already proving a success on the ITV network.

The only problem was that Disney was not always the easiest partner to work with. On its home turf, in contrast to its wholesome image as a purveyor of children's entertainment, it had a reputation for determined belligerence, ruthlessly exploiting every angle and shaving every margin. (The distinctive Disney approach had even spawned a string of coarse jokes in media circles. Such as: two Disney executives walking in a film lot pass a beautiful starlet. 'I fucked her,' says one. 'Out of what?' says the other.) Dyke, however, was unperturbed.

First he phoned Etienne de Villiers, the tall South African who ran Disney's international sales operation out of an office in London's Soho Square. De Villiers, Oxford-educated and a former management consultant, had become a familiar face on London's media circuit. With his taste for expensive cars and top-of-the-line Boss suits he was every inch the international media executive. ITV chiefs who bought off him spent hours speculating on his salary. (American television salaries were a constant source of envy to their poorer British counterparts.) As he was one of the most powerful Disney executives outside America, enjoying the title of president of international television, it must top £300,000, they thought – bigger even than Gatward's or Gyngell's. Dyke thought the eminently clubbable de Villiers was the business.

He had worked with him before, buying Disney family movies for the network and helping him get his toe in the water on the ITV business circuit. Likewise de Villiers had been careful to cultivate ITV's rising star, making sure Dyke's children were invited to Disney launches and promotions and frequently socialising with Dyke and other media noteworthies. When de Villiers said he liked the idea of the breakfast bid, and would put the proposition back to 'Burbank', Disney's head office, Dyke was confident he would bring the company in.

Next he told Pile to approach Broadcast Communications, the *Guardian* newspaper subsidiary run by Michael Braham, another former LWT producer. Broadcast Communications held the contract for televising the House of Commons, and also provided *Business Daily*, made at LWT's studios, for Channel 4's breakfast service.

Braham, a soft-spoken, bearded man, was sitting in his Covent Garden office when the call came through. As Pile, whom he had known at LWT, sketched out the proposition he was surprised that LWT wanted only to provide facilities for the new station, not programming. Then he saw the logic. It was another way of utilising its huge studio complex on the South Bank.

After meetings between Bland, Dyke, Braham and Harry Roche, the *Guardian*'s chairman, Broadcast Communication was in. The first steering group meeting took place under conditions of utmost secrecy in Disney's Soho Square office in October. Bland and Dyke explained that the consortium must not look like an LWT-instigated bid – like Leach, they did not want to draw a reprisal bid from TV-am. Roche agreed to chair the consortium.

It took Dyke until January to find out about the NBC bid. He and Bland had been trying to get a news provider on board, the only missing piece of the jigsaw. The guidelines which had already appeared made it clear that any breakfast service had to provide a competent, stand-alone news service. Like NBC's Cox, Bland had already put out feelers to Reuters, which owned a stake in Visnews, a global news service in which the BBC owned a stake. At the same time Dyke approached ITN – co-owned by the ITV companies – where he was a board director.

It had been announced in October that Bob Phillis, the Carlton group managing director, was to take over at ITN from February. Phillis, who had already taken soundings from NBC on Carlton's involvement, knew about both bids before either knew of each other. He never let on; he listened intently when

Dyke called and promised to give him an answer after Christmas. He made it clear that he would prefer ITN to take a stake in any breakfast bid, though it had no money to pay for it, and base the service in its spanking new but half-empty headquarters in London's Gray's Inn Road. Otherwise he was enthusiastic.

At a meeting in January in Carlton's Hanover Square offices, on Phillis' last day with the company before joining ITN, Dyke, de Villiers and Braham tried to thrash out a deal with the new ITN boss. Immediately they noticed the tone had changed. Phillis and Stewart Purvis, ITN's editor-in-chief, were cool about the prospect of joining LWT.

'Tell me, why should we go with you as opposed to someone else? Give me a reason,' asked Phillis.

Braham looked at Dyke and smiled. 'Because we are going to win,' he said. Phillis smiled back.

'Yes,' he said slowly.

Dyke and Braham drove back together after the meeting. The LWT boss was apoplectic. It was the first sign they had had that another breakfast bid was being prepared. But it was not so much the competition as what ITN might do that upset him. As he saw it, *he could end up subsidising the rival bid as well*. LWT was a 6 per cent shareholder in ITN, and he was convinced the news company would put in an artificially low costing for any news service it provided. It was already asking ITV companies to stump up more cash than budgeted to pay off the debts incurred covering the collapse of Communism. He had to do something about it. The famous Dyke grin was fast disappearing.

Phillis, a plump, good-humoured manager much liked by other ITV bosses from his time at Central, was pleased to get out of Carlton. However much he admired Michael Green's achievements, he knew first-hand that he was not an easy man to work for. Sometimes he had felt swamped by Green's desire to control everything. He had been poached from Central on a salary close to £200,000 with the promise of leading Carlton into the next franchise round. It had not quite worked out like that. Now he was leaving, he felt like a weight had been lifted from his shoulders.

Everyone knew, however, that ITN was no soft option. The news provider faced a number of make-or-break decisions over the next three years. Despite its illustrious reputation, it had been hamstrung by haphazard management, overrunning its budgets, and getting its fingers burnt dabbling in the London property market. Its new headquarters, designed by Norman Foster, all cream concrete and grey glass, was twice as big as it needed. It had hoped to make a killing renting out the spare space. Instead, the property collapse left it contemplating a huge hole in its bottom line.

It could not have come at a worse time. Iraq's invasion of Kuwait and the imminent war in the Gulf meant another strain on the news gatherer's resources. The ITV companies, which provided its budget every year, were in no mood for charity. Many had had enough of ITN's arrogant inability, as they saw it, to face commercial realities.

Much of the bad feeling hinged on ITN's efforts to shake free of ITV control. ITN senior management, in particular David Nicholas and Alastair Burnet, the veteran newscaster, had lobbied the Government vociferously to end ITN's ownership. The new legislation included the stipulation that 51 per cent of the company must be placed outside the ITV network by 1994. For many ITV bosses, all of whom took turns sitting on ITN's board, it was treachery of the worst order, especially as the stations had consistently bailed the news organisation out. They put it simply: if Nicholas and Burnet had spent more time worrying about how badly ITN was run, and less time playing politics, matters might not look so grim for the news gatherer.

They sent for Phillis to sort it out. It was well known that he was unhappy at Carlton. His appointment to replace Nicholas, a renowned journalist who had little management experience, was designed to reverse the losses and prepare ITN for life without ITV support. Top of the list of priorities was to increase ITN's income, and make it attractive to outside investors. It was not an easy task.

Bidding for the breakfast licence was one way to do it. A successful bid would increase ITN's income and fill some of the empty space in Gray's Inn Road. It would also make up for losing the breakfast bid last time round to TV-am – a decision that still grated with senior managers.

Ironically it was Green who had first suggested it in October. Phillis had been sitting in his first-floor office at Carlton with Piers Inskip, Green's financial adviser, and Patrick Cox discussing the NBC breakfast bid. Green, as was his habit, walked in without knocking and asked what was up. Cox explained.

Green turned to Phillis. 'It's very simple, Bob. When you go to ITN you can bring them in; then we'll come in too.'

Phillis's face fell. 'Patrick doesn't know I'm going.'

'I do now,' said Cox with a grin. 'And it sounds a great idea to me.'

Even so, Phillis still had to persuade ITN's senior management. A number automatically resisted, not wanting to be rushed into any ready-made consortium. But Phillis won them over. His power of persuasion was one of the strengths he was hired for. Green even chipped in, helping to convince an uncertain Nicholas.

Phillis, however, knew that discussing a possible deal with Green was one thing; getting him to sign on officially was another, especially if someone else was lurking with a different tempting offer. Green's endless indecision had been one of the contributing factors behind his determination to leave Carlton. He did not want to end up the wallflower at the dance again, waiting for Green to make up his mind.

The problem was LWT. Right from the moment Dyke approached him about ITN's involvement, he had suspected, correctly, that it was only a matter of time before LWT tried to pull Green in as well. It made sense. Bland and Green went back a long way, both having cut their teeth in the print industry. And Phillis knew something the rest of ITV was unaware of: that Carlton and LWT had been holding regular meetings at the highest level since 1989 to discuss whether the two companies could co-operate if Carlton won the London weekday licence.

The secret talks, codenamed 'Lions and Tigers', were conducted between Green, Phillis, Bland and Dyke. They explored the possibility of Carlton sharing LWT's facilities, and operating a joint venture to handle local news for both stations. The traditional rivalry between LWT and Thames had precluded any such co-operation before; Bland in particular was keen that if a new contractor came along, a compromise could be reached with benefits for both sides. It was also a way of ensuring that Green did not bid against his old friend – something which many at LWT thought he was quite capable of.

It was a highly sensitive area. Advertisers would have been the first to cry foul if they thought there was any excessive cooperation between the London contractors. The reason the region had been split in the first place was to diminish London's hold on the advertising market. Two contractors working together would clean up. Then there was Thames. If Richard Dunn suspected that LWT was helping Green on a regular basis, he might be tempted to take a stake in a reprisal bid. So the talks were kept strictly under wraps.

In January Phillis rang NBC's Cox again and asked him to make ITN a presentation. Cox and Hollingsworth, who had learnt at Christmas that Yorkshire was now unwilling to participate, agreed to meet him at ITN's new headquarters one evening the week after. Phillis, still working out his notice at Carlton, held the meeting in an unfurnished room opposite his new office on the second floor. The presentation over, he then took Cox and Hollingsworth by surprise.

'What about Carlton?' he asked. He was still group managing director of the company, and even he did not know what Green was planning.

Phillis had already rationalised the choice facing him. He had little doubt that the NBC bid, with Carlton, was the better one for ITN. Cox and Hollingsworth were willing to base the station in ITN's studios, give it a stake in return for services, and let it take a lead role in shaping the bid. All LWT needed was a 'feed', a news service for which they would pay a straight fee. Nor could ITN go it alone. Without help, it was hopelessly ill-prepared – one of the surprises waiting for Phillis when he joined was how little work ITN had done on a possible breakfast application – and it had no cash. No, if ITN wanted in, it had to be with one of the two groups being formed. But Phillis knew Michael Green would not choose Cox and Hollingsworth over

Bland and Dyke unless he had a very good reason to do so. Luckily there was one; it was called Conrad Black.

Cox and Hollingsworth had signed the Telegraph up before Christmas. Black was now an enthusiastic backer of the NBC bid and had spent much of January trying to persuade Green to come in too. It was gradually becoming clear how closely Black and Green were working on broadcasting. The two had tried to link up before; both had been touted as potential investors in BSB during 1990. Green was offered Alan Bond's 37 per cent stake in the ailing satellite venture, but said no, because the other shareholders would not give him managerial control. Black had been a willing partner with Green. He respected Green's broadcasting nous, and by 1991 had pledged the Telegraph to taking small stakes in Green's regional ITV bids as well. Like Phillis, he did not want to end up bidding against him for the breakfast licence.

By the end of January, however, it was clear that Green was now getting overtures from Christopher Bland to join the LWT consortium. Hollingsworth thought Green wanted to go, but only if he could take ITN and Black with him. Phillis was reluctant, but equally would not fully commit ITN to the NBC bid while Green vacillated.

Black, who prided himself on being an honourable man, was beginning to get impatient. He had already given a commitment to another potential investor, the Taylor Woodrow construction group, that the Telegraph was a willing partner in the NBC bid. He could hardly jump ship and leave it in the lurch. The consortium was in danger of collapsing into a complex, angry mess.

On the second Thursday of February Carlton and ITN asked for a final presentation from NBC and the Telegraph. Cox and Grabiner met Phillis and Nigel Walmsley, newly appointed chief executive of Carlton TV, in Carlton's boardroom. Hollingsworth was left kicking his heels in Grabiner's office waiting for them to return. With Yorkshire out of the bid, he was now excluded from the crucial shareholders' meetings.

When Cox and Grabiner returned they looked disconsolate. 'That's it,' said Grabiner, flinging down his papers. 'It's all fallen apart.' Cox looked shattered. He could not speak. Walmsley had torn his business plan to shreds, showing that he was wildly overestimating the station's potential ad revenue, and confusing 1991 figures with projected data for 1993, when the new licences start. Cox acknowledged he had made a mistake; he had used figures which were gross revenue estimates – anyone with media experience knew you had to deduct ad agency commissions from the totals to get the real revenue. But the figures were not even his; they had been supplied by the Advertising Association. He still felt humiliated. Phillis and Walmsley had said they would have to reconsider their involvement. The NBC bid looked over.

Green confirmed their worst fears in a call to Black only hours later. He wanted out. He was going to join LWT and wanted the Telegraph to move with him. Black, to Green's surprise, would have none of it. He told Cox later that his response had been short and to the point: 'No,' said Black. 'I don't behave like that.' He insisted he would stand by Cox. 'This is a hiccup; we can sort it out.'

Cox told friends afterwards that with that response Black had earned his loyalty for life. Most businessmen would have left him high and dry.

The phone lines went red hot that weekend. NBC's Holsten rang Green from New York to tell him they would go on regardless. Hollingsworth, devastated at the thought of two years' work disappearing down the drain, rang Phillis to plead with him that he should reconsider. They talked for two hours. Both had been at Central together. Hollingsworth tried to call in any credit points he might have with Phillis. Cox rang John Whitney, the former IBA director general now heading Andrew Lloyd Webber's Really Useful Group. He had done some early work on the bid, before RUG had lost interest, but Cox still drew on his experience and had lined him up, along with Sir Paul Fox and Sir Robin Day, as a non-executive director of the bid. Whitney told him not to give up hope; the bid he and Hollingsworth had put together was a winner. If he was judging it at the ITC he would have to give it very strong consideration. Cox agreed, and reworked his figures till he got them right.

On Sunday Phillis rang Hollingsworth back. He was blunt: 'OK, I will pull the bid together but Patrick has got to take a back seat.' You could not have a chief executive who had lost control of his figures, he said. By Monday he had sorted it out with the other shareholders. Green rang NBC's Holsten in New York to ask cheekily: 'Are you still in our consortium?' Everything appeared to have been smoothed over.

A week later Phillis asked to see Cox in his Gray's Inn Road office. Hollingsworth drove Cox there, reminding him to ensure that his role in the bid was defended, and waited in a café opposite.

Face to face, Phillis laid down the terms for Cox. ITN, the Telegraph, NBC, Carlton and MAI, which had signalled its interest to Phillis in December, would be shareholders. Taylor Woodrow might come in later. Dick Emery, the former Central sales chief, would be chief executive of the consortium if the bid was successful. Until then, ITN would run it, with new consultants and lawyers to handle the bid. 'That's the way it is going to be from now on,' he said. In effect, the NBC bid for the breakfast licence was to become the ITN bid.

Cox went back to Hollingsworth. 'What happened?' said Hollingsworth as he walked into the cafe. 'He said I fucked it and he's taking over,' said Cox. He was not too disappointed. Right from the start he had acknowledged that the man who represented the Americans in this was unlikely to remain as boss.

'What about me?' said Hollingsworth.

'Oh, you're all right,' said Cox, absently.

He was wrong. Stewart Purvis, who remembered dealing with Hollingsworth in the past, had argued strongly that his role should be kept to a minimum. Hollingsworth could not continue as a director of the proposed new venture. He kept a consultancy on the project, but now someone else was running with the ball. He was watching from the touchline. It typified the mutual mistrust that was gnawing away at the consortium. The partners did not have long to wait for the next bombshell.

Three weeks later Phillis and Grabiner organised a dinner at the

Telegraph for all the partners to discuss the bidding strategy. The others already knew that Phillis was perturbed about something, but presumed it was pressures elsewhere. That evening, in a meeting room near Grabiner's office in the Telegraph's black glass and steel headquarters, eight of them sat round a table discussing the bid: Phillis, Grabiner, Cox, Emery, Simon Olswang, the lawyer ITN had appointed, Roger Laughton, representing MAI, Lord Bellwin, representing Taylor Woodrow, who had now agreed to take a 5 per cent stake in the bid, and Piers Inskip for Carlton.

Then, shortly before they were due to break for dinner, Phillis took Inskip into an adjoining room. The other partners raised their eyebrows but presumed it must be about old Carlton business. Ten minutes later they returned. Inskip, a tall, slender man with tight curly hair, looked upset. He excused himself from dinner and rushed off.

Nothing was mentioned during dinner, then, at the end, Phillis made an announcement. 'I have just had a conversation with Piers Inskip,' he said. 'I told him I was worried that Carlton is going to hold the price of our bid down. What should we do about it?'

The assembled partners were stunned. They quizzed Phillis and asked what it was all about. In fact Phillis was worried not just about Carlton but also about NBC. He thought neither company was really prepared to endorse a big bid to get the breakfast licence. But they had to bid high to win. He took Cox's promise that he could deliver NBC in New York on trust. Carlton was trickier. He had had clear hints that Carlton would not underwrite a big bid; it was consistently arguing for lower projections on advertising trends and revenue growth. Inskip, a former Classics scholar who did the brainwork behind most of Green's deals, had listened to Phillis's complaint that Carlton was out of line, but could not offer a way out of the impasse. Everyone had seen his concern. A company's first loyalty had to be to its own shareholders, not to any prospective partners in a new venture. If Carlton could not justify a big bid, the consortium was in real trouble again.

Eventually Cox spoke up: 'There is only one thing to do. Put it fair and square to Conrad Black and get him to put it to Green. They are both entrepreneurs. They understand each other. Let them sort it out.'

The next day Black rang Green and told him of the partners' fears. Green's reaction, Black told them later, was astonishment. *'Why should I hold the bid down? Why on earth should I do that?'* 'Fine,' said Black.

He told the other partners that Green had given him his word that Phillis's suspicions about Carlton were misplaced. Phillis put it down to the difficulties of holding a consortium together. Each had their own interests to look after. All he wanted was everyone pulling in the same direction so they could put in the most competitive bid possible. They agreed to leave it at that. But the mistrust remained.

LWT never lost hope of luring Green away. Christopher Bland kept up the pressure on him right the way through till April, long after Carlton had signed heads of agreement with the other shareholders in the ITN consortium. Despite his refusals, he knew that Green had been sorely tempted to cross the river earlier in the year. The logic was clear: if Green beat Thames and put Carlton TV in with LWT, it made sense for them both to have an interest in the same breakfast bid as well.

He also knew that the rumours about Green's uncertainty were having an unsettling effect on his partners. They were already finding Green's behaviour curious. Despite his and Bland's involvement in rival bids, they were making no attempt to avoid each other, meeting socially and frequently speaking on the phone. Black in particular was perplexed by it all.

Once it was clear that ITN was committed to NBC and the Telegraph, Bland and Dyke wasted no time in signing up Visnews to supply news for LWT's Apollo consortium. But the conflicts of interest were mounting. Not only was Dyke a director of ITN but NBC was a stakeholder in Visnews. Assurances on confidentiality had to be given. Every time the ITN board discussed the progress of its bid, Dyke faced the indignity of having to leave the room and wait for the discussion to finish.

By April Bland had realised that Green was not going to be prised away from Conrad Black. At least one more investor had to be found. Tentative approaches to Hanson and Reuters had also fallen through. Instead, Scottish TV was invited to join the Apollo consortium, with a further stake earmarked for City institutions if the bid was successful. STV was an obvious fit; it already worked with Disney, and its senior executives, Gus MacDonald and Bill Brown, were on friendly terms with Dyke and Bland. It also provided a counterbalance to the three founding shareholders, who were all suppliers to the venture.

MacDonald, a former Granada executive and ex-presenter of Channel 4's *Right to Reply*, had suspected the bid was on long before it was confirmed. He had received a visit from Hugh Pile, LWT's bid co-ordinator, in the autumn of 1990. Pile would not reveal his backers but asked if STV would supply regional news to his consortium. MacDonald had immediately written to Dyke to warn him that Pile might be putting something together. Only later did he realise Dyke had sent him. He had then made it plain to Dyke that STV would be an asset to the LWT consortium, especially as it wanted to make regionalism one of the quality aspects of the breakfast bid. By then many ITV bosses knew that Dyke had asked his old TV-am colleague, Clive Jones, now at TVS, to do some costings for individual ITV stations providing local news opt-outs in the breakfast service.

Cornering Dyke at a network controllers' lunch, MacDonald had told him frankly: 'Remember, if you are planning a breakfast bid it would do you a lot of good to have a Scottish component – that way it would look like a British breakfast bid.'

For MacDonald it was a chance shot that had hit home. Dyke's partners already knew how paranoid he was about the press portraying the bid as 'Mickey Mouse Meets Roland Rat'. Dyke had smiled enigmatically and countered: 'Are you really serious about joining such a bid?'

'Of course,' said MacDonald.

Dyke phoned him back the next day. 'I've talked to my partners about it. You're in.'

The letter was on ITC-headed notepaper, addressed to Bruce

Gyngell and signed by George Russell. It commended Gyngell on TV-am's coverage of the Gulf War. Gyngell showed it proudly to his senior executives. So much for the press coverage criticising the station, he said.

Added to the phone call he got from Russell last year, congratulating TV-am on being a contender for The Training Agency Investment In People award, it showed just how much the regulators appreciated what TV-am were doing. The phone call had been a private one but, according to Gyngell, Russell had been positively eulogistic. His message had been clear: *with a training record like yours, you can't possibly lose your franchise.* (The station might not need his approval anyway. Gyngell had harnessed higher powers in its defence. Decals saying 'TV-am, the winning team for 1993' were affixed to all the station's doorknobs. He told the staff that every time they touched a decal, their energy would flow through it and bolster the licence application . . .)

The Old Mill conference centre in Minster Lovell is a small, discreet venue, tucked away on the edge of the Cotswolds. Across the road lies the Old Sun pub, a popular meeting place for locals and weekenders alike. At the back runs the river Windrush, setting for *The Wind In The Willows*. When the varied members of LWT's Apollo consortium threw open their windows that sunny Saturday morning, they were taken aback by the beauty of it all.

The meeting, to finalise the range for the LWT breakfast bid, had been organised by Dyke's office. Originally it had been booked for Hever Castle the weekend after, but they had had to switch to accommodate the different schedules of those involved. Hever was booked this weekend, so they had plumped for Minster Lovell instead. It was perfect for their needs; with nearly thirty people attending they filled the whole complex.

Everyone was there, including the two executives lined up to run the station if the bid was successful. Both had to keep their interest secret from their current employers: Chris Stoddart, earmarked for the chief executive slot, was running Satellite Information Service, the TV service that supplied racing coverage for Britain's bookies; Lis Howell, the prospective programme director, had been co-ordinating Sky News' Gulf War coverage.

Also there was a large contingent from Disney in America. Heading it was Rich Frank, one of the company's most senior executives in Los Angeles. (Bland had grinned on being introduced. 'To have one adjective in your name is unfortunate,' he quipped. 'To have two is really excessive.') Throughout the previous nine months, the reactions of the Disney team had been under intense scrutiny from their partners. Their serious manner and rigorous adherence to research had already surprised some of them. Mischievously, a new word had been coined to capture their demeanour: 'the Disnoids'.

Michael Braham, boss of the *Guardian*'s Business Communication subsidiary, could never quite get over it. After hours of dour negotiations and humourless trawling through statistics, Disney executives would suddenly pick up Mickey Mouse phones to make deeply serious calls. Their approach was so different from the casual, creative world of independent production. He had to keep pinching himself: *these are the people who make cartoons; we are the people who make the serious documentaries.*

Disney's internal politics had become a spectator sport for the other partners. By April it was apparent that the decision to join the LWT bid had caused waves within Disney way out of proportion to the size of investment involved. Decisions were being constantly referred back to Burbank. Disney officials would moan: 'We tried this on Burbank. Burbank doesn't like this. Burbank is unhappy.'

The others started to envisage Burbank as a huge grumpy animal that occasionally woke in a bad mood. Either executives would be questioning why the financial risks were worth taking if they did not even have control, or they would be implying that it was such a potty little investment for a company of Disney's size, why go ahead with it?

But that weekend they seemed reconciled to the investment. The mood at the centre was up-beat. As presentation followed presentation, all the participants felt more confident. STV's

MacDonald and Brown looked particularly pleased with themselves. Dyke was already ribbing them about how little they would have to bid for their own Scottish licence. After an initial flurry of interest from Conrad Black and Murray Johnstone, the investment bank, there was now no sign of any opposition north of the border. 'Hey,' said one of the Disney executives, looking impressed, 'I must buy some shares in Scottish when I get back.'

The presentations covered everything: the range of projections for advertising revenue, the impact of other media like satellite television, even the likely moves of potential rivals. Much was, by necessity, finger-in-the-wind speculation. The guidelines for bidders laid down by the ITC necessitated projections for advertising revenue over a ten-year period – an impossible task given that most ITV sales directors did not even know what revenue was likely to be a month ahead, let alone ten years ahead.

The array of assumptions that had to be made was staggering: what the growth in the economy would be, what the size of total advertising revenue would be, what share TV advertising would take of that, and what share one station would take of that. The only consolation was that everyone had to do it, and that the ITC had promised to rule out overbidders who had deliberately chosen optimistic estimates to back high bids. A lot of research also overlapped with LWT's own, so there were savings to be made.

It was not long before the Apollo partners narrowed their bid down to between £32 million and £36 million for the licence at 1993 prices. Their projections of TV-am's likely range showed that the station could not bid more than £30 million without carrying out the sort of major capital reconstruction that LWT had. In fact, because of the huge cost of servicing its equity, it was likely to bid a lot less. For that reason, Dyke vetoed the consultants' suggestion of a £40 million bid. He had to ensure that the consortium made a decent return from it over a prolonged period of time.

Only one thing bothered them all as they motored home early on Sunday afternoon. *If they found it this easy, so would the likes of Conrad Black and Michael Green.*

Five days later Gus MacDonald wrote a private letter to every ITV boss threatening to take ITN to the Office of Fair Trading if it proceeded with its bid for the breakfast licence. It conflicted with the interest of ITN's shareholders, he argued. Especially as he had 'anecdotal evidence' that ITN was offering its breakfast news service 'at marginal rates' in return for equity participation.

The letter was faxed to every ITV station, including (by mistake) TV-am. It faxed the letter on to the Sunday papers. TV-am's senior executives were jubilant. Maybe if it just stood back a little, the other two bidders would simply knock each other senseless.

9

*'Like medieval barons, they rode up to
the capital from territorial fiefdoms to
show their faces in the corridors of
power, pay court to their sovereign lords
and plot among themselves.'*

Jeremy Potter,
Independent Television In Britain,
volume 4

Clive Leach smiled. It was the toothy, satisfied grimace of a man
proved right. Gus MacDonald's fax had just landed on his desk
in Leeds. He was well out of that one, he thought.

The Yorkshire TV boss had paid Hollingsworth's expenses for
four months in 1990 while he researched the breakfast bid but
something had not seemed right. Gyngell was too unpredictable
and there were too many interested parties. Gus MacDonald's
fax showed that STV was now grinding its own axe, meaning
only one thing: that it was joining the LWT consortium and
lining up against ITN. What a mess, thought Leach. At least
Yorkshire were out of it. He had, he felt sure, made the right
decision. There was enough to attend to in his own backyard.

Leach, a dark, intense man who practised a jovial charm
honed by years on the ITV airtime sales market, worked hard at
the big decisions. He put it down to his training in marketing. He
always tried to make decisions on rational lines, weighing up
the benefits against the disadvantages, making sure the reasons
were unmotivated by self-interest. Just like his golf: you have
got to get the right line, select the right club and then it all fits
into place. At heart, though, he was a schemer, always
instinctively trying to chisel an angle on a deal and keep
Yorkshire one step ahead of the competition. His secret involvement in Hollingsworth's initial research was par for the course.
Like many of ITV's £150,000-a-year bosses, he believed that to

survive, Yorkshire had to have more. His board called it 'dog eat dog'. He called it reality.

At a time when most ITV companies were run either by programming men or accountants, Leach was one of only three bosses – along with Harry Turner at TSW and Charles Romaine at HTV – with a sales background. He knew many of the programme-makers round the ITV Association council table sniffed at the salesmen, always junketing or chasing clients round the golf course. But, after all, they brought the money in, not the programme-makers. And they were just as well, if not better, equipped to guide an ITV station through the harsh commercial realities of the 1990s. Programme-makers thought the quality of their programmes excused everything. Salesmen knew that quality was important, but that the market was more so.

Leach had mapped out an aggressive expansion strategy for Yorkshire right from the start. He wanted to rebuild its old links with the north-east, and from there expand to defend itself against the strength of richer stations in the south. Yorkshire became a far more attractive prospect for advertisers if linked with the Tyne Tees area. The two areas had been linked before, run by a joint holding company, Trident, from 1970 to 1980. The IBA had broken that up, unhappy that both regions were being run from a London head office. Leach wanted to put it back together again. His mouth watered at the prospect. Combining YTV's transmission area (from the Tees to the Wash – far bigger than just the county of Yorkshire) with Tyne Tees's grip on the north-east would give it an audience of over 3.5 million homes, close to Central's 4 million and far more than Granada's 2.8 million. The regional services could still be run separately, but the benefits from joint sale of airtime and economies of scale on production were huge. Best of all, Yorkshire would no longer be the runt of the pack among the larger stations.

There were hurdles to overcome, of course. The government's guidelines on ownership allowed the top six – Thames, London Weekend, Central, Granada, Yorkshire and TVS – only a limited interest in other stations. Each could control one smaller one and take a 20 per cent stake in any other. Then there was the complication of the Government's 'contiguity' restrictions, which forbade stations taking majority stakes in stations with whom they shared a significant border. But the issue for Leach was not which smaller station Yorkshire would target; that was clear from the start. If it could not bid against Tyne Tees, it would buy into it, restrictions permitting. More intriguing was where it might take a 20 per cent stake.

Leach started the franchise preparations in 1989. He had little doubt Yorkshire would face a fight for its licence on its home ground. The station had had a turbulent history, with frequent bouts of industrial action in the 1970s and a bitter franchise battle in 1980 against a consortium put together by some of its own employees and led by two MPs, Jonathan Aitken and Austin Mitchell. There were enough old Yorkshire hands around to consider making a challenge. So, like other ITV bosses, Leach responded to the threat of the competitive tender by reorganising the company into separate profit centres, reducing overheads and ruthlessly cutting back on staff. Happy he was well set up to make a huge bid, if he needed to, at home, he began looking elsewhere for opportunities.

Investment in the south was attractive for all northern contractors. They had long suffered from advertisers' preference for the more affluent audiences in London and the south-east. A financial interest there would be a useful bolster against any further drift of revenue in the same direction. Besides the breakfast licence, Anglia was an obvious target. The region adjoined Yorkshire, but was far enough south to have benefited from the boom in the mid-1980s. Leach opened talks with EMAP, the publisher, which was already putting a consortium together to bid against the incumbent. He also kept in touch with Virgin, which had approached Media & Airtime Sales, a Yorkshire subsidiary, for help in its ad revenue projections. A stake in a London weekday bid, or a bid against TVS, were all considered.

Then in December 1990 Leach got the news he was waiting for. Yorkshire's brokers told him that Vaux, the Sunderland brewer, was finally willing to sell its 19 per cent stake in Tyne

Tees. Leach had consistently denied that Yorkshire was in the market for the stake. But when the news came through he pounced. The stake cost Yorkshire £5.1 million and journalists immediately speculated that Leach's long-term aim must be to mount a full takeover bid for the company. Leach denied it but the message to the rest of the broadcasting world was clear: hands off, this one is ours. Then came the bombshell from Granada.

Leach had heard the rumours that Granada might back a bid against Tyne Tees for some months. But speculation about Granada was rife in the network; there did not seem to be a bid going that Granada was not negotiating with. And he believed he had a pledge from Andrew Quinn, Granada TV's koala-eyed managing director, that they would work together in the north (Granada executives later insisted that Leach misinterpreted the agreement, which was to work together *until* there was a conflict of agreement). He put it all down to the rumour mills working overtime. It was his first serious misjudgement.

Just days after he had done the Vaux deal, Granada suddenly confirmed it: it was linking up with Border to co-ordinate a bid against Tyne Tees. Leach was humiliated; his purchase of the Vaux stake now looked like a rather dangerous investment. Tyne Tees, a small station racked by internal feuding, was losing a stream of senior executives and appeared to be on the rocks. Granada was one of the most respected programme-makers on the ITV network. Any application it made was bound to pass the quality threshold and hence increase the sheer amount that Tyne Tees would have to bid to stand a chance of winning the licence. What price Yorkshire's 19 per cent then? So by February Leach had plumped for a new course of action. He would bid against Granada.

He told colleagues later that it was a rational decision. He had sat at his desk in mid-February trying to finalise Yorkshire's bidding strategy. In his mind, the station was perfectly placed. It was well defended at home; it had a foot in the door at Tyne Tees. It had all the numbers crunched and data documented to make itself a very attractive partner for anyone looking for a 20 per cent backer against another major region. But where?

He took a blank sheet of paper from a pile in front of him and drew three parallel lines down it. In each of the four columns he had listed the key factors he was looking for in choosing an area that might be vulnerable to a Yorkshire-backed bid:

- it must be an area where the incumbent is financially unstable;
- it must be an area with some programming weaknesses;
- it must be an area in which a contribution from Yorkshire would have obvious benefits;
- it must fit in with Yorkshire's long-term strategy.

Down the side he wrote the names of all the other ITV companies, putting crosses in each column as the criteria fitted. When he finished he looked at the sheet. Only Granada had four crosses against it.

The next day he had a meeting scheduled with Leslie Hill, Central's chief executive, in Central's Nottingham studios to discuss network arrangements. He took John Fairley, Yorkshire's experienced director of programmes, with him and on the way down told him what had happened. Sitting in the back of his boss's white BMW, Fairley listened thoughtfully as Leach spelt out what they should do.

Leach ran through the financial difficulties of Granada's parent company, the speculation over the future of its boss, Derek Lewis, the obvious weaknesses of its regional programming, and the geographical synergies. Not only that, but the Granada TV chairman David Plowright had been going around boasting that he would bid low because the quality of the station's programming would see it through. He clearly remembered Plowright saying it at the Prix Italia awards in Capri last year. It had been under their noses all along, but so close they could not see it. 'It has got to be Granada,' said Leach. '*It's an absolute sitting duck.*'

Fairley was half smiling. 'Christ, you're right,' he said.

'Ring Redmond,' said Leach, picking up the car phone in front of them. Fairley punched the numbers.

Later people would say that Leach was not just getting angry over Granada. He was getting even.

Bingo! thought Phil Redmond as he put the phone down. He turned from his desk and stared out of the huge windows that dominated his office in Childwall, Liverpool. In the distance the Winter Hill transmitter rose from the skyline. He had a fair idea what Yorkshire wanted to talk to him about. Ever since Granada had got involved in the bid against Tyne Tees, he thought it was only a matter of time before Yorkshire came looking for revenge. He felt a tingle of excitement run through his lanky frame. With an ITV partner on board, he was really up and running.

At the age of forty Phil Redmond was in danger of becoming an institution. Running the biggest production independent in the north, he had spent five years railing against the complacency of ITV, the lack of imagination in broadcasting, the southern bias of the media, the iniquity of Manchester's domination over Liverpool in the north-west. His detractors said he was perfectly balanced: chips on both shoulders and an inferiority complex to match. They called him The Professor, a derogatory reference to his honorary professorship in media studies at Liverpool Polytechnic. Redmond gave them two fingers.

With his dark eyes peering out of a mop of long, greying hair, Redmond was a familiar and distinctive figure in the pages of the media press. One of the few writers in television to emerge as boss of his own production company, Mersey Television, he was rarely short of a flip and dismissive opinion about anyone or anything. For him, ITV was a carve-up; much of its programming 'crap'. He spoke in the nasal scouse of his birthplace, frequently ending his tirades with a questioning 'hnnh?' It had become a familiar sound in the question-and-answer sessions on the media conference circuit.

At times his quotability overshadowed his talent. He grew up on a council estate on the edge of Liverpool, a keen viewer of the wide range of programmes that defined TV in the 1960s and early 1970s – *Plays for Today, Monty Python, Coronation Street.*

After training to be a quantity surveyor he chucked it in for script-writing. He got his foot in the door at LWT, contributing scripts for the *Doctor In Charge* sitcom before persuading Anna Home at the BBC to let him write a series for kids about life at a comprehensive school. He called it *Grange Hill*. By the second series it was a runaway success, pulling large audiences and worrying adult viewers with its realistic depiction of school life. It was a radical departure from the traditional 'Billy Bunter'-style of kids' programming, acknowledging that bullying, swearing and sex were now commonplace among young teenagers. No one was quite sure if it should be shown on television. It defined the Redmond approach for years to come. 'They say it won't work but in the end it always does. Hnnh?'

Grange Hill spin-offs and a series on council bureaucracy, *City Hall*, followed. Then came *Brookside*, the Channel 4 soap that made him one of Britain's richest independents. The Redmond version of how it came about was typically flip. He accosted Jeremy Isaacs at a public meeting before the channel had launched.

'Are you serious about catering for minorities?'

'Yes,' said Isaacs.

'Would you put a teenage drama on at 8 p.m. which used the word "fuck"?'

Isaacs hummed and hawed and told Redmond to come round and see him. Redmond remonstrated with him about Channel 4's lack of a popular soap opera series. He explained how it could be used to examine complex issues without losing a mass audience.

'We can't afford it,' said Isaacs.

'I'll show you how,' said Redmond.

Raising £1 million through his own company and spending over £2 million of Channel 4's, Redmond promptly built his own estate of thirteen modern houses, complete with working wiring, bathrooms and kitchens, in Liverpool. '£3m RIVAL FOR THE STREET!' announced the *Sun* in August 1982. Redmond, described as a '32-year-old whizzkid', was typically confident: 'If, when we are nine months into it, the viewers are staying away, then I shall start to worry.'

He did not have to. The twice-weekly series consistently topped the Channel 4 ratings, with audiences well over the five million mark. It made Redmond a rich man. By 1990, when Channel 4 decided to increase its frequency to three times a week, with an omnibus repeat at the weekend, he was a millionaire. His company, Mersey TV, was taking in over £7 million from Channel 4 alone. He had two houses, two smart cars – a Range Rover and a Volvo Estate – and a new wife, Alexis, who had been seconded to Mersey TV from Arthur Andersen, the accountant, to put in new costs controls and management systems. Redmond had been bowled over by her, leaving his first wife and two children, marrying Alexis and making her managing director of the company. Now no one could complain that he was neglecting his family for his work. Along the way he developed a reputation as a formidable autocrat. As he told one journalist later: 'I gave up the hippy school of management after six weeks.'

Yet he never lost his oddball tag. His politics were hard to pin down. The social realist streak that ran through all his work appeared aggressively anti-Tory, yet he was one of the most ardent supporters of Thatcher's broadcasting reform. He wrote a paper for the Home Office advocating the dismantling of Channel 3, and its replacement with a privatised version of Channel 4. He portrayed the pleas for quality and public service broadcasting as patronising bleats from the Oxbridge set. What he wanted was more access, both for a wider range of programme-makers and the general public. Most of all, said the cynics, he wanted more access for himself.

He made no secret of the fact that his number one target was Granada. He was so open about it – he told colleagues he had been planning a franchise bid since 1982 – that many concluded it was a bluff, just more of Redmond's 'Liverpool blag'. Granada TV was surely unshiftable. It had a thirty-five-year track record of outstanding productions such as *Brideshead Revisited*, *World in Action* and *Coronation Street*, and an enviable reputation in training young programme makers who had gone on to fill some of the most senior positions in ITV. The Granada mafia was everywhere. Redmond was too small to be serious competition. His tirades were those of an angry youth throwing bottles against a tank.

Ironically, by the beginning of 1991, Redmond had reached much the same conclusion himself. His attention had turned to the opportunities offered by Channel 5, the mooted fifth national channel to be auctioned after ITV, or a possible bid against Border, the tiny northern contractor based in Carlisle. Its smaller size and negligible importance to the network made it a much easier, and less politically sensitive, target than Granada (even its ITV colleagues joked that its audience was 620,000 viewers and 5 million sheep). Its £10 million turnover was similar to Mersey TV's own and, the cherry on the cake for Redmond, it was thought a likely target for Granada itself once the takeover restrictions were lifted. A Redmond bid against it would get right up Granada's nose. It was almost as good as bidding against Granada itself – but not quite.

Then came the call from John Fairley. Redmond had got to know Fairley the year before when Yorkshire commissioned Mersey to produce an innovative science series. The production had been fraught with difficulties and not been recommissioned, but the two had kept in touch, fully conscious of the opportunities that 1991 might bring. Redmond, however, hearing the gossip that Yorkshire had agreed a no-compete pact with Granada, had already concluded that it was an unlikely partner. Granada's decision to organise a bid against Tyne Tees, and the subsequent rumours that it was helping potential bidders in the Yorkshire region with advertising data, changed all that.

Redmond agreed to meet Leach, Fairley and Allan Hardy, Yorkshire's commercial director, at the Holiday Inn in Leeds two days later. Leach had told his secretary to make sure that Redmond went straight up to the meeting room. He did not want any eagle-eyed media spotter wondering what the *Brookside* boss was doing in Leeds. (He had reckoned without the hotel's efficiency. When he arrived at 11.30 a.m. the hotel's bulletin board in the foyer carried the announcement 'Yorkshire Television welcomes Mersey TV'. He swiftly ordered the manager to remove it.)

They sat around a table in an airless, windowless room on the first floor. Redmond brought his wife, Alexis, whose steely grasp of their company's finances impressed Leach, and his newly appointed public affairs chief, Phillip Reeval, a former publisher on *Televisual* magazine. They were late, stuck in traffic coming over the Pennines. They exchanged pleasantries before getting down to the hard bargaining. Most of the initial questioning went one way: the Yorkshire team quizzing Redmond on his bid plans. How far has he got? How is he going to put the programme schedule together in the time left? Who has he already spoken to?

They talked for two hours, eating sandwiches and taking notes. Then they broke to discuss it among themselves, the Mersey team heading for the coffee shop downstairs. Back together again, they agreed they had a deal. Yorkshire would provide advisers, know-how and contacts, but Redmond had to write the bid, sort out the programming and plan a prospective schedule. It must be seen to be a Mersey bid, not a Yorkshire one.

There was one proviso, said Leach. 'If there is a leak of our involvement before 15 May the whole deal is off.' Their best chance of winning, he said, was to catch Granada on the hop. It would not expect a fully funded, ITV-backed bid from Redmond, and so would bid low, safe in its belief that Mersey will either fail the quality threshold or Granada will be offered exceptional circumstances. If Yorkshire's involvement is kept secret till the last moment, it will not have time to reorganise its bid.

They had a deal. Redmond already had a company name registered for the eventuality: North West TV. Leach put Fairley and Hardy on the board, and told Hardy to sort out the business plan. He added Yorkshire's merchant bank, Barings, to the team, and signed up Arthur Andersen, the accountant, to help put the bid together. Within weeks Redmond would have a smoothly oiled, franchise bidding machine at his finger tips – yet to outsiders, Yorkshire's involvement would be invisible. They shook on it. The Yorkshire team swept off in their BMW 7 series saloons. That's the way to do it, thought Redmond as he clambered into Reeval's Volvo for the drive back across the Pennines. It was like having the Jeddae Knights on your side. *Granada won't know what's hit it.*

Scoffers called it 'Hollywood on Irwell', after the canal that ran behind the Granada TV's Manchester headquarters. It was more than just a TV station; it was a whole vision of regeneration for Manchester's run-down warehouse area. Just a half-hour walk from Piccadilly station in the city centre, it included Granada TV, museums, cafés. At its heart was a celebration of the very skill that had provided the impetus to revive the area: making programmes. The Granada Studio Tour complex, the first of its kind in Britain, included mock-ups of the sets for Coronation Street and Sherlock Holmes, a replica of the debating chamber in the House of Commons, special effects displays, 3-D film shows and even a 'Motionmaster' cinema. 'Feel your seat propelling you in synchrony with the action on the giant screen,' trumpeted the Studio Tour guide. To the rest of ITV, it was all a trifle ambitious.

The man behind it all, David Plowright, chairman of Granada TV, had an awesome reputation within the network. Irascible, arrogant, but probably the most talented producer of his generation, Plowright had become one of ITV's main strategists, arguing continually that the protection of quality should be the chief concern within any broadcasting reform. Granada's track record backed that up: it supplied a quarter of ITV's peaktime schedule, churning out everything from up-market drama like *Prime Suspect* to soaps like *Coronation Street*. It even produced critically acclaimed feature films such as *My Left Foot* and *The Field*.

Plowright had joined Granada in 1957, working his way up from programme controller to become managing director and then chairman. But whereas other ITV chairmen took a back seat, Plowright, with Andrew Quinn, his managing director, at his right hand, ran the company with a drive for quality that inspired intense loyalty among its long-serving employees. For them, he provided a consistency of vision that set Granada apart from other ITV companies. Its adoption of the role of crusader and its defiance of authority – its radical documentaries in the 1970s had frequently brought it eyeball-to-eyeball with the IBA – were rooted in the socialist ideals of its founder, Sidney Bernstein, and protected by the financial weight of its parent company, the Granada group, a theatre and cinema chain which had since diversified widely.

To that Plowright added his own political clout. Brother of Lord Olivier's widow Joan, he had formidable connections in the arts and political establishments, particularly in the northwest. Nor was he frightened of throwing his weight around. It raised the hackles of some of the younger ITV executives. They saw him as the last of the 'old guard' of TV bosses, men who ran their stations, for better or worse, with a mixture of charismatic bullying and scheming diplomacy – men who, for all their programming achievements, fiddled while the unions nearly burned down the network in the late 1970s and early 1980s.

Christmas 1990 was not an easy time for Plowright. His problems were twofold. In front of him he had a potential rival, Redmond, whose intentions were difficult to gauge. Behind him, he had a holding company which was swiftly running into trouble. The £1.4 billion Granada group, for so long the bedrock on which the TV subsidiary built its achievements, was feeling the effects of a series of ill-fated diversifications. Since the 1960s, when it had successfully moved into TV rentals, it had grown rapidly into a conglomerate handling bingo, bowling and motorway service stations as well. But in the 1980s unsuccessful excursions into electrical retailing, the holiday trade and computer maintenance hit the bottom line hard. So had the £200m bill for propping up BSB, of which the Granada group was a founder shareholder. By 1991 it was clear that the group, while in no danger of collapse, would need a rights issue to reduce its debt gearing. That would not be popular with its major shareholders. Speculation about the future of Derek Lewis, the group's chief executive, filled the financial pages.

There was little Plowright could do about it. A slide in Granada TV profits was contributing to the group's difficulties, but the station was operating in the middle of a worsening recession. He had already introduced widespread staff cuts and cost reforms, in line with other ITV companies. He was not going to turn it into a publisher-broadcaster, commissioning most of his programmes outside Granada, just when the franchise round was demanding quality output from the bidders and when he had huge studios round the back to fill. That went against the grain for him and, anyway, no one was asking him to do so. He was confident Granada could ride out the storm.

Redmond was harder to plan against. The two had met for an hour in Plowright's office the year before. For all his aggression, Plowright had rather liked him. He had drive. Yet Granada had never worked with Mersey, which was surprising, as it was on its very doorstep. A number of possibilities had been discussed, but none of Redmond's ideas had been good enough. There was a case, at least politically, for finding some kind of joint venture they could work on, if only to stop the speculation that there was bad blood between the two companies. But he was not going to buy Redmond off just to stop him bidding. Redmond had met Quinn as well and been blunt: he *would* bid if he was not given an output deal by Granada. *He's just busking*, thought Plowright. Everyone knew Liverpudlians were great buskers.

To some extent, Plowright had been through it all before in the last franchise round. The 1980 contract renewal had been fought against a background of growing criticism that Granada neglected Liverpool, one of the only principal cities in Britain without its own television station. Granada had promptly built a news and production centre in Liverpool's Albert Dock. It had still been challenged for its franchise by a group calling itself Merseyvision, founded by academics from Liverpool University and Polytechnic. Its application had distinguished itself by being the most vituperative of the 1980 bids, savagely condemning the other ITV contractors to the extent that the IBA wondered why Merseyvision wanted to join the network at all. Granada had won easily, but not without deepening the divide between the two cities, already forcefully expressed in the bad feeling between its two most famous football teams, Manchester United and Liverpool. The arrival of 'Professor' Redmond, trotting out some of the same arguments as his Merseyvision predecessors and opening the old wounds, must have seemed like *déjà vu* for some Granada executives.

Plowright had other things on his mind anyway. The initial

projections on the growth of satellite and cable meant more competition for Granada TV in the long term. He had decided that to maintain profits the broadcasting division had to expand. As the rules covering multiple bidding emerged, he and Quinn studied Granada's options. A stake in a southern licence-holder was obviously attractive. Through Simon Albury, an old Granada hand, a meeting was set up between Quinn and Clive Hollick, the MAI boss. For Hollick, whose wife had also worked at Granada, the station's quality image made it an obvious fit in an MAI bid against TVS.

That left the possibility of a stake in a smaller station. A short list was drawn up: Anglia was an obvious target, but Yorkshire and Central lay between it and Granada. Tyne Tees was more intriguing, overlapping with Granada on only a small front, between Yorkshire and Border, but close enough to make economies of scale seem a real possibility. Quinn, a shrewd, uncomplicated man, decided to check it out.

He roped in Stewart Prebble, Granada's director of regional programmes and founder of the Campaign For Quality Television. Prebble, who had worked as an on-screen reporter for the BBC in Newcastle and whose in-laws still lived in the north-east, knew the area well. 'Let's have a little run-up and look around,' Quinn told him before Christmas. 'It helps me get a grasp of these things.'

So for three days Granada's managing director and regional programming director had driven round the major cities of the north-east in Prebble's company car. They made no attempt to conceal their identities, but then no one was exactly looking for them. Ironically on their second night they walked straight into Tyne Tees's boss, David Reay, in the bar of the Gosforth Park Hotel. Reay knew Quinn well – after all, the ITV bosses met every month in London to discuss network affairs at the ITV Association. He had smiled and stuck out a hand.

'Hello, what are you doing here?'

Quinn, without blinking, replied: 'We're thinking of bidding for your franchise, David.'

Reay, slightly taken aback, had laughed. Quinn's propensity

for straight talking was well known on the network. 'Oh . . . well, you must come in and have a drink then.'

Prebble was open-mouthed. 'That was a bit of a surprise,' he remarked as Reay walked off.

'Well,' said Quinn, 'it's just business.'

The next day they were given a guided tour of the Tyne Tees offices and studios in Newcastle. Reay, it was clear, was still not sure if Quinn had been joking. Nevertheless, the atmosphere was good-humoured. Later, as they motored back to Manchester, Prebble expressed his enthusiasm for bidding. Quinn was not so sure. A lot would depend on Yorkshire, which at that stage had still to take its stake in Tyne Tees. It was clear from talking to Reay that Tyne Tees thought Leach might still bid against the station, rather than buy into it. If it did, that would make the area an infinitely tougher proposition to win.

When Yorkshire revealed its hand in December, Granada gave Prebble the green light. First he called Paul Corley, programme director of Border, and an old friend. Corley had worked with Prebble at the BBC in Newcastle – both had played in a staff rock band called (appropriately) The Cringe – and knew the area as well as Prebble. Ironically he had just been approached by both Tyne Tees and Clive Leach to take the vacant programme director's job at the Newcastle station. Corley said no. He took Border into the Granada bid with a 12.5 per cent stake.

By April it was like the War of the Roses all over again. On one side of the Pennines Granada and Border plotted an attack on Yorkshire's flank through Tyne Tees, while on the other Leach persuaded Tyne Tees to retaliate by joining Yorkshire behind Redmond's bid. It was the final battle for control of the north: its outcome could determine who ran commercial TV from Liverpool to Newcastle for decades to come.

For Tyne Tees, already rocked by a collapse in its ad revenue and a seemingly never-ending exodus of programme-makers, it was an extraordinary situation. It had avoided what it saw as the Doomsday scenario: both Yorkshire and Granada bidding against them. The sale of the Vaux stake had proved to be an asset; it had at least got one of its powerful neighbours on its side. But its future still hung in the balance in the battle between the two of them. At the same time the station seemed to be falling apart as it approached the franchise round. A new programme director could not be found. And to add irony to the situation, its new chief executive, Ian Ritchie, who took over from David Reay in 1991, was an old Granada hand and close friend of Stewart Prebble's.

Faxes were now flying between Yorkshire's Leeds head office and Redmond's Campus Manor headquarters – a former further education college which he had bought and refurbished on the outskirts of Liverpool. Redmond was working round the clock to put the programme proposals together. The initial drafts were raising eyebrows in Leeds. They had agreed that Granada's weak point was its regional programming, but Redmond's response was to suggest nearly sixty hours a week of regional programming as against the ITC's specified minimum of eight. Much of it was cheap access programming running through the night. After hurried consultations, Leach and Fairley agreed that Redmond's innovative approach was the best way forward. He would not tolerate anyone else writing the bid, anyway. Better to make a virtue out of the fact that it was going to be different from most of the rest of the bids that went in.

Other partners had now been brought into the consortium; as well as Tyne Tees, who agreed to take a stake on winning, Trinity International, 3i and Causeway Capital had joined too. But Redmond could not persuade the biggest fish, Guardian and Manchester Evening News. Talks were opened with Michael Braham's Broadcast Communication, the GMEN subsidiary, over programme supply. They broke down after Redmond refused to pay for development work. The Broadcast Communication team left with the impression that Mersey TV was hopelessly ill-prepared.

At Granada's Manchester office Redmond's sudden flurry of activity was ringing alarm bells. Rumours that Redmond was preparing a bid against Border had been confirmed in January when Plowright had poached Jane Leighton, a Mersey TV

163

director, to be director of public affairs at Granada – a move that had infuriated Redmond. Leighton believed that Redmond was looking north and was simply not geared up to make a bid against Granada unless he got a lot of help. Now it became clear his intentions were slightly closer to home. But still Granada did not know about Yorkshire's involvement.

As Leach paced his office that April he knew he would have to be careful. Redmond could be an asset or a liability. He wanted to keep his options open right up until the last moment – hence the proviso that he would pull out if Yorkshire's involvement in North West leaked. Whacking off faxes like Gus MacDonald, and announcing your interest to every other ITV boss in large neon lights, was not his style.

Anyway, things were beginning to look pretty good for Yorkshire. At the beginning of April it launched a new network series, *The Darling Buds Of May*. Just once in a while a series catches the nation's imagination. *Brideshead Revisited* had done it. So, after a slow start, had Central's *Inspector Morse*. Now, with perfect timing, *Darling Buds* was picking up huge audiences, and Fleet Street was leaping on the bandwagon.

As Leach ploughed through the cuttings he realised the press was going *Darling Buds* crazy, spinning out endless articles about Pop Larkin, its central character played by David Jason, and his family. By May the weekly audiences had topped 18 million and nearly 5000 column inches had been devoted to the series. Even the broadsheets were discussing what the popularity of the roguish tax-dodging farmer said about the British character.

ITV had never had a success like it. The show had gone straight to number one in the ratings and never budged. The network was now so consistently wiping the floor with the BBC in the ratings battle that the corporation called crisis meetings. Yorkshire, in the meantime, lined up a £17 million deal to sell the series to America. The mood at the station's Kirstall Road headquarters in Leeds as it put the final touches to its bids was close to euphoric. With form like this, it was going to blow its rivals apart.

'The last month has been nothing
to do with business. It has
been nothing to do with television.
It has been pure poker.'

Greg Dyke

The headquarters of the East Midlands Electricity Board sits low
and squat atop a hill in the Arnold suburb of Nottingham. To
one side sweeps a view of Nottingham city centre, on the other
endless rows of semi-detached houses. Surrounded by well-
manicured gardens, lily pond, and flagpole, the three-storey
block reflects the stolid civic confidence of the post-war era.

Leslie Hill, standing outside next to his dark, chauffeur-
driven Ford Scorpio, was impressed. It was a sunny afternoon in
early April. The Central TV boss, a thin, determined-looking
man with dark hair drawn up and back in a low bouffant, was in
fine spirits. Looking around, he smiled. He suspected he was
about to get some good news.

The meeting with John Harris, the East Midlands chairman,
had been set up a week or so before. The call had come in from a
director at Goodall Alexander O'Hare, the consultancy which
was helping East Midlands put together its bid. Would Hill like
to come round for a chat on areas of mutual interest? It could
mean a lot of things, thought Hill, but surely not that East
Midlands was following through its bid against Central. More
likely it was pulling out, but wanted something in return. He
buttoned up his jacket as he walked slowly towards the front
entrance.

Hill had known about the East Midlands bid for months.
Michael Green, so surprised at East Midlands' initial approach,

had told him about Harris's intentions after Christmas. The news had been a blow, as Central had been hoping to get a clear run. But how seriously should Central take it? It all depended who went in with East Midlands. It needed local programme-making expertise, and a major media partner. Despite doing the rounds, there was little indication that it had found anyone yet.

Hill knew that a number of potential bidders had been put off by the sheer size and diversity of the Central region. Of all the transmission areas carved out of Britain as ITV developed in the 1950s and 1960s, Central was the most incongruous. Stretching from the east coast to the Welsh borders, it included parts of Wiltshire, Gloucestershire, Oxfordshire and the Potteries, and cities as different as Birmingham, Nottingham and Oxford. With close to 9 million viewers, Central's franchise was the largest of the seven-day, regional licences on offer, but also the most complex to operate. Given the requirements of the competitive tender, any bidder faced a formidable workload in putting together a comparable rival service to operate in the area.

The station had learnt the lessons well from the last franchise round. Operating under the ATV tag and controlled by Sir Lew Grade, it had faced two rival bids and fierce local opposition from the Labour-controlled Birmingham Council, who had appealed to the IBA to take away its franchise. Much of the complaint centred on the station's neglect of the region, in particular the siting of the ATV's main studios in Elstree, outside London, where it made most of its network programmes. Other areas within the region also wanted their own service. The IBA considered offering two franchises, east and west, but backed away because of fears that it would deprive the network of a powerful programme-maker. Instead it insisted that the one franchise holder must split the service in two, providing separate regional programming, local news and weather for the two areas.

ATV won, but only on certain conditions. It had to tackle its image problem by changing its name, locating its headquarters more fully in the midlands, and putting at least half of its shares on to the open market. After doing this at the end of 1981, renaming itself Central Independent TV, it then went a step further. By the mid-1980s it started operating three regions, splitting off the south midlands for its own local programming as well. When the ITC issued its invitations to apply for ITV licences, it stipulated that the three-way split had to be maintained. By 1991 the split, which made the region into an expensive and complicated licence to bid for, was looking a very shrewd move indeed.

Hill joined in 1987. An accountant by training and a former boss of EMI Records, he was the surprise choice to replace Bob Phillis, then on his way to Carlton. Many in the industry expected Central to lure Andrew Quinn from Granada. But Central's headhunters pitched Hill's name on to the chairman's desk. Hill was remembered in media circles as the man who had hastily offloaded the Sex Pistols after their notorious appearance on the early evening magazine programme, *Today*. His decision, judging that the band would be more trouble than they were worth, was proved right in business terms, if damaging to the company's image among other artists. From there he moved into industrial services before being pitched into unemployment by a hostile takeover bid. He got two offers, from Polly Peck and Central. He took Central.

His lack of TV experience proved no disadvantage. His principal problem in the run-in to the franchise round was Central's costs and its shareholdings. In 1990 he laid off 500 staff and closed Central's facilities section in a highly publicised move designed to send a message to potential rivals. He also worked hard on his shareholders. Green's 20 per cent had appeared a threat, but once he had declined to take over the company it became clear that it was better to have him on board than leading any rivals outside. Robert Maxwell was a different matter. Although the *Daily Mirror* boss had made it plain since 1990 that he wanted to sell his 20 per cent stake, he could never find the right price. Eventually Hill organised the sale through Central's own brokers and surprised even himself by persuading Maxwell to distribute the stake through City institutions without even a quibble.

Central's ITV rivals were more difficult to second-guess.

Ironically Hill had been the leading advocate for multiple bidding – other bosses, fearing they would be swamped by the larger stations, had hoped that the Government would stop ITV companies bidding for each other. More than a few would have seen it as a just come-uppance had Central then become a prime target for others. But Hill had diligently worked the ITV social circuit to gauge his rivals' intentions. Conversations were noted, like the one with Yorkshire's John Fairley, who had led a bid against ATV in 1980. 'You're safe,' Fairley told Hill during a chance meeting at the Cheltenham Races in 1990, 'No one's going to want to go for triple regions.' Bruce Gyngell, a former ATV boss and another obvious rival, was collared at a Downing Street charity function for Age Concern. 'Are you bidding against us, Bruce?' asked Hill bluntly. Gyngell looked him straight in the eye. 'No, of course not.'

Hill was determined Central would not make the same mistakes as ATV. In late summer 1990 he set up a special Licence Campaign Unit under Central's corporate strategy director Marshall Stewart to PR the station to the local community. It bombarded 'opinion formers' in the region with Central literature, inviting them to presentations and briefings. In early 1991 it also launched a press advertising campaign highlighting the controversial issues facing the TV industry, such as racial stereotyping, minority programming and sponsorship. The innovative campaign, which asked readers to telephone their views for publication the next week, looked bizarrely inappropriate to Central's rivals, who had long held the station to be one of the old-fashioned monoliths of the network. For those outside TV, however, it gave a new image to a station previously best known as the producer of *Crossroads*. No bolshy councils could accuse them of not caring this time round.

By April 1991 the station looked in a strong position. Nearly all its rivals, apart from East Midlands, appeared to have been eliminated. Its final worry, MAI, had been eliminated after a chance meeting between Hill and Roger Laughton at a dinner held by McKinsey's, the consultant. Hill had questioned Laughton about speculation that MAI would bid against TVS and then, with typical bluntness, had asked if it was bidding against any other regions. Laughton said no. Hill believed him and had been impressed. 'We should speak to these MAI people,' he told Kevin Betts, Central's finance director, the next day. Weeks later Central pulled out of Virgin's bid against TVS and jumped into MAI's. It was not just based on Hill's feelings that MAI stood a better chance. It also made sure that MAI was not a late arrival into any consortium challenging Central.

That left East Midlands. Hill was confident that Central could fight off the utility. It had performed miserably during the freak snowstorms that winter leaving many villages in Derbyshire and Nottinghamshire without electricity for up to a week. Hill himself had been cut off for three days. Yet, apart from a hitch with one transmitter, Central's TV service had continued. The station's public relations experts were rubbing their hands in anticipation of the fight. Who were East Midlands to go into television when they could not even provide their own electricity service properly?

Harris met Hill at the door of his office. His welcome was warm. He came to the point quickly, speaking in the nasal, flat tones of the region he so proudly represented. He was looking at putting together a Midlands Development Corporation to bring more business into the area. It was not a philanthropic gesture: more business meant more users of electricity. It was the only way East Midlands could expand its core business. Would Central be interested in coming in with them?

But first, said Harris, there was one thing he should clear up. East Midlands had looked at bidding against Central in the upcoming franchise round, but had now decided not to. The research they had done showed that the station was too strong to take on. 'We don't think we can beat you,' said Harris. (He could have added that East Midlands had also found it impossible to find a major media partner to go in with. Discussions with CLT, the Luxembourg-based media group, had broken down only a fortnight previously. CLT thought it had more chance bidding against Anglia. That meant East Midlands was still on its own, ill-prepared, with less than two months to go before bids had to be handed in.) Hill smiled.

'Can you confirm, then, that you are definitely not going to bid?'

'Yes,' said Harris, 'that's right.'

Hill relaxed and let the rest of the conversation wash over him. The opportunities facing East Midlands, the chances of setting up a development corporation, how Central could help. They chatted for an hour and Hill promised that Central would look at the possibility of helping put together the corporation. Harris had asked for nothing in return for his promise not to bid. Hill surmised that he was right; Central simply *was* too strong for a company like East Midlands to take on. But the very fact that people thought East Midlands was still looking at a bid might yet prove useful. For a start, it would deter others who might want to move into the region at the last moment. He pointed out to Harris that, from Central's point of view, a 'no comment' to reporters would be a lot more useful than a straight denial in the run in to 15 May. Harris said he understood. All he wanted from Central was goodwill.

As he left the building for the drive home, Hill felt an extraordinary sense of relief. It really did look as if Central, one of Britain's biggest ITV stations, might be unchallenged in the forthcoming franchise round. If it was, that opened up the possibility of bidding not just low, but the minimum, £2000 (Hill in fact wanted to bid £1000 but was warned by his lawyers that the broadcasting legislation said bids must be in *multiples* of 1000). It was an option the board had already discussed. The station would also, of course, have to pay the extra tax devised by the ITC, a percentage on revenue (in Central's case 11 per cent), but that part of the process was out of their hands. No other major station was likely to have the opportunity of bidding so low. It was a decision that could turn Central into the most profitable company in ITV – but he had to call it right.

Central's interest in the south was already well known to TVS. The fact that two senior Central executives, Bob Southgate and Laurie Upshon, had worked at TVS in the early 1980s and knew its regional programming inside out always made it a likely ally for a major bidder. But the TVS team working flat out on the station's own bid had enough on their plate without counting all the potential rivals. Every one of the major ITV stations had evaluated possible bids against TVS. James Gatward's determination to be different from the other ITV companies led others to see TVS as fair game; its financial vulnerability made it even more attractive. At TVS's London head office they had only one thought: proving the snipers wrong. They were working on a plan that would blow all the rivals, however big, out of the water.

In the confusion and euphoria that followed Gatward's exit in February, Agnew had put forward a bold strategy. Under the old franchise system, he argued, TVS would have been a certain loser – it had made too many mistakes and antagonised the regulators too often. But this was a very different franchise round. As he understood it, the whole point of the process was to maximise income for the Government while ensuring that programme quality did not suffer. So if they took it as read that TVS would pass the quality threshold for programmes, regaining its licence might be easier than they thought. They simply had to bid more than anyone else and prove to the regulators that the bid was 'sustainable'. And to do that while carrying the heavy losses made by MTM, its subsidiary in America, it had to get help. In short, a reorganisation of its shareholding structure to bring in new heavyweight backers who would guarantee it could meet its commitments. Simple.

The strategy made sense. TVS's senior team were already convinced that the station would have to bid high as it was likely to face more competition than anyone else. The difficulty was always going to be affording the bid. What if the recession got worse and the station ad revenue collapsed? It might find itself committed to paying an annual sum for its bid which it could not find. Agnew's optimism, and his determination to bring in others to underwrite the TVS bid, gave them heart. They could use the franchise round to turn the tables neatly on all those hoping to profit from their misfortunes.

Agnew saw few dangers in a high bid. His experience in the mining industry told him that so long as you were confident in the quality of your research, there was nothing dicey in

171

projecting revenue for five, ten or fifteen years ahead. In gold mining, companies regularly sent geologists out into the wilds looking for a square mile of gold deposit in an area four times the size of Great Britain. If they find anything they then have to work out if it is worth developing – that involves projecting the price of gold seven-to-ten years ahead. They did it all the time. It was taken for granted that you could choose the figures to suit your purpose. The important thing was the overall trend and to make sure the company had back-up to cover an unforeseen eventuality.

Agnew had already been bowled over by the quality of the staff work on the bid. It was one of the essential paradoxes he was finding out about the company; at board level it had failed to respond to the MTM crisis when it should have. Yet the television company, run by Tony Brook and Clive Jones, appeared in excellent shape, and the teams working on figures for the franchise bid were churning out research of a calibre far beyond what he expected. In particular their forecasts of advertising expenditure in the region went right down to the minutiae, tracking seventy-five key product groups in the region and forecasting advertising growth based on the likely shifts in demand for those groups. The figures surprised even some of those working on the research. Whichever way you looked at it, the region's growth in advertising expenditure looked set to continue for some time into the future.

At a meeting in February a TVS team working on revenue projections put forward 4.5 per cent as the median figure to be used as the growth rate between 1993 and 2002 for total television advertising revenue. It was the key figure in every bid – just how fast a bidder presumed overall revenue would grow determined the limits for how much he or she could bid. Agnew asked what the other figures were. This, he sensed, was the company's chance to put together an unassailable bid. He threw out 4.5 per cent and told the team to use a higher one. Any short-term difficulties would be ironed out in the long term, he argued. The licence was awarded on a rolling basis. That meant that so long as programme quality did not deteriorate, the licence would be consistently re-awarded to the incumbent.

Over twenty years worries about revenue in 1993, 1994 or 1995 were negligible – especially if you had heavyweight backers to underwrite you.

Schroders, TVS's financial adviser, lined up two new investors who would not conflict with the company's French shareholders, Canal Plus and Générale des Eaux. In London it approached Associated Newspapers, the *Daily Mail* owner which had previously held a stake in Southern TV and badly wanted to get back into television. In New York it presented to Time Warner, the American media giant whose Home Box Office subsidiary had already made a number of internationl co-productions with TVS. The two were already linked through their joint ownership of Whittle Communications, an American specialist magazine house. Both said yes. The deal proposed committed all four companies – the two French, Time Warner and Associated – to putting £30m into TVS if it won, leaving the new investors with stakes of between 16 and 20 per cent each, depending on how many of the new shares issued were taken up by existing shareholders.

Incredibly, the deal was done in less than two months, with teams charging between London, Southampton, where the main computer work on the bid was being done, and New York, to show the latest projections to the company's prospective American partner. There was only one hitch on the horizon: the Stock Exchange was insisting that the size of the bid and the business plan would have to be revealed to existing shareholders before they could approve the plan. That meant that during the summer, while everyone else's bid was still under wraps at the ITC, TVS would have to make its bid public. So be it, thought Agnew. What harm can come of that?

The same frantic scenes were being enacted all over the country. By the middle of April forty bids were being prepared by thirty-seven different companies or consortia. Computer runs were being finalised, projections polished, the final ink put on deals with eager production independents. Soon each bidder would have to settle on a figure that would be sealed inside a separate envelope for delivery to the ITC with the rest of the applications on 15 May. The bid, an index-linked sum to be paid annually, determined not just whether you won, but also how profitable a company you would operate. It was the toughest decision of the whole process.

Interest was split equally between the large and small licences on offer. More than twenty bids were being prepared for the smaller licences, with rivals trying to outsmart each other by registering names that ranged from the distinctive to the plain unimaginative. Grampian in the north of Scotland (0.5 million TV homes) faced two bids from independents, C3 Caledonia and North of Scotland TV. Ulster in Northern Ireland (0.5 million TV homes) faced another two, Lagan TV and TVNi. TSW in the south-west (0.7 million TV homes) lined up against West-country TV and Telewest. HTV in Wales (2 million TV homes) was challenged by three, Channel 3 Wales & West, C3W and Merlin. Even little Channel TV, the smallest ITV contractor with only 40,000 homes, faced a rival, C13, headed by *Bergerac* actor John Nettles.

In London and the south deals were being put together with a rapidity that surprised even seasoned observers. MAI had fallen out with Granada over terms but lured Central from Virgin with an offer of a 20 per cent stake in its TVS bid. It had also pulled SelecTV, the production independent responsible for *Lovejoy* and *Birds Of A Feather*, out of Carlton's clutches with the offer of another equity stake. Carlton had responded by signing Noel Gay TV, another independent, to an exclusive development deal and taking Paul Jackson, its joint managing director, as programme director designate for its London weekday bid.

Virgin had little time to mourn the loss of Central from its team. It was now working flat out on three bids – against Thames, TVS and Anglia – in a consortium that included Frost, Charterhouse Bank, BHC Communications, Electra, a venture capital specialist, and Island World, the film and TV subsidiary of Island Records founder Chris Blackwell. Responsibility for writing the Virgin bid was given to John Gau. Papers were flying back and forth between his Putney office and Virgin's Notting Hill headquarters as the programme proposals were worked out. Gau had already settled on a distinctive, discursive style, similar to that used by applicants in earlier franchise rounds, in writing the licence bids. According to Levison, the decision stemmed from a meeting he and Gau had had with the ITC in February to clarify points in the 'invitations to apply' for an ITV licence. Did the ITC want specific answers to specific questions or more of an 'extended essay' describing what they intended? They believed that the ITC signalled it would be happy with the latter. (The ITC later denied it.)

At Thames' head office on the Euston Road the tension was beginning to bite. With no official confirmation from either Carlton or the Branson/Frost team as to where they were bidding, anxious Thames executives had to trawl the media world for gossip. The deals being done by both potential rivals implied that at least two London bids were on the cards, but there was little indication of who might be in with them. Always there was the fear that London Weekend, Thames' great rival, might be lurking behind one of them.

Richard Dunn, the Thames boss, and John Handley, chief executive of Euston Films, the Thames subsidiary, co-ordinated the bid work. Dunn had known from the start that Carlton would bid as a 'publisher-broadcaster', minimising its overheads and enabling it to put far more in the envelope than Thames with its current high overheads. Coopers Deloitte, the giant accountant whose media consultancy was helping Thames put together the bid, had already warned him that the Carlton bid would top £40 million. And Dunn also believed that Carlton, which had already invested so much in Green's broadcasting ambitions, would never be failed at the quality threshold. So, he reasoned, Thames faced two options: it could match the likely Carlton bid by slashing its workforce, selling off its studios and transforming itself into a similar, Channel 4-style operator. Or it could call the ITC's bluff, bid low, put more money into its programming proposals, and rely on winning via the 'exceptional circumstances' clause.

The decision hung on just how willing Dunn thought the ITC would be to use exceptional circumstances. He was in no doubt. He had worked closely with George Russell, the ITC chairman, throughout 1990 on the Broadcasting Bill lobby. And, he told his board, Russell had repeatedly assured him that the Home Office saw exceptional circumstances as something to be used, not just a makeweight. If he had not believed that, Dunn told his colleagues, he would have continued to lobby for further safeguards.

Few on the Thames board disagreed. There were dissenting voices elsewhere, however. One school of thought argued that the level of cuts needed to underwrite a £40 million-plus bid was not as drastic as many Thames executives were making out – probably only £8–10 million. These critics contended that virtually any ITV company could sustain cost cuts of at least 20–30 per cent, such was the extra weight that many of them were carrying. Thames itself had a PR budget alone of over £1 million. Indeed some of Thames' consultants argued that in theory the station could even outbid a start-up: the problem was that the massive income from its programme library was being offset by bad management of resources elsewhere.

Dunn, however, appeared to have painted himself into a corner. Lousy investments like the £57 million purchase of Reeves, an American distribution company, in December 1989 were draining the balance sheet. It was bought at a time when TVS's problems with MTM were already apparent. The resulting interest payments on the loans raised to buy Reeves cost Thames £6 million a year. At the same time the company was inevitably distracted by the attempts of its shareholders Thorn EMI and BET to sell their stakes, and by Dunn's role (which he had asked for) as head of the ITVA. When Thames should have been busy preparing its own application and assessing its rivals, Dunn was either trying to sell the company or leading the lobby over the broadcasting legislation.

By early 1991 it was too late to start remodelling the company in order to make a competitive bid. Better to concentrate on the strengths the company had – a formidable track record in programme production – and rely on the ITC's discretion. Dunn argued that, as the biggest ITV station and one of the largest providers of programmes to the network, Thames was far more difficult to cast aside than any of the smaller stations. The ITC had to ensure that ITV continued with a comparable service in

1993, when the new companies started. It could not just butcher most of its current suppliers and expect a whole batch of new boys to slot smoothly into the system.

Dunn was backed up by his programme director, David Elstein. He had little faith in the publisher-broadcaster system, and argued that you could not guarantee programme quality without a core set of creative and technical people working for you on a permanent basis. He warned the board not to get too fixated by the licence process. Thames already ran a profitable production business; it also ran a power distribution company and held a library of programmes of good commercial value. Why bid a fortune to win a licence that might offer you annual profits of less than £10m when you can make more without it?

The arguments swayed Thorn, Thames' majority shareholder. Colin Southgate, the Thorn boss, was close to Dunn, and readily believed his arguments that the ITC would secure the company's future. At the same time Thames executives produced a series of bullish forecasts of what the company was worth without the licence. Known internally as the Next Best Alternative (NBA) plan, it valued Thames at £140 million without the licence, £169 million with. Although some in Thorn doubted the estimates, the bid strategy was waved through. Discussions centred on how much to bid in order to make the ITC feel comfortable about awarding Thames the licence on exceptional circumstances. Dunn wanted to bid low. Thorn wanted more. A ludicrously low bid – £1 million, £2 million? – could look like cheek. It had to look like Thames was competing, even if it knew it would come last.

Tom Guttridge had asked Thames for help earlier on in the year. Would it be interested in a small stake in the Palace/Polygram bid against LWT? Thames had swiftly said no – to move aggressively against its London neighbour might discourage the ITC from awarding it exceptional circumstances for its own licence.

Guttridge had been stumped. The Palace/Polygram bid, which been christened London Independent Broadcasting (LIB), was finding it hard to get a clear idea of how the ITV network operated. The ITV Association, the trade body which represented the interests of the sixteen ITV companies, was blocking moves by outside bidders to get access to crucial network data, such as the size of the jointly held programme library controlled by the ITVA. Without the help of a network insider, a bidder was hopelessly disadvantaged.

Andy Birchall, LIB's bid director, had approached Granada's Andrew Quinn, whom he knew from his BSB days. Would Granada be interested in a stake? 'No,' came the reply, 'we're still not sure what we should be doing up here, let alone anywhere else.' Quinn, Birchall later realised, was being somewhat disingenuous. But LIB ploughed on regardless.

Guttridge took over the writing of the bid in April. Much of his time had already been spent on bizarre counter-espionage tactics, spreading misinformation in the hope of keeping LWT off the trail. He even went as far as pinpointing where LWT's consultants drank. He then sent in staff to talk unguardedly about their preparations for a TVS bid. He also regularly surprised his partners with what he claimed was reliable information on LWT's plans.

The on-the-hoof nature of the LIB bid was continually throwing up difficulties, however. Without a fixed base the group had hired rooms at the Groucho Club in Soho, now just a short walk from both Mentorn and Palace. In an office on the top floor Guttridge and Birchall started putting together the research for the application. It was a hopelessly indiscreet place to base such confidential number crunching; nor did it really offer the right image for any serious applicant. Cynical journalists quickly labelled LIB 'the Groucho bid'.

The difficulties reached a head in late April. Guttridge, Birchall and John Needham, a Mentorn manager, were putting in fifteen-hour days trying to get the application together. One night, taking a break from work upstairs, they sat in the Groucho's ground-floor restaurant. They had just ordered dinner when a manageress approached them.

'Do any of you have portable phones?'

(It was, thought Birchall, a pretty stupid question to ask in a place like Groucho's.)

'Yes,' they all replied in unison.

'Well, somebody's been caught in the street with two portable telephones. The police think they've been stolen from here.'

They rushed outside. Pinned to the railings next to an expensive-looking bicycle was an extremely drunk writer, held by two burly policemen. His story spilled out. Representing a national newspaper at a book launch on the first floor, he had got lost trying to find the way out, gone upstairs instead of down, walked into LIB's unlocked offices, and helped himself to two portable telephones and six small pots of jam belonging to a maid. He had been caught outside trying to wrench the bicycle free of its lock. It was not his fault, he pleaded. He was on 'medication'.

Birchall and Guttridge were open-mouthed. All LIB's work on the franchise bid had been laid out in the office, yet of all the things to steal he had taken two telephones and some jam. Thankfully the man was too drunk to have read anything.

Why had they not locked the office? The door did not have a lock.

Michael Green: *'Why are you
in this breakfast bid?'*

Lord Bellwin (Taylor Woodrow):
'I don't know . . .'

Greg Dyke came back from Minster Lovell, the planning
weekend with his breakfast bid consortium, with a changed
perspective. Working out the bidding strategy against TV-am
had convinced him of one thing: if somebody was planning to
do the same thing to LWT there was no point in bidding high. A
station like LWT, however stripped down, just could not match
a greenfield bidder proposing to operate as a publisher-
broadcaster.

That left two ways to win: making sure the opponent failed at
the quality threshold or gaining the licence through 'exceptional circumstances'. Either way, he had to know more about
the opposition. He knew the rumours about Powell and
Guttridge targeting LWT, but there was no confirmation. And
he was confident Thames was not involved: LWT had researched a bid against Thames as a way of hedging its bets in the
London region but backed away because of the high cost of a
winning bid (it estimated £45 million at 1993 prices) and
because it did not want to bring Thames down upon it. Thames,
he believed, had done likewise. Now he needed to find out just
how strong LIB was.

So for a week, from 8 to 12 April, Dyke went back to being a
reporter. He made a list of all the people he knew who had
worked with Mentorn, Palace, Polygram and Working Title,
and rang them up. He tracked down people who might have

been offered jobs by them. Eventually the information started to roll in. By the end of the week he felt better about it. If these people were going to make a convincing bid, he thought, they had a lot of work to do.

That weekend Dyke had organised another strategy session, this time for the LWT bid team, at Hever Castle in Kent. The castle, now a moated conference centre complete with mock Elizabethan village at the back and real Roman statues round the front, had been the venue for LWT's initial strategy meeting in the autumn of 1990. The LWT team liked it; despite the castle and gardens attracting thousands of tourists every day, the conference facilities were discreet and the food good. It smoothed over the tough talking. It was at Hever the year before that Dyke had told LWT's production division that it had to hit breakeven by 1993. At the time it was losing £15 million a year. Perhaps the baronial majesty of the place made the blow easier to take.

That Saturday the twenty or so executives, consultants and accountants ran through a variety of bidding strategies for a number of different ITV companies, just to get a feel for what might happen elsewhere. They looked at TVS – a franchise with similar revenue to LWT but far greater overheads because of its dual region split and local programming commitments. They concluded a bid of between £35–40 million was necessary to win the licence.

In the discussions about LWT that followed it soon became clear to Dyke that many of his executives had reached the same conclusion as him: there was no point in bidding high to regain the licence because life afterwards would be a misery. *Who wants to spend the next ten years having nothing to spend, scrabbling along, making a profit of one or two million?* (Later, others would offer a different reason: the complicated share option scheme devised by Bland to lock executives into the company meant they had to bid low. They would get the maximum rewards only if the share price, then below £2, hit 278p in autumn 1993. To do that, they had to achieve sizable profits. If the low bid came off, men like Bland, Dyke and Melvyn Bragg, LWT's arts supremo, need never work again. It was some incentive.)

The next day they finalised the LWT bid range. All the senior executives had to write on a piece of paper what they thought LWT should bid. The highest call was £28 million; the average between £21–22 million. Both Dyke, who wrote £15 million, and Christopher Bland, his chairman, thought that was too high. They returned to London determined to do more work on it.

Bland was already considering a bid of less than £15 million. He was convinced that any rival bidder would probably offer something over £30 million, say £32–36 million a year. LWT could not match it. But more than that, the probable opposition, LIB, looked unlikely to pass the quality threshold on any criteria. The balance sheets of Palace and Working Title in particular were weak; they did not have broadcasting experience in any depth; they did not have a strong slate of people associated with them. So if LWT could not outbid them, surely it should just put more money into its local programming and network schedule to give itself the strongest possible chance of getting exceptional - circumstances. And to heighten, by contrast, the chances of LIB failing the quality threshold. After all, the bids would be assessed by the same executives at the ITC who LWT had worked with for so long at the IBA. Their views on quality must coincide.

Dyke's sleuthing was also pulling in more information that supported a low bid strategy. A conversation with an executive who had turned down an approach from LIB revealed that the consortium's capital base was only £20 million. Dyke reckoned that the most they could borrow on that was another £20 million. That gave them £40 million to set up a new station, run the service, and pay off the bid costs. It was not enough.

By the end of April Bland was convinced that LWT should bid lower. One Saturday, coming in after walking his dog, he rang Dyke at home.

'I've just thought of something. If we are not going to be the highest bidder, why bid £15 million? It might as well be £1 million.'

Dyke pointed out that it had to be something that did not embarrass the ITC. 'So what's respectable?' asked Bland.

The LWT bid dropped to £11 million, then lower still.

Eventually the argument swung between a £2000 bid, and £8 million. The latter guaranteed the station similar profits to those it made in 1990, taking into account the bid and the new levy the Government was introducing from 1993, a percentage of revenue dependant on the size of the licence area (in LWT's case, 11 per cent).

The week before the applications were due in, the LWT team prepared both bids. But they had to know for certain that LIB were going to bid against them, and not TVS as had been rumoured. On Friday 10 May Dyke gave the go-ahead for LWT to make Working Title a proposition: a £300,000 film development deal which offered the company the full fee whether they made a movie or not. All they had to do was sign a no-compete clause which barred their involvement in a bid against LWT.

Tim Bevan, boss of Working Title, made a panic call to Guttridge that afternoon. He explained the proposition.

'What are you going to do?' asked Guttridge.

'I'm going to turn them down,' said Bevan.

They offered it to the wrong company, thought Guttridge. Working Title, part-owned by Polygram, could just about afford to turn away that kind of money. Palace might have had to think longer. And Mentorn? A seven-figure offer would certainly have been hard to resist.

A few days earlier TVS had finalised its bid. At a full board meeting on the sixth floor of the company's Buckingham Gate offices, Agnew had led the discussion. 'The key point is that we will be starting as a new company. Do we want to start at breakeven in year one, 1993? Or do we want to get a higher return by going for £10 million plus profit, or even a £10 million loss?'

The directors looked at the research in front of them. Their own models of what their rivals might do predicted that the MAI bid would fall below £40 million, but that Carlton and Virgin would bid more. It all depended on how badly they wanted the licence. Green, in particular, was a worry, as they had no idea what information he had gleaned during his takeover talks with James Gatward. To win, the research made it clear that TVS had to bid over £50 million. It would leave hardly any return for shareholders for a number of years, but without the licence, all the company had was a large loss-making subsidiary, MTM. It was worth less than nothing.

Agnew asked each executive director to name his bid figure, and then withdraw. The non-executive directors were then each asked the same question. The figures ranged from £45 million to £62 million in 1991 prices. Inflation then had to be added to get a bid for 1993. He settled on a consensus figure of £54.1 million (£59.8 million in 1993 prices), which was approved by the non-executives. With optimistic forecasts, that would allow TVS TV to show a projected profit of just over £1 million in its first year of the new licence. It was a lot less than its 1990 profit of £22 million, but a fair performance if you saw it as a start-up.

The non-executives, Agnew noted, had wanted to bid much higher than the executives. But then many of them sat on the finance committee, and they had looked long and hard at the alternatives to winning. They were not attractive.

The weekend of 11 and 12 May was a long one for all bidders. Final decisions loomed. Most had completed nearly all the paperwork, allowing themselves one or two options. They could not leave it for too long. The mass of supporting documentation linked to the final bid meant that the key numbers had to be fed into the business plans at least a day before the 15 May noon deadline.

Michael Green paced the top floor of Zenith's Baker Street offices, cleared to accommodate the Carlton TV bid teams. Banks of computers and piles of printer's proofs now covered the desktops. Green had tried going home but he was too anxious. He checked the proofs for the Carlton applications and looked at the figures for the umpteenth time. He trawled his team for the latest rumours about who was likely to do what. That weekend he knew he had the knowledge. No one could have amassed more information on people's intentions than Carlton. His team knew more people in the business than anyone else, his organisation had more tentacles. That's why he was going to be successful.

Carlton TV had already done a full model of the likely Thames bid, taking into account its intention to remain a producer-broadcaster and analysing the finances of its principal backer Thorn EMI. That forecast a Thames bid of between £30 million and £35 million. But Green knew Branson and Frost were likely to bid a lot more for the licence. As the weeks before the 15 May deadline went by, Carlton's London bid had crept higher and higher. By contrast the team organising its application against TVS were under instructions to bid low; that region was always going to be Carlton's second choice, and Green did not want to give the ITC any encouragement to save Thames through exceptional circumstances. The regulators might just think that if Carlton lost in London but could be given the south in compensation, it would find it difficult to challenge exceptional circumstances. Green did not want to be fobbed off, but he wanted to keep his options open as well and keep rivals like MAI from concentrating on London too. (Some of his team later argued that targeting LWT would have been a better business decision as a second choice after Thames, but that was precluded by Green's friendship with Christopher Bland.)

By that weekend Green had drawn up two separate bids for both Thames and TVS, high and low, and decided to leave it till the last moment before making a decision. The final power rested with him. Despite pressure from a number of would-be investors he had let in only two stakeholders: Conrad Black, whose Daily Telegraph group had wanted 20 per cent but took 5 per cent, and Rizzoli Corriere della Sera, one of Italy's largest publishers, with another 5 per cent. Characteristically, Green kept 90 per cent for Carlton plc.

Elsewhere the bidding strategies varied wildly. In the north-west Phil Redmond pushed through a massive £35 million bid. Yorkshire, his partner in North-West TV, facing two rivals for its own licence but brimful of confidence, bid even more, £37.7 million. That big bid confidence spilled over into Tyne Tees, 20 per cent owned by Yorkshire, as well. It tabled a £15 million bid, a vast sum when the company was only making pre-tax profits of £6 million the year before.

It had gambled on major cost cutting and a reduction in levy

185

to make its bid achievable. It also believed it had to bid high to beat off Granada's rival bid. In the event Granada did not attempt to oubid Tyne Tees, but made its own gamble – that Tyne Tees would bid so much its application would be judged unsustainable. In its own region, too, it saw little point to trying to match Redmond's bid. By April, with its own brand of confidence, it had narrowed its options down to three bids, £7 million, £9 million and £11 million. In May it plumped for £9 million. (Granada's confidence appeared to falter slightly just before May 15; Stewart Prebble tried to persuade his fellow Campaign for Quality Television directors to co-author an open letter emphasising again that quality must prevail over cash. They declined, suggesting Prebble was using the Campaign for Granada's purposes.)

There was little consensus. In London Thames bid £32.7 million, LWT £7.6 million. The LIB stakeholders, meeting at Guttridge's house in Barnes on Sunday morning, scribbled their bids on the back of wrapping paper and averaged them out: £35.4 million. Representatives from MAI, SelecTV and Central, christening their bid for the south Meridian, met in Clive Hollick's spartan riverside office and chose £36.5 million. Richard Branson and David Frost, deliberating over a dinner for shareholders in the Charterhouse dining room on Monday night, chose a massive £45.3 million for the London weekday licence. They bid less for their second and third choices – £22.1 million for the south and £10.1 million for the east. They too had their eyes on the main prize: Thames.

Some ITV companies facing more than one opponent bid high: HTV, facing three, bid £20.5 million; Anglia, facing two, bid £17.8 million, TSW, also facing two, bid £16.1 million. Others bid little more than what would maintain their profits: Ulster settled on £1m, Grampian chose £700,000. They knew they would be outbid. They hoped the quality threshold or exceptional circumstances would save them. At its core the broadcasting legislation was like any popular religion – you could interpret it in a variety of ways. The ITV companies, with a better knowledge of the individuals involved, thought they knew how the ITC would interpret it. That was what counted. But for many, it was a wing-and-a-prayer job.

On Monday morning the shareholders' representatives behind the ITN breakfast bid met at the news provider's concrete and glass headquarters in Gray's Inn Road. The atmosphere round the table was tense. Bob Phillis, ITN chief executive, surveyed the faces: MAI's Roger Laughton, NBC's Patrick Cox, the Telegraph's Stephen Grabiner, Taylor Woodrow's Lord Bellwin, Dick Emery, the consortium's chief executive designate. There too was Michael Green, who had replaced his representative, Nigel Walmsley, at the last moment. A posse of advisers and accountants completed the group.

The consortium, which had named its bid Daybreak, had fought off Gus MacDonald's impetuous threat to take ITN to the OFT over the rates it was charging the group for its news service. Phillis thought the accusation was ludicrous and had demanded an apology from Scottish TV. He got one. He knew, however, that it was meant as a shot across the bows. ITN had enough difficulties without that kind of aggravation from its own shareholders.

Despite the difficulties, the Daybreak partners were happy with the programming side of the bid. The final submission had retained some of the original Hollingsworth ideas but added a harder-edged news element. This fitted in with research which showed the staple housewife-and-children audience of TV-am would soon shift to populist satellite services, leaving the network breakfast shows with a more up-market audience of working adults. The proposed Daybreak service could make that shift as satellite TV viewing grew.

The friction between the individual consortium members had worsened, however. At Cox's instigation, both Sir Paul Fox, the retired BBC boss, and Sir Robin Day, the famous interviewer, had been invited on to the Daybreak board (his third suggestion, John Whitney, had been rejected). Fox, an aggressive, domineering man, was also a former ITN chairman, and was immediately pencilled in as chairman designate of the Daybreak bid. This infuriated Green who had fallen out with Fox earlier in the year. He had approached him to chair Carlton TV's London weekday bid and had been outraged when, after discussions had started, Fox had suddenly said no and accepted a seat on the Thames board instead. Not many got one over on Michael Green like that.

Then in late April, as Daybreak's chairman, Fox gave an intemperate interview to the *Observer*, describing TV-am as 'garbage', and declaring that he never watched breakfast TV, but preferred to listen to the radio. To many it appeared as if Daybreak had shot itself in the foot. Fox's comments on how he would not run against other bosses who were his 'friends' smacked of an old-boy network that was distinctly out of fashion. Green, up early as usual on a Sunday morning, had been appalled at the article. He phoned round, waking all the other shareholders up, demanding an urgent meeting with Fox in Carlton's offices the next morning. They all turned up, even Clive Hollick, whose ennoblement to Labour peer was announced that morning. There was no time for congratulations. Green had laid into Fox, telling him this was the last time he opened his mouth to the press.

Fox, a former paratrooper, had squared up to him. 'Are you telling me you are muzzling me?'

'Yes,' said Green.

'I'm not going to be told what to do,' retorted Fox, now equally angry. In the end Phillis patched it up, and Fox agreed to keep a low profile. But the tension simmered on. There were now clear suggestions that Green resented being told what to do by his old employee, Phillis. For his part, Phillis was desperately trying to hold all the parties together so that they could at least get the application in.

By 13 May, however, there was still little consensus on how much to bid. Phillis had spent the weekend canvassing the shareholders with his preferred range, £34.5 million to £35 million at 1993 prices. Green had made it plain he thought it was too high. Cox was also nervous. Research which NBC had done in New York showed that any bid over £34.5 million would probably need refinancing. If that was what they had to bid, so be it. But NBC for one would prefer less.

Cox and Grabiner, the Telegraph's marketing director, had discussed a common strategy first, as they always did before

Daybreak meetings. Both had decided that they would go in at £32.5 million, and might allow themselves to be pushed to £33.5 million or higher. They were conscious that Phillis wanted more. Cox also had an additional piece of information that he planned to tell the shareholders. Two weeks before, an NBC executive at the Cannes Film Festival had been given a fax by mistake at her hotel. The fax, intended for one of the Walt Disney team there, was headed Evaluation Of Breakfast TV Bid Price. It appeared to list the bid range for the rival LWT–Disney bid: 'target bid – £26 million; highest bid – £28 million; furthest bid prepared to look at – £30 million'.

That morning Phillis presented again his research which showed that Daybreak could bid up to £40 million and still make a profit on the breakfast service. Green was unconvinced. He resolutely refused to allow the bid to be shifted above £32.5 million. Laughton backed him up. Cox then told the group about the Cannes fax. There was a sharp intake of breath. Was it a plant? Why else would Disney fax confidential figures to a hotel (ironically the Carlton Hotel) in Cannes where they knew rival executives were also staying? Both Green and Phillis seized on it. It shows we are already bidding too much, argued Green. No, said Phillis, this was two weeks ago. We have got to bid more to be sure.

The arguments swung back and forth. Eventually it became obvious that Phillis just could not carry the other shareholders with him. It would have to be £32.5 million. He threw up his hands.

'I am not happy with this. I am being railroaded.' He turned to Laughton.

'Is this your final word, Roger?'

'Yes,' said Laughton, 'but Clive Hollick will take a phone call.'

'OK, let's adjourn,' said Phillis. He phoned Hollick and explained that he thought the bid was too low to win. Hollick in turn rang Conrad Black. There would have to be another meeting. They all agreed to check their figures again and reconvene at Price Waterhouse, the bid's accountants, late on Tuesday afternoon, less than twenty-four hours before the bid had to be in.

At the final meeting Phillis again pitched for a higher bid. Black and Hollick had already given the go-ahead for £33.3 million; Green stuck to his arguments that it was more than the licence was worth. On a satellite link to New York, NBC's JB Holsten III said he would support Black and Hollick's final figure. It was agreed; Phillis looked disappointed, but accepted defeat gracefully. Cox, waiting till he thought Green was out of earshot, made a mischievous suggestion.

'If Bob feels so strongly about the bid, why don't we give him permission to substitute another figure. On his neck be it . . .'

He had meant it only half jokingly. Green heard, swung round and gave him a withering look.

The figures would return to haunt the Daybreak consortium. At a one-and-a-half-hour board meeting the Sunday previously, Gyngell had persuaded TV-am's directors to endorse a bid of only £14.1 million for the breakfast licence. Against the advice of the station's own consultants and the worries of some non-executive directors, he argued that TV-am was impregnable on quality. That was the message behind every communication from the ITC, from Sarah Thane's speech the year before to George Russell's letters and calls. Others could bid the earth. They would still not get it.

At the same time the LWT consortium, now calling itself Sunrise, had agreed a £34.6 million bid.

Patrick Cox was not the only one getting messages from Cannes. Leslie Hill, sitting in his ground floor office at Central's London headquarters in Portman Square that Monday, found his hands were shaking. In front of him lay a note from his secretary: 'Ring Richard Creasey in Cannes. He has got news of someone who is bidding for Central tomorrow'.

For a moment Hill was too shocked to pick up the phone. Following the confirmation that East Midlands Electricity would not be bidding, he had assumed Central would get a clear run. It had prepared four bids for the Midlands licence, ranging from £2000 to £15 million, but the £2000 bid was the one they were all hoping to make. Now this.

Creasey, Central's director of special projects, was in his hotel bedroom when Hill rang. Breathlessly he told Hill what had happened. He had just been to lunch with a journalist from the Rome office of *Variety*, the TV and film trade paper. While sitting in the restaurant a man had walked past and the journalist had remarked, 'That is the man who will be bidding against Central on Wednesday.' Creasey's jaw had dropped. He chased after the man and tried to introduce himself. The man, an Italian, spoke little English, but appeared to confirm to Creasey that his company, RCS, was bidding against Central. '*Si, centrale, centrale . . .*'

Who with? Carlton.

Hill tensed. The rumours of a Carlton bid against Central had been in the press the day before. Most at Central dismissed them as ludicrous. Michael Green sat on the Central board and owned 20 per cent of the station. He was hardly likely to bid against it. Unless something was happening that Central had not accounted for. Hill put the phone down on Creasey and rang Green. He got straight through.

'Michael, I've just got a report in from Cannes that you're planning to bid against us with someone called RCS.'

'What?' laughed Green. Hill felt uncomfortable. It was hardly easy for a chief executive to suggest to his major shareholder that he was committing corporate high treason. 'I think you have got it mixed up,' said Green. He explained: RCS was his partner in Carlton's bid against Thames. Creasey must have misheard. Hill said he would check. Sure enough, by '*centrale*', an Italian adjective meaning 'at the centre', he had meant the London station, Britain's biggest ITV company; much of Cannes thought he meant Central. Hill breathed a long sigh of relief.

The next night, in his suite in a small hotel behind Sloane Square, Hill finalised the Central bid. He had already recommended £2,000 to the Central board. They had approved it but gave him *carte blanche* to alter it if circumstances changed before 15 May. Ever cautious, he had devised a system which left the ultimate choice till the last possible moment. At 8 p.m., he had to choose two bids from the four they had prepared. At breakfast the next day, he had to choose one. The appropriate paperwork would be gathered to support the chosen figure. It left a safety net for any last-minute shocks.

That evening he could take the tension no longer. With his inner circle of three – Kevin Betts, finance director, Andy Allen, programme director, and Marshall Stewart, corporate strategy director – sitting around his bedroom, he argued for a final choice to be made. Surely it was clear now that Central was unopposed. They would have heard of any deals with local production independents. Without the production independents you could not make a credible bid. After some debate, they decided unanimously that it had to be the minimum: £2000. They celebrated with drinks but it was a tense night for all of them. What if they were wrong?

At Mentorn's headquarters over in Soho, the LIB bid was going from bad to worse. For the final week Tom Guttridge had moved the bid back to his Wardour Street base, putting the bid team into offices above the dry cleaner opposite Mentorn's main building. But the actual writing of it had fallen way behind schedule. Each application consisted of three sections, tagged A,B, and C, which detailed the programme schedule proposals, the bidders and the business plan respectively. Difficulties over the proposed number of hours to be broadcast had forced Guttridge to rip up LIB's section A and start again. The other members of the team were also having difficulties with Guttridge's visceral writing style. His dislike of Dyke was beginning to become an obsession, and too much of the application was being coloured by invective about LWT's performance. By Tuesday night it looked, yet again, as if the bid was falling apart.

Guttridge was sitting in Mentorn's second-floor meeting room working on a portable computer. He had just finished a draft of the three-page statement of intent that had to accompany each bid. He still had to write the eight-page summary also demanded. He looked at his watch and cursed. It was 10 p.m. The whole lot still had to go to the printers – the ITC wanted over fifty copies of sections A and B for distribution to public libraries. And the printing deadline was 9 p.m.

A panic call was put in to the printers. They would run late if penalties were paid. Guttridge agreed – they had no choice. The room was now heaving with despondent-looking consultants and lawyers; most thought they could not make it. Guttridge and Andy Birchall went back to the computer. Together they worked painstakingly through the eight-page summary. Outside they could hear the engines and shouts that signalled throwing-out time from the local pubs. Still they worked on. At midnight, Guttridge sat back with a sigh of relief and pressed the word-count button. The length was spot-on. 'That's it!' he shouted.

'Anyone like a cup of coffee?' asked one of the lawyers, getting up out of his chair by the window and heading for the door. He was halfway out when his foot hit the computer's power lead. The plug whipped out of the socket, leaving the computer screen blank. 'Shit!' Guttridge looked on in horror; it felt like his heart had hit the pit of his stomach. They plugged the computer in again but the summary had gone. He had forgotten to save it. Cutting off the power had wiped it out. The other team members had warned him repeatedly to save what he wrote as he did it. This time it was all too much. He fell apart.

Right on cue, Polygram's Michael Kuhn walked in to check the bid had been completed. He listened in horror to what had happened. 'Get a secretary. I'll dictate it. It's quicker.'

Guttridge rang round, hauling a Mentorn secretary out of bed. Kuhn and Birchall took the secretary across the road and dictated the summary. Guttridge finished off the statement of intent. Half an hour later Kuhn popped his head round the meeting room door. 'We've done it,' he said proudly.

'There's no way you can have finished eight pages,' said Guttridge.

'Look, Tom, it's not really part of the bid. It's only for people who don't want to read the whole thing. They say it should be eight pages long but they don't say how much should be on each page.'

He grinned as he showed Guttridge what he had done. He had spaced out a summary of the bid in bullet points over five pages, and added three pages listing some of the awards won by those associated with the bid. It would have to do. They reached the printer by 2 a.m. By 6 a.m. it was ready. They agreed the consultants from Arthur Andersen's would hand it in, and headed for bed.

12

'George is loaded with experience in changing businesses . . .'

An associate on George Russell

Wednesday 15 May dawned cool and cloudy in London. Leslie Hill was already up. He had woken at 4 a.m. to scrabble outside his hotel room for the newspapers. He scanned the headlines: Winnie Mandela's jail sentence – six years for her part in the kidnapping and assault of three men and a boy, who later died – and Edwina Currie's libel award. The Tory MP had won £5000 damages after the *Observer* likened her to a character in a film who put political gain above her family, took a young lover and resorted to murder. The intrigue in the television world was still inside-page news.

The Central boss, sitting in his pyjamas, skim-read till he found the stories he was looking for. His first reaction was relief; still no indication of a bid against Central. Then he caught his breath. 'Challenge For Granada TV Franchise On Eve Of Bid Deadline'. He read on. Yorkshire and Tyne Tees were believed to have joined forces with Phil Redmond to bid for the northwest of England ITV franchise held by Granada. He wondered how many other bids would be revealed today.

The ITC's underground car park was swarming with press by 8 a.m. The authority, hoping to avoid an unseemly scrum outside its Brompton Road front doors, had told bidders to deliver their applications via the back entrance. Early risers were not disappointed. Carlton Television's Nigel Walmsley and Paul

Jackson strolled in at 8.02 a.m., their applications for the London weekday and south and south-east licences following in two separate vans.

Thames boss Richard Dunn was next, waving regally from a chauffeur-driven Ford Scorpio. 'Sock it to them, Dicky!' shouted a Thames News cameraman, almost caught changing his videotape. All morning the bidders kept rolling in. TV-am's Bruce Gyngell by foot, after unveiling his company's financial results at a press conference nearby; Leslie Hill and Andy Allan, Central's programme director, by car, with a van in convoy. (Central had hired two in case one broke down.) Allan winced as he saw the mob of press and muttered to Hill: 'Now I know what it's like to be Madonna.'

Many bosses decided against turning up in person. Greg Dyke sent the company secretary, Graham Howell, with LWT's application. The bid envelope had been sealed in wax by Christopher Bland, LWT's chairman, with his father's signet ring. Others had taken more elaborate security precautions. Yorkshire TV had organised a five-vehicle convoy, co-ordinated by a security firm, to drive the documents from Leeds to London the day before. The TVS application was carried in a fleet of Escort vans – plans to use heavy duty security vans had been quashed only when the company found out that the clearance of the ITC's back entrance was just six feet two inches.

Not everyone was benefiting from such meticulous planning. Guttridge and Birchall's LIB bid hit yet another last-minute hitch. Birchall had been woken at Kuhn's house at 9 a.m. by a journalist's call on his mobile phone. Only then did he realise that a vital table had been left out of the LIB application. After a frenzy of phone calls, copies of the missing table were stapled in by the Arthur Andersen team before the applications reached the ITC. If Birchall had not forgotten to switch his mobile off the night before, he would never have remembered.

Pandemonium reigned behind the ITC. Journalists ran back and forth, up and down the car park ramp, desperately trying to coax car window comments from rival bidders. Most remained tight-lipped. Thames' Dunn managed a mouthful: 'We have put in the highest bid we can in order to maintain the high-quality diverse service not only that the ITC requires but that we want to offer our viewers.' Only TSW's Harry Turner seemed prepared to lighten the tone of the occasion. He leaned against his limo, grinning for photographers, a fat cigar in one hand and a toy rabbit in the other. 'This is the TSW mascot,' he told reporters proudly. 'He's called Gus Honeybun.' It was the picture that filled the business pages the next day.

By 11 a.m. most of the bids were in, except the one that many were waiting for: Branson and Frost. Their celebrity guaranteed them top billing. They had already held a photocall in the City on the steps of St Paul's to announce they were bidding for no less than three licences. But at the ITC, there was no sign of the applications. Ironically they were stuck behind the trooping of the colour at Buckingham Palace. The bids, for the London weekday, south and south-east and east of England licences, arrived in three separate taxis with half an hour to spare.

Ten minutes before the noon deadline the last bidder shot past the press scrum in another taxi. 'It's Andrew Neil!' shouted one journalist. It was not. It was the C13 bid for the Channel Islands – the fortieth application to arrive. The journalists drifted off to lunch. In less than four hours they would get official confirmation of the bidders from the ITC.

For bosses like Central's Hill and Scottish TV's MacDonald, both expecting no opposition, it was a nerve-racking day. MacDonald had pushed through a £2,000 bid convinced that no one could have assembled a rival application without Scottish hearing about it. He even put the application in on Tuesday. He was sitting in his Glasgow office on Wednesday morning when he got a call from his broker, Alan Tracey at Kleinwort Benson.

'This is a call I don't like to make, Gus, but we've just heard from sources in the City that someone has gone into the ITC with a bid against you.'

MacDonald's heart sank. 'Well, I don't think it can be a serious bid,' he replied, more for his own benefit than Tracey's. It was not the best of lunch hours for MacDonald. Eventually the news filtered through. It was a crank bid. An inventor with a machine that bleeped out swear words on television had put in a spoof application for Scottish as a publicity stunt. He did not

197

enclose a cheque with his envelope. (It was the wrong tactic, mused MacDonald later. If the inventor had gone round the stations saying 'Buy this machine or I'll bid against you' the response might have been different. Like: 'What a wonderful machine, my man. How much do you want for it?')

Leslie Hill was in his car on the way back to Birmingham when he heard that Central was unopposed. Marshall Stewart, Central's corporate strategy director, rang through on the car phone at around 4.30. Hill was ecstatic. The next day he gave Kevin Betts, Central's finance director, the biggest hug he had ever had.

George Russell strode into the ITC after the scrum had finished. Taking the lift to his office on the eighth floor, he pondered what he might find. Already the indications were that the ITC was going to get more bids than it expected. More bids meant more work, and he badly wanted to get the licensing process wrapped up by October. That gave everyone more time to prepare for 1993, when the new licences started. Any foul-ups and he could have some major delays on his hands.

Russell, fifty-six, was a broad, grey-haired man. His pensive, slightly lugubrious face was testimony to half a lifetime's experience of boardroom politics; his small paunch to the dining demands exacted by the 'great and the good' circuit. He had been involved in broadcasting, both as regulator and board director, for fifteen years. For a day-job, he ran Marley Tiles, the massive building products group. A video installed in his BMW allowed him to view programmes as he sped between Marley's Kent headquarters, his central London home and the ITC's Knightsbridge offices. Despite his high-flying lifestyle, his manner was resolutely down-to-earth. Colleagues nicknamed him 'Geordie', after his Tyneside birthplace. They plucked out words like 'workaholic' and 'straight-forward' to describe him. For the task ahead of him, he needed to be.

Russell's roots were solidly in manufacturing. He started his career at ICI, working his way up from junior managerial rank before joining Welland Chemical in Canada. From there he moved back to the north-east, taking charge of Alcan's

Northumberland aluminium smelter. In 1981 he became managing director of Alcan Aluminium UK. In 1986 he moved to Marley.

He often described himself to the press as a 'turnaround' man. Reorganising Welland after a takeover, merging Alcan with British Aluminium, restructuring Marley. As a northerner, a manufacturer and a man interested in the arts he was a natural choice for the IBA when, in 1979, it realised that too many of its members reflected the media's southern bias. Russell did not even know what the IBA was. The day he arrived the ITV companies went on strike. Suddenly, with his years of experience in industrial relations as a manufacturer, he was the most knowledgeable person there.

He served for eight years, before moving to Channel 4 as deputy chairman in 1987 to help find a successor for Jeremy Isaacs. In 1988 he became chairman of ITN, the first outsider to hold the position. While never a fully paid-up member of the broadcasting establishment he was seen by many as a good compromise man, well liked by the ITV bosses he worked with. His no-nonsense manner and gritty manufacturing background also impressed the Government. Few, however, realised just how much.

Russell was sitting in an ITN board meeting in October 1988 when the message came through. He was slipped a piece of paper by a secretary. Would he come at once to the Home Office to see the Secretary of State? His brow furrowed. He had no idea what it was about. When he got there Douglas Hurd and Timothy Renton, the broadcasting minister, were waiting for him. They explained that, as he knew, they were looking for a successor to George Thomson, someone who would take charge of the dismantling of the IBA, and build, in its place, the ITC. Would he do it? Russell was stunned. He had three weeks to think it over. He returned to the ITN board meeting perplexed. No one at the meeting was any the wiser.

Eventually, after getting permission from the Marley board and discussing it with Thomson, he said yes. He never found out why he was approached. He suspected he had been Renton's choice. He had recently spent an evening with the minister in deep discussion about the future of broadcasting during a Channel 4 board dinner. Others suggested he was Thatcher's man, but he had hardly met her, only once as boss of Alcan five years previously and once briefly as chairman of ITN. Even after his appointment he had only a ten-minute audience with her at 10 Downing Street. He was never asked what he thought of the Government's proposals for broadcasting, which appeared in the White Paper that autumn.

Russell laid down only one precondition on taking the job: that he should not be forced to sack all the IBA staff, but be allowed to take those who wanted to come into the new authority, the ITC. The politicians waved it through. He started in January 1989 with no job definition and no terms, other than to oversee the transition from IBA to ITC and organise the competitive tender for the licence round. The key change was the legislative shift from broadcaster to regulator. The IBA had operated as a broadcasting body, supervising franchises held by regional ITV companies. The ITC would operate solely as regulator, while the ITV companies themselves were now the broadcasters. Russell spelt it out bluntly for the IBA staff. 'You're going to be asked to build your own gallows. Why don't you make them the best gallows you've ever seen built in your life.'

He had no trouble taking the helm at the IBA. He had worked there, after all, since 1979. He then began a campaign of attrition against some of the White Paper's more radical proposals for the licensing mechanism. What he could not get behind closed doors he used publicity to achieve. At one press conference he threatened to resign if there was no 'exceptional circumstances' clause written into the competitive tender. At another he deliberately raised the quality threshold by likening it to 'Beecher's Brook', the most formidable jump in the Grand National.

His vision was a realistic one: to create a mechanism that would help the inevitable restructuring of the industry occur, while leaving much of the quality associated with public service broadcasting intact. He believed the industry was already overextended: hours of commercial broadcasting had expanded on the back of strong advertising growth by more than 200 per cent in the 1980s. The competition for revenue and talent posed by the new satellite channels, as well as the proposed fifth terrestrial channel, would prove a tight squeeze for ITV.

He did not, in the end, get the licensing mechanism he wanted. IBA proposals for a minimum lease price for the licences plus a percentage of an applicant's net advertising revenue were rejected. But he got something fairly similar; and most important of all, he won a greater deal of discretion for the ITC in interpreting the mechanism than anyone expected. By the time David Mellor had reshaped the legislation as it went through committee stage in the House of Commons, Russell was confident he had something he could work with.

Standing in his office that May afternoon, waiting to open the sealed bids that had arrived that morning, he was conscious that the next five months would provide the real test. The eleven members of the Commission, each appointed by the Home Secretary, would sift through the applications. Each would be assigned specific regions to monitor, working closely with different teams of in-house specialists. Some would vet the business plans, others would assess the programme proposals, to see who passed the ITC's 'quality threshold'. The financial bids themselves, enclosed in separate sealed envelopes, were to be opened by Russell, checked, and then locked into the ITC secretary's safe. Only when applications had passed the quality threshold would they be considered. The whole process would take place in utmost secrecy. The bids would then be revealed to the public, if bidders gave permission, when the winners were announced in October.

Four of them gathered to check the sums bid: Russell, David Glencross, the ITC chief executive, Jocelyn Stevens, the ITC deputy chairman, and Kenneth Blyth, ITC company secretary. There were forty envelopes and applications in front of them, four more than the ITC had anticipated. Russell opened the biggest bundle first. It was TVS's application. Later he opened the accompanying envelope. It read:

STRICTLY CONFIDENTIAL

1. Name of Applicant: TVS Television
2. Licence applied for: South & South-East
3. Cash Bid: £59,760,000

He swallowed hard. This was far higher than he expected.

He had predicted that the sums bid would be mere 'topping up' of the 'percentage of qualifying revenue' (PQR) – the replacement for the old Levy which the stations also had to pay. In TVS's case it was 11 per cent of its ad revenue, or around £20 million. The bid was nearly three times that.

Hastily they read the other envelopes. Some of the bids seemed huge. Others, in particular the two at £2000, restored his humour. This was going to be more interesting than he had thought.

'Richard, I've got an idea.'

Richard Branson's brow furrowed slightly as he listened to the voice on the other end of the phone. Michael Green was not a frequent caller at his private office in his Holland Park house. The bids had just gone in. What was he up to?

'Don't you think it is sensible that we reveal the bids to each other?'

Branson thought about it. The arguments were convincing: he and Green were bound to have outbid Thames. Why wait all summer to find out which was the highest?

The ITC had specifically said they did not want the bids revealed publicly until the end of the process. If it got out, it would inevitably antagonise them.

'I'll take advice on that one, Michael,' said Branson, smiling.

The boardroom of the Independent Television Commission runs along the back of its Knightsbridge headquarters on the eighth floor. A thirty-foot oval table, hollow in the middle, dominates the room. Twenty featureless chairs fit around it. Another fifteen rest against the walls. The only windows, overlooking an office block occupied by Texaco, stretch down one side. Outside, beyond the office block, the top of the Knightsbridge barracks, the Albert Hall and the Albert Memorial can just be seen. Inside, a vermilion carpet and four nondescript modern prints hanging desultorily on the end walls provide the only decoration. It was here that the future of ITV was decided.

The ten Commission members sitting round the table at 9 a.m. on the morning of Thursday 13 June – the ITC's first full meeting to discuss the applications – were not exactly a disparate bunch. Besides Russell, no less than seven were involved in education in some form, either as teacher, lecturer or governor. The eighth was a businessman, the ninth an earl. The *Sun* described the decision makers as 'telly toffs'.

The best known was Russell's deputy chairman Jocelyn Stevens. Rector and vice-provost of the Royal College of Art, and a former executive with Beaverbrook and Express News-papers, Stevens had a reputation from his publishing days as a man with a prodigious temper. He had also experienced a franchise round from the other side, as a director of one of the losing breakfast TV bids in 1980. He was joined by three members based in specific regions: the Earl of Dalkeith, a former Border TV board director, now director of Buccleuch Estates, who was the ITC member for Scotland; Professor John Fulton, pro-vice chancellor of Queen's University, Belfast, who was the ITC member for Northern Ireland; and Eleri Wynne Jones, lecturer, psychotherapist and former Channel 4 board director, who was the ITC member for Wales.

Two women and three men completed the Commission: Lady Popplewell, JP, magistrate, council member of Open University and a governor of several schools; Pauline Mathias, former headmistress of Morehouse School in London and chairman of governors of St Felix Southwold; Pranlal Sheth, Kenyan-born businessman, lawyer, governor of the Polytech-nic of North London and former deputy chairman of the Commission for Racial Equality; Roy Goddard, business consul-tant and chairman of the Dyslexia Institute; and Professor James Ring, emeritus professor of physics at Imperial College, and the most experienced member of the Commission, who had served as an IBA member and later as a Cable Authority member since 1974. Five of the others, including Russell, had also served as IBA members.

Each had been asked to declare any links to the companies involved in the bidding, and pledge themselves to a period of social purdah while they were considering the bids. Even arm's-length links were monitored – Russell wrote to the manager of his pension scheme asking him to make sure there were no investments in ITV companies (there were not). He also declared his daughter's interest. She was working on a short-term contract as a researcher at TVS.

Even so, before the applications were received, the Commission had an early scare. Lord Chalfont, chairman of the Radio Authority and a member of the ITC since 1990, was found to be a director of a security company which numbered TVS among its clients. Chalfont claimed he had no idea of the client list. Before the press could make anything of it, he resigned from the ITC in the first week of May.

The resignation forced a reshuffling of responsibilities. Russell had already assigned different members to oversee specific licences. Following Chalfont's exit the responsibilities had to be redivided. Chalfont had been assigned Yorkshire. That was now given to Popplewell, along with Midlands and north-east England. The rest were divided as follows: Dalkeith took north and central Scotland; Wynne Jones, Wales; Fulton, Northern Ireland and breakfast; Goddard, borders and south-west England; Mathias, east of England and north-west England; Ring, south-east England and Channel Islands; and Sheth, London weekday and weekend. Many had already researched the areas, attending the viewer consultative councils set up by the ITC. Russell and Stevens did not have specific areas of responsibility.

The plan was for ITC specialist teams to report to those members, who would then present their findings to the rest of the Commission at the official meetings. The specialists' job was to scrutinise the financial, programming and technical aspects of the applications and advise whether the services promised were sustainable by the financial plans. This was the Beecher's

Brook promised by Russell. Only those that got through would have their financial bids considered by the ITC members. The bids would be ranked in order of size. Finally the members would consider whether to invoke the 'exceptional circumstances' clause, if it was thought that a lower bidder was offering a 'substantially higher quality' programme service.

On the morning of 13 June they took their seats amid an atmosphere of tense anticipation. They sat in the same manner as for their regular monthly meetings: Russell and Stevens in the centre, backs to the window; David Glencross and Peter Rogers, the ITC deputy chief executive, on their right; Kenneth Blyth, ITC company secretary, and his secretariat on their left. Opposite: Dalkeith, Fulton, Goddard, Wynne Jones, Mathias, Popplewell, Ring and Sheth. Senior ITC officials sat round the walls.

There were no introductory speeches. This meeting had been set aside to confirm procedures and give members a flavour of the applications received. Each would have to produce position papers to lead the discussions on their individual areas. They noted that forty applications were rather more than had been expected: extra bids in Wales, Northern Ireland and the north of Scotland, not to mention Branson and Frost's triple bid, had caught the commission by surprise. It was going to be a long, hard summer. They finished after lunch in the members' dining room. Another meeting was pencilled in for 18 July. So far, so good, they all thought as they packed their papers and headed for the lifts.

The idea first came to Ray Snoddy over lunch in July. His guest leaned forward conspiratorially. 'You know Scottish bid less than a million, don't you, Ray?' Snoddy, as senior journalist on the *Financial Times* and one of the country's most experienced media reporters, raised his eyebrows. The bids had already been the subject of some speculation but no one had got close to establishing the real figures. The ITC was adamant that they would remain under wraps until October. He returned to his food with the idea spinning round his head: if he could make the low bid lead stand up, that would be some scoop.

Media reporting was one of the major journalistic growth areas of the 1980s. Much of it was fuelled by the job boom in media and creative industries in the early part of the decade. Jobs meant classified ads for newspapers. Classified ads needed editorial around them. By the end of the decade every newspaper had its media specialist, given a brief to report on TV, newspapers, magazines, publishing, sometimes even advertising itself. Older journalists mistrusted the coverage; for them it seemed to have a self-serving, navel-gazing quality to it. Too often it lacked bite; the stories were either too specialist or the reporters were too cosy with their contacts to come up with real exclusives.

Snoddy had worked the *FT*'s media beat for nearly a decade. A tall, garrulous, sandy-haired Irishman, he was a familiar figure at media conferences and events around Britain. He had served his apprenticeship on provincial newspapers, sharing an office with a young Greg Dyke along the way. Through a mixture of easy-going charm, tenacious reporting and an assiduous working of contacts, Snoddy had established himself as one of the most consistent journalists covering the sector. He used the *FT* shrewdly, turning it into a trusted bulletin board for media announcements, endlessly doing deals with contacts, holding off on stories in return for major exclusives at a later date.

By the end of the 1980s he was a key figure in the media world. Major players like Robert Maxwell rang *him* to find out what was happening, rather than vice versa. He even had his own Channel 4 programme, *Hard News*, which investigated the behaviour of the press. With his rumpled suit, steel-rimmed glasses and almost boyish enthusiasm, he had a growing group of fans, among them most of Britain's newspaper editors, who had at one time or another tried to lure him off the *FT*. His colleagues liked the fact he had no airs and graces. His gallant attempt to dance the lambada on TV at the end of one *Hard News* show brought the house down in the *FT* offices.

By the summer of 1991 there was talk in media circles that the *FT* wanted to move him on to another sector. The paper had a policy of not allowing specialists to remain in one area for too

occasion. Russell was unperturbed. Both he and Glencross had decided that, as some of the predictions were off the mark, the leaks could not be coming from inside the ITC. If bidders chose to help journalists, there was little they could do. The ITC would just keep its head down and get on with it.

The paperwork was already beginning to pile up for the members. A public consultation period had drawn in over 2000 written comments on the bids to add to the reports of the ITC's own viewer consultative councils. Among the written comments were some from the ITV companies themselves. The stations with their hopes pinned on the quality threshold and exceptional circumstances – in particular Granada, LWT and Thames – took apart the services offered by their rivals. LWT's submission ran to five different sections, commenting on its rival LIB's 'inaccurate assertions about LWT', its lack of management in depth, and its inadequate staffing, finance and capital. All of these were summarised for members by Sarah Thane, the ITC's controller of public affairs. The summaries sat in front of the members that morning, as well as the first staff assessment papers.

Russell had already decided that they would kick off by looking at the three applications which were uncontested: Border, Central and Scottish. That, he felt, would give the members a good feel for the issues at stake, without the worry of whether they were being unfair to one group or another. Dalkeith, Goddard and Popplewell offered their preliminary assessments, speaking to papers that detailed which requirements of the Broadcasting Act the bidders were considered to have satisfied or not satisfied. That established the pattern for all their future discussion. The members could then decide where they wanted more work done for the next session. Their reaction to the applications was broadly favourable. Russell pointed out that they could not take any decisions, as they still had to check that none of the three had done anything in other applications that might disbar them.

Papers on five other licences were also presented that day: north-west England; London weekday; London weekend; south and south-east England; and Yorkshire. The possibility that both Phil Redmond's North-West TV and the London Independent bid might fail the quality threshold was raised.

They agreed to take a break in August for the summer holidays and return in September. There was no shortage of material to take with them. Russell packed the Tyne Tees application and that of its rival, North-East TV, as holiday reading for a trip to Canada.

Rudolph Agnew confirmed TVS's bid at the beginning of August. Because of his decision to raise an extra £30 million and bring in two new major shareholders, Home Box Office and Associated's Daily Mail and General Trust, TVS had to reveal the details of its application. Sitting in a stifling conference suite on the first floor of the Tower Hotel in London on 5 August, Agnew fielded questions from a sceptical press. They had swiftly decided that £59 million was a bid too far. Seated with him behind the press conference table was a grim-faced quartet of TVS senior executives. From their looks it appeared as if some of them had the same doubts.

The company was having a rough summer. A month earlier a long article in *Private Eye* had appeared, alleging that Claire Enders, TVS's corporate development director, was 'running the clapped-out station single-handedly', having 'worked her magic' on Agnew. It also accused her of helping James Gatward with the acquisition of MTM, then disassociating herself from the planning when it went wrong (in fact she had joined TVS after the MTM acquisition). Enders took the piece to be a typically misogynist broadside; she was one of the few women to hold a senior position in ITV, and was used to the snide innuendoes from junior male colleagues. But the piece rubbed the scabs off some old wounds inside TVS. Not only that, now its bid was released as well, the company was firmly in the media spotlight during what was traditionally for newspapers one of the slowest months for business news.

For three weeks, up until TVS's extraordinary general meeting for shareholders on 30 August, newspapers debated the bid. Many concluded it was unsustainable. Rivals were astounded by it. They focused on its projections, such as the

5.5 per cent forecast for national advertising revenue growth in 1993–1997, to claim that the station was being wildly over-optimistic. MAI's Meridian launched a prolonged public relations campaign on the issue of 'over-bidding'. TVS would be financially crippled if it won, Meridian argued. By then it knew that if TVS was knocked out, it would be next in line.

Agnew was unfazed. He cited the intention of the four major shareholders to back the station with more cash. 'All my experience tells me that if you are starting at a zero base in year one with all the safety nets in place, then you are giving yourself the optimum chance to win.' But he was losing the PR battle.

At the end of the month shareholders assembled in the Abraham Lincoln suite at the Savoy to vote on the capital raising. Agnew ran the session with arrogant poise. The capital raising was voted through. The meeting over, he relaxed, lighting his customary Gitane. He was flanked by the twelve-strong TVS board, six either side. They were sitting behind a long table, strewn with papers, pens and mineral water bottles, on a raised dais facing the room. It looked for all the world like a tableau out of *The Last Supper*.

Phil Redmond was furious. By mid-August Granada's head office was telling anyone who would listen that Redmond's bid had already failed the quality threshold. The implication was that it had received 'a nod and a wink' from the ITC. The ITC strenuously denied it. Redmond went on the attack. He had already organised public meetings and press conferences in the north-west to back the bid, and presentations to City analysts in London to prepare the way for raising money when he had won the licence. Now he added extra press conferences to explain why he believed he would win. His argument was simple: there can be no 'hidden agenda' within the ITC to safeguard Granada. North-West TV had bid far more – that already was plain – and a bid with Yorkshire and Tyne Tees in it could not be failed at the quality threshold, nor could Granada rely on getting 'exceptional circumstances'.

'Even if they could,' Redmond told one interviewer, 'it's going to take a hell of a lot of bottle for George Russell to go back to David Mellor in the Garrick, or wherever it is they drink, and say, "Dave, me old mate, I'm going to deprive the Treasury of £150 million in the north-west because we'd like to see Granada get back in." '

When, later in August, Redmond got a letter from the ITC asking him to clarify the details of a co-production deal with Yorkshire mentioned in North-West TV's application, he was chuffed. The fact that the ITC was still asking questions convinced him that North-West had passed the quality threshold and was on the way to winning.

The Commission met again after its summer holidays on Thursday 5 September, and discussed the north of Scotland, Northern Ireland and Wales licences. At a two-day meeting a fortnight later, on 18–19 September, they completed the assessment papers, working through the applications for the east of England, north-east England, south-west England and the Channel Islands. Between meetings, the individual members continued working with the various specialist teams checking the programming and business plans. Draft assessment papers were continually revised.

By the end of 19 September, sixteen bids faced the axe. Three – TVS, TSW and TVNi in Northern Ireland – were judged by the ITC staff to have failed the quality threshold because their business plans would not sustain the promised service over ten years. The members backed those recommendations. Russell asked Peter Rogers, the ITC deputy chief executive, to prepare a paper comparing the three high bids with two others, Yorkshire and Tyne Tees, who had also both bid high, and whose applications were thought to be 'marginal' by ITC staff. That would allow the members to check their decisions on the overbidders for consistency.

Thirteen were judged to have failed because their programming plans did not meet the requirements laid down in the broadcasting legislation. Among those failing at the fence were Redmond, Branson and Frost, and the London Independent bid. Their cash bids were not even considered. That left only the ranking of the remaining bids and the consideration of exceptional circumstances. It was to be the most trying part of the process.

The legislation demanded that in every region where more than one bid passed the quality threshold, the ITC had to decide whether any were worthy of exceptional circumstances, regardless of what was bid. Seven areas had to be considered: London weekday; Yorkshire; South and south-east; Wales; east of England; north-east England; and breakfast. Although the cash bids had not been officially revealed to all the members yet, most knew that Thames and TV-am had been outbid. It was already clear that knocking them out was going to be the toughest decision they had to take.

They ran through the arguments in all seven regions. Russell led the discussion, outlining the case for exceptional circumstances in each instance. Members then spoke to the arguments he had laid out. In five of the regions, as they expected, those arguments were slim. They agreed the highest bidders should win. They returned to Thames and TV-am, both of whom appeared to have a more convincing argument for exceptional circumstances. With help from the lawyers who had sat through every meeting, they debated whether a decision in favour of either could be sustained against any form of legal action. They agreed they would return to both of them at their final meeting.

'You'll like this one,' ran the memo from Barry Cox, LWT's director of corporate affairs, to the rest of the station's bid team. 'John Gau told me today that he had heard (from Andy Birchall) that Tim Bevan's friend's* daughter works for the ITC – and that she had told her father, who told Bevan, that LIB had failed to pass the quality threshold.'

By mid-September, when Cox sent his memo, most bidders were climbing the walls with tension. The two big industry shindigs that summer, the Edinburgh TV Festival and the Royal Television Society conference in Cambridge, had been nervy affairs. With little hard information to go on, every nuance,

* changed to protect identity

every inflexion on the statements that occasionally slipped out from the normally tight-lipped ITC staff was studied. Titbits were passed around like bottles between parched men. Anything, however tangential, was gratefully received.

(Christopher Bland, LWT's chairman, was unimpressed by Cox's memo. He wrote back:

'My accountant's wife's gynaecologist's window-cleaner told her that he was cleaning Tom Guttridge's windows the other day and couldn't help seeing that Guttridge was reading a letter from the ITC. He was just about to see what it was when he fell off his ladder but he thinks it was about failing to cross the quality threshold. This confirms it!'

But Cox was right.)

Michael Green had done such a good job at fending off Ray Snoddy and the packs of hacks trying to wheedle out the Carlton bids that he had presented himself with a problem. By the end of September most were convinced that Carlton had won the London weekday licence. But for the wrong reason. They believed that Carlton had outbid Virgin and Thames. Green knew differently. If his projections were right about the Branson and Frost bid, he had outbid only Thames. Not knowing if Branson and Frost would fail the quality threshold, or if Thames would get 'exceptional circumstances', he started to feel very sick indeed.

Green had brooded on this since the bids had gone in. A month after his call to Branson, suggesting they tell each other their bids, he had buttonholed David Frost at a private view of the new Constable exhibition in the Tate Gallery.

'This waiting is endless, David. Maybe we should merge our bids? . . .'

It was said as a joke but Frost got the hint. There were obvious mutual advantages: a number of television insiders had already said they thought the Branson and Frost bid might fail the quality threshold. It was only loosely put together, and lacked the rigorous attention to detail of other bids. But Green could not depend on that and was fairly sure Carlton had been outbid. Folding the Branson and Frost bid into Carlton's would offer all of them the chance of winning. There was nothing in the legislation to say that a bid could not be withdrawn. Frost rang Green the next day and suggested lunch. Green had no hesitation in saying 'yes'.

They met in Victor Blank's private dining room at Charterhouse Bank's offices opposite St Paul's in the City. Only Blank, Frost and Green attended. The lunch was a light-hearted affair, with both Frost and Green exercising their considerable capacities for personal charm. Underneath the bonhomie, however, the talk was serious. By the end of the lunch they realised there were two major obstacles: Green was unwilling to hand over more than 20 per cent of his bid and there appeared to be little way in which the executives already signed up by Branson and Frost could be accommodated in the Carlton bid. Frost concluded it was a splendid idea, but highly impractical. They agreed to leave it at that. (It had, however, given Green a fair idea of the level of the Branson and Frost bid. They, for their part, never stopped believing that he had bid more. He knew he had not, and the worry never stopped nagging at him.)

By October Green was a bag of nerves. On the evening of the tenth, at a Jewish Film Festival reception at the NFT on the South Bank, Green bumped into David Elstein, Thames's director of programmes. Both were with their wives. Green knew Elstein was a fierce critic of Carlton and had written a scathing critique of its London weekday bid as part of Thames' official comment to the ITC earlier that summer. Even so, Green did not like making enemies. So he started chatting pleasantly to Elstein, confessing that the tension of waiting for the ITC's decisions was unbearable. He added that he was very upset about the rumours of rifts and bid leaks within the Daybreak breakfast consortium, and that he intended to sue anyone who accused him of doing anything underhand.

Elstein, a tall man with dark curly hair, smiled sympathetically. He was not sure why Green was going on about it; few in the industry took the rift rumours seriously. But Green looked genuinely hurt by it all. Then he added: 'Look David, whatever happens, I hope you'll still count me as your friend.'

Elstein shrugged. Green's charm cut little ice. 'That *does* depend on what happens,' he said, and, turning on his heel, walked away.

The film both attended that night was called *Homicide*.

Earlier that day the Commission had assembled for its last meeting to discuss the ITV licences. It was scheduled to run for two days. At the end of it, the members hoped to make their final decisions on winners and losers. The press had already been informed that if exceptional circumstances were invoked, then that decision would be delayed while the ITC interviewed the bidders in the region concerned. If there were no exceptional circumstances, the results would be faxed to bidders at 10 a.m. the following Wednesday. The press were quick to dub it 'The Fax Of Life'.

In front of them that morning the Commission members not only had details of the cash bids for each region, they also had Rogers' paper on the high bidders. The issues laid out in the paper were of particular concern. The members had been advised by Allen & Overy, the ITC's solicitors, that a decision to block a high bid either through exceptional circumstances, or through 'unsustainability', was more likely to be challenged in court than any decision made on the basis of the programming plans. Angry losers had the right to take the process to judicial review. The members knew that any decision they took had to be absolutely watertight.

The problem of 'sustainability' had already proved to be the most contentious issue discussed by the members so far. Just when did a projection move from being 'reasonable' to being clearly over-optimistic? Rogers' paper pulled together the five separate financial assessments on the bids by TVS, TSW, TVNi, Tyne Tees and Yorkshire. It ran through the staff recommendations – that the first three should fail on financial grounds and that the latter two were 'marginal' – and used a series of twenty graphs and charts to compare projections for ad revenue, costs, profits and tender payments.

The paper concluded that the staff recommendations to fail TVS, TSW and TVNi, and leave Yorkshire and Tyne Tees in the balance, *were* consistent. It pointed out that the problems with the TVS and TSW applications recurred throughout the analysis and on a greater scale than for the other three applicants. TSW looked worse than TVS, but the MTM dimension of the TVS application had yet to be fully taken into account. The Yorkshire and Tyne Tees bids raised 'substantial concerns', Rogers added, but less ones of revenue and profit than simply of the sheer size of each bid.

The staff recommendations were not easy to push through. There was no problem with the programming proposals put forward by either station, and both had kept their TV services in profit for years. The arguments swung back and forth. Roy Goddard, the member who had been assigned the south-west region, was vociferous in his contention that both TSW and TVS should be blocked. Goddard was the only member, Russell and Stevens aside, to have real business experience, having set up his own recruitment consultancy which had specialised in the broadcasting sector. His authority carried weight among the educationalists. Russell too admitted that he had been surprised at the TSW bid; it was almost greater than the balance sheet value of the company. If something went wrong, there was little to fall back on.

TVS, with its £30 million of new capital and four cash-rich major shareholders, was more difficult. Its bid was more than double that of two of its rivals, Carlton and CPV-TV, the Branson and Frost consortium, and nearly twice as much as Meridian's. There was no guarantee that its shareholders, however rich, would endlessly underwrite a loss-making service if the projected ad revenue failed to turn up. In the end Russell and Goddard's business experience and the strength of the arguments in Rogers' paper held sway. Both bids were axed unanimously. Yorkshire and Tyne Tees were saved. Likewise the decision to block thirteen bids deemed deficient on programming quality was finally confirmed.

That left Thames and TV-am. All were conscious of the fact that the exceptional circumstances clause had been left for them to interpret. The only guidance given by the Government had been a statement by David Mellor which emphasised that a lower bid would have to be 'exceptionally better' than its higher bidding rival(s) to win. But what did that mean? It could not include a judgement on past performance; only the proposals in front of them could be considered.

Papers had already been prepared on the reasons for and against awarding exceptional circumstances in each case. Russell again led the discussion, laying out the reasons for using exceptional circumstances in each case. The discussions went on for hours, filling the morning and afternoon sessions that Thursday. Everyone – ten members, eight ITC senior staff and a lawyer – contributed. It was not a question of judging which was the best bid. That was the old system. Nor could they take into account factors like TV-am's popularity, with over 70 per cent of the breakfast TV audience. If that was an issue, no one could have won against TV-am. All they could ask themselves was whether either of the services proposed by Thames and TV-am were exceptionally better than that offered by their higher bidding rivals, Carlton and the Daybreak and Sunrise consortiums.

In TV-am's case it was easier to decide: the proposals and the teams put together by both breakfast consortia looked capable of matching the service proposed by Bruce Gyngell. Thames took longer. The members picked over every inch of the Carlton application. But try as they might, they could not justify the judgement that Thames' proposals were exceptionally better. Carlton's financial clout, its executive team and its commitment to areas like new writing were clearly strengths. Its schedule planning was too close to Thames' own to differentiate it. By proposing 'more of the same', Carlton had put up the perfect defence against exceptional circumstances. The members concluded, reluctantly in some cases, that they could not award the licence on that basis. Thames and TV-am were out.

It was, Russell reflected later, one of the most trying times he and other members had ever worked through. In one sense the old franchise system was far easier, as the IBA members simply had to decide which applications they liked best. With the system he inherited and modified, a number of highly complex judgements had to be made, while all the time the expectation was that the highest bidder should win. And some of those judgements were about companies run by individuals with whom he had already built up close friendships. The decision not to save Thames was the hardest. Greenfield bidders could shrug off disappointment. Thames had been going for twenty-three years, with thousands of staff, many of whom had given the best years of their lives to the company. He never wanted to go through anything like it again.

The decisions made, they voted it all through by 1 p.m. on the Friday. In a bizarre quirk of arrangements, the Archbishop of Canterbury and his wife had been invited to lunch with the ITC members that day. The Primate did not offer any blessing on their efforts. 'Wisely, perhaps,' wrote David Glencross later, 'we did not seek it, nor did he volunteer it.'

As soon as the ITC confirmed that the results would be faxed to bidders the next Wednesday, Thames knew it had lost. The Wednesday fax meant there would be no exceptional circumstances. Few at Thames believed both Carlton and CPV-TV would fail to cross the quality threshold. Many Thames senior executives also believed the ITC were briefing the press as to the likely outcome; it made sense as a damage limitation exercise. When they saw the press consensus on Saturday morning that four incumbents were going to lose their licences – Thames, TVS, TSW and TV-am – they concluded that the Cassandras who had forecast the station's doom all summer were right.

It was an uncomfortable weekend for all the bidders. By chance Branson and Green were pitched together in a box at the Albert Hall on Sunday to watch the sumo wrestling. Branson, convinced CPV-TV had been outbid, spent the day winding up the Carlton boss by loudly describing him to others as 'Mike Green, the man who has won the London weekday TV licence'. Green's misery was complete when Branson used the sobriquet to introduce him to Mick Newmarch, the Prudential's group chief executive. Green was mortified. The Prudential was a major shareholder in Carlton; bragging about winning TV licences before the award was unlikely to endear him to so important a backer. He rang up Newmarch the next day.

'Look, I have to apologise about yesterday. I just want you to know because you're shareholders in Carlton that we do not know that we have won. We do not regard the papers as authoritative. We are under a confidentiality agreement with the ITC not to reveal anything. I couldn't say anything yesterday but I didn't want to mislead you either way.'

'I quite understand,' replied a surprised Newmarch.

Others started preparing for the big day. Rudolph Agnew, so confident all summer, was finally beginning to realise that he had got it wrong. Lunch with Ray Snoddy at the Savoy the week before had convinced him. It was not even Snoddy's cogent arguments that high bidders would be thrown out. It was his whole body language. Snoddy knew the industry inside out, and had as good a feel as any bidder for how the legislation would be interpreted. He seemed to be convinced that TVS would lose. Agnew decided he would wait for the news at home. He had never liked standing by faxes.

Bruce Gyngell, who acknowledged he had been outbid but still did not believe that the ITC would let through either the Daybreak or the Sunrise bid, agreed to order crates of pink champagne in advance of the result. Even if TV-am lost, his executives reasoned, staff would still want a drink.

At LWT Greg Dyke was giving his chairman heartburn with his confident plans to celebrate the station's impending victory. He had already printed posters, badges, rosettes and banners for the occasion.

'Honestly, Greg,' pleaded Christopher Bland, 'you can't do that, I'm too superstitious.'

Dyke had been at his ebullient best. 'Look, if we lose we are going to have a lot more to worry about than a few wasted posters and poster sites.'

On the Monday evening, just thirty-six hours before the results were due, many of the bidders assembled in a private room at the Savoy for a party to honour David Nicholas's retirement from ITN. Most of the ITV bosses were there and a sprinkling of media celebrities: Richard Branson, Alastair Burnet, Robin Day, David Frost, Michael Grade. Dyke chatted animatedly in a corner, exuding confidence from every inch of his diminutive frame. Other bidders watched nervously as George Russell and David Glencross circulated. It was a difficult occasion for everyone.

13

'It's time we told the old bat what's what. Anyway, she's gone, finished. She can't touch us no more.'

Greg Dyke on Margaret Thatcher

That Wednesday George Russell got into the ITC early. His first task was an 8 a.m. interview for the BBC *Today* programme. The interview previewed the decisions that were to be announced at 10 a.m. Russell sat in the corporation's brand new radio van giving little away. On the street outside Sky News had already set up an outside broadcast unit, conducting vox pop interviews as background trailers for the press conference, which it was showing live. (ITV had decided against offering similar coverage; for a start, the housewife audience of the *This Morning* show simply was not interested enough. Later it changed its mind and dropped excerpts of the conference into the show as it was running.)

Inside the ITC Russell, back from his interview, phoned the Home Office and relayed the results to Kenneth Baker, the Home Secretary, as had been prearranged. Baker listened as Russell ran through the winners and losers, but made no comment, saying simply 'Thank-you for phoning.' Downstairs the ITC prepared for the media circus. Staff were expecting over 150 journalists. The TV crews were early, setting up in the huge conference room on the first floor. Elsewhere in London journalists gathered in the drizzle outside Thames, London Weekend and TV-am, hoping to get the first reaction from ecstatic or dejected staff. Around Britain anxious bidders began to assemble near their designated fax machines, less than an hour away from corporate life or death.

On the seventh floor of the ITC, behind the newly installed electronic door locks, the Commission secretariat began to prepare the faxes. The sheets of paper had been typed out, checked, and locked away the day before. Now a bank of twenty-four fax machines awaited them. Teams of secretaries and clerical staff stood by each. There were not enough machines to fax every bidder simultaneously. So it was decided that the sixteen winners would be faxed first, then the losers. Just after 9.40 a.m. Ken Blyth, the ITC company secretary, gave the signal and the first faxes started stuttering out.

Christopher Bland was pacing the corridor outside his thirteenth-floor office at LWT when he heard the cheer go up. *That can't be too bad*, he thought, as he pushed his way back in through the throng of executives and consultants. Dyke, a big grin splitting his bristly face, was standing by the fax machine, reading the fax out loud.

Six floors up in the Sunrise offices in the same building Hugh Pile, LWT's breakfast bid director, was sitting behind his desk theatrically smoothing out a similar fax. Around him a hushed group waited, representatives from Disney, Broadcast Communication and Scottish TV. He looked up. 'We've got it,' he said, smiling as pandemonium broke out. The call was put into Bland's office. Already the balloons and banners were being distributed. It was going to be one long party at the station's South Bank offices that day.

Less than a mile along the river a smaller party was breaking out on the first floor of MAI's five-storey block behind Southwark Cathedral. Bill Cotton, the former BBC managing director and deputy chairman of MAI's Meridian bid, pulled the sheets from the fax machine. Roger Laughton, already on the phone to Simon Albury at the ITC, and a shirt-sleeved Clive Hollick stood next to him; SelecTV's Alan McKeown and Michael Buckley and others waited in front. A cheer went up as Cotton read out the fax. Hollick's wife hugged him.

Phil Redmond was watching the press conference trailers on

Sky News in his first floor Childwall office when Yorkshire rang. Alexis, his wife, Philip Reeval, his public affairs chief, John Fairley, the Yorkshire TV programme director, and Rod Farley, the North West TV Chairman, were with him. It was Allan Hardy, Yorkshire's commercial director, for Fairley. Fairley took the phone, listened and grinned. 'They've just got the fax. Yorkshire has won.'

As he said it the fax machine outside Redmond's office started sputtering into life. Redmond stood by it, still confident he was going to win too. Fairley was on the phone when Redmond took the first two sheets off the machine and muttered, 'Didn't get it.' He walked back to his office and sat down. He did not look surprised, nor did he seem disappointed. Coolness under pressure was one of Redmond's attributes.

Downstairs at the entrance to the building the journalists and TV crews were gathering. Eventually Redmond put on his jacket and said he had better go and talk to them. He and Reeval walked downstairs. Pushing through the double doors that led to the ground floor, they found the corridor blocked with press and photographers. Redmond took it in his stride. He smiled and shrugged, lifting both hands. 'That's the way it goes.'

In the executive suite on Thames' fourth floor Roy Addison, the station's head of corporate affairs, watched the colour drain out of Richard Dunn's face. He was still standing over the fax machine outside his office, reading the fax upside down as it lay there. Addison knew it was bad news. 'I'm sorry,' he said, and shook his hand. Dunn's secretary gave him a kiss. He took the sheets off the machine and walked slowly across the corridor to where the Thames board awaited him.

The panelled boardroom was silent as Dunn walked in. The directors, a mix of employees, non-executives and representatives of Thorn EMI, Thames' controlling shareholder, knew immediately.

Dunn stood at the head of the table clutching the sheets of paper. On his left sat his chairman, Lord Brabourne, and six non-executive directors. On his right sat his programme director, David Elstein, and six Thames executives. They all waited for Dunn to speak.

'I've now received the fax from the ITC,' he said slowly. 'I will read it to you.' Carefully, he began: 'The Independent Television Commission will be announcing today its decisions, in accordance with Section 17 of the Broadcasting Act 1990, on the award of the Channel 3 licences. The Commission recognises, and is grateful for, the time and effort that went into the preparation of the application from Thames for the regional Channel 3 licence for London Weekday. I regret to have to inform you . . .'

There was a quiet gasp. Dunn read on but few round the table were listening. They sat in shock. So it is true, they thought: Thames has lost; Green has won. It took him six years but he got it in the end. Thames had been outbid and nothing could save its franchise now. *Minder, The Bill, This Is Your Life, This Week* – the Thames successes that for so long had been the bulwark of the ITV network. None of that mattered any more. Two words were all they needed to confirm it. 'I regret . . .'

Dunn finished reading the fax. It was signed: 'Yours sincerely, George Russell'. He sat down. He was speechless, filled with a great, numbing, cavernous emptiness. No one said anything. They could see that Dunn was stupified. Again and again he was asking himself the same question: *How could Russell do this to me?*

Never mind Thames' award-winning programmes – Russell was a friend. As head of the ITV Association, Dunn had led the ITV companies' fight against the Government plans to auction off the ITV franchises. And Russell, newly appointed chairman of the regulatory body that controlled ITV, had helped him.

He had even asked Dunn to stay on as head of the ITVA for an extra six months while the Broadcasting Bill was being finalised – time he could just as easily have spent helping prepare Thames' bid. Dunn had trusted him.

He sat, turning it all over in his mind. At the end of the room, someone had switched on Sky News. Russell's press conference at the ITC was just starting. The irony of it all – that much of the world should hear of their fate via satellite TV – did not escape those watching. Mike Metcalf, the Thorn finance director, slipped out of the boardroom and crossed the corridor to ring his boss, Colin Southgate, at Thorn's West End head office. 'We've lost,' he said.

Rudolph Agnew, chairman of TVS, received the same message in his Belgravia sitting room. Grey hair swept back, hawk eyes narrowing, he stood as he held the phone.

'Your fears have been confirmed, Rudolph.' It was Tony Brook, managing director of TVS. His voice was shaky with emotion. 'They've turned us down for overbidding.'

'Damn,' said Agnew. He had known for at least a fortnight. Somehow he had got it all terribly wrong. But what else could he have done? He had bid to win. *Damn the ITC. Damn James Gatward*. Maybe he couldn't have won.

He lit another Gitane.

Three miles away across town, on the first floor of TV-am's determinedly modern Camden headquarters, a different scene was being acted out. Bruce Gyngell had all but collapsed. The TV-am boss had been so stunned by his fax from Russell that he had had to be physically supported by his directors.

He, too, could not believe his station had lost. How could it? It was not only the most profitable in ITV, it was also one of the most popular. It wiped the floor with the rival BBC service. And now this?

His secretary got him a glass of water. Someone else found him a cigarette. He had given up years ago, but in the weeks before the franchise result was due, had started again, cadging off his staff. Typical Bruce, they thought. On £280,000 a year, he could have bought his own.

Outside, in the drizzly TV-am forecourt, a pack of journalists waited. Gyngell, for so long the most charismatic figure in ITV, would not disappoint them. Despite having prepared a statement to hand out, he resolved to talk to them himself. As he walked slowly down the main stairs to the reception and out through the swing dooors, the news was already round the building. Two bodyguards and his senior press officer, Jane

Ironside-Woods, went with him. They were swiftly engulfed by the scrum.

'What's your reaction, Bruce?' 'This way, Bruce.' 'Over here, Bruce.' Gyngell bit hard on his top lip and composed himself. Defeat etched on his features, Ironside-Woods holding one arm and a security man behind him, he provided the picture that dominated the front pages the next day. His speech was short and bitter. He derided the decision to give the breakfast franchise to a consortium, Sunrise, that had bid more than twice as much as TV-am. 'I do not believe Sunrise will be a profitable company,' he snapped. 'I predict they will be bankrupt by 1994.'

Eventually he broke off and pushed his way back into the two-storey building. At his insistence, staff had already broken out the pink champagne ordered for the victory celebrations. Except now it was a wake.

On the second floor of the ITC in Knightsbridge, in the large circular room that used to hold the IBA's broadcasting museum, two screens had been set up to relay the press conference to representatives of the bidders. It had been felt diplomatic to keep them away from the main gathering. After the event, they could either speak to the press or slip out undetected. The room was nearly full by the time George Russell, Jocelyn Stevens, David Glencross, Peter Rogers and Sarah Thane took their seats downstairs in front of a seething mass of press. By then, many knew the results already. They had been flashed on the Press Association wire. Thames and TV-am had lost for not bidding enough. TVS and TSW had lost for bidding too much. The other incumbents were safe.

For Russell it was three years to the month since he had accepted the job of ITC chairman – three years of inexorably growing pressure. Despite the sense of relief that it was all coming to an end, the tension showed on his face as he took the first questions about the results. He summed it all up: 'Quality has won on this occasion and the viewers will win.' He defended the results by forecasting that the Treasury would only gain an extra £40 million from the process. That, he argued, would be balanced by £45 million worth of savings for the ITV companies which would no longer have to pay for the Welsh fourth channel SC4. So money that would otherwise have been spent on programming was not flowing out of the system. 'It may not be a better way,' he said emphatically. 'But this will be the last way it is done.' The ITV licences were now on rolling contracts. There would never again be a one-off franchise round for all of them.

David Keighley, TV-am's head of corporate affairs, returned from the ITC's offices in Knightsbridge to find the breakfast station in shock. Everyone was grey. Some were in tears. Gyngell was trying to console them.

Walking upstairs to his first-floor office, Keighley, a former BBC press officer, pondered the winners: Michael Green's Carlton, Clive Hollick's MAI, Westcountry, and, of course, Greg Dyke's Sunrise consortium that had beaten TV-am. How ironic that Greg, one of the men who had saved the station early on, should now destroy it. Just as the press had said at the weekend. *They had got it so right, it was uncanny – almost as if they knew the results in advance.* And TV-am had got it so wrong.

Pausing he noticed Carol Thatcher, who worked on TV-am's *Sunday* show, in animated conversation on the phone. She was standing in the middle of the open-plan newsroom. She turned and waved at Keighley, gesturing urgently for him to come over. 'Can you get Bruce?' she asked. 'Mummy's on the line.'

Keighley returned with Gyngell. He took the phone and talked briefly, then put it down. 'What did she say?' asked Keighley.

'Well,' said Gyngell looking dazed, 'she's very upset about it.'

'I want to know why they failed us.' Richard Branson's voice was angry. 'I want to know why, and I want a meeting fixed up with the ITC as soon as possible. Get the lawyers in.'

Charles Levison, holding the phone in Victor Blank's fifth-floor City office at Charterhouse Bank, nodded. 'They're on their way.' He noted how fast the Virgin boss's mood was changing.

Branson, at his home in Holland Park, had been phoned with the news by Will Whitehorn, his public affairs director, as soon as the fax had come in. 'Ah well,' he had joked, 'at least I don't have to find the money for that one.' He thought he had simply been outbid. Then Whitehorn explained why they had lost. All three of his bids had been thrown out after failing the quality threshold. Branson was furious.

The door of Blank's office swung open and David Frost, looking grim, walked in. His normal gregarious charm was muted. He was not the kind of man who enjoyed losing. The office was a sea of coffee cups and papers, with people hanging off phones, as the bid team relayed out the ITC's decision.

Turning on the TV, they gathered to watch the news. Outside London Weekend they were hanging huge banners proclaiming victory. Frost's face showed no emotion as he watched himself on screen, stepping into his Bentley in Camden after the TV-am board meeting. The film showed him turning to address the reporters. His sound-bite was caustic.

'When I was at school I was told the important thing was not the winning but taking part. I did not believe it then and I certainly do not believe it now.' The crowd in Blank's office murmured assent. *Given how much this whole thing has cost,* thought more than one of them, *he's got a point.*

Elsewhere winners mugged it up for the press. In Birmingham Leslie Hill, pinstripe and floral tie, held aloft a huge cardboard cheque made out for £2000 while punching the air outside Central's headquarters. In Manchester David Plowright received a smacker from actress Julie Goodyear – Bet Lynch in *Coronation Street* – as Granada staff celebrated his gamble of bidding only £9 million. In London Michael Green, who had received the fax with his two teenage daughters at his side, eventually appeared on his company's Hanover Square steps in his shirt sleeves, holding a giant sign with CARLTON TELEVISION written on it. Nigel Walmsley, the Carlton TV boss, had had to coax him down from his office. As he came out through Carlton's front entrance he had been confronted by a sea of journalists, all screaming questions at him. 'How do you feel, Michael?'

'Are you happy?'

'Look this way, Michael, this way, this way . . .'

He took it like a pro, lifting the sign above his head and smiling smoothly.

The TV cameras caught most of it. On the *News At Ten* that night they showed ITN's own fax coming through, telling the news provider that its Daybreak consortium bid for the breakfast licence had been just pipped at the post. Sir Paul Fox pulled it off the fax and read it; Bob Phillis peered over his shoulder. Neither looked surprised.

At Thames Richard Dunn was receiving commiserations from Colin Southgate, the Thorn chief executive. Southgate was bullish. 'Don't be downhearted. You did the right thing,' he told the Thames board. 'You didn't overbid. You're all in business to make calculations. We're sorry but there's no regrets – let's press on.'

Dunn went down to Studio 5 to make a prepared speech to Thames staff. Hundreds had gathered to hear what he had to say. Others watched on the station's closed-circuit system. The mood was angry. Dunn told them that the new franchise system was unfair and warned that a thousand jobs would have to go by 1993, but at least the company had a future, as Britain's largest independent production firm. It was little consolation. Hostile questions were asked about the level of the bid and the likely redundancy terms. At the end, though, Dunn was applauded. Not all the staff thought he deserved it. 'I think it was the herd-habit,' said one. 'They thought they were a studio audience.'

At TV-am a stricken Bruce Gyngell was still trying to make sense of Margaret Thatcher's phone call. Her commiserations were welcome enough, if a little rich, given her role in pushing through the broadcasting legislation. It was her final words that puzzled him. 'I am going to write to you.' Why?

He discussed it with David Keighley, TV-am's head of corporate affairs. Keighley immediately thought of the public relations value. It was a private conversation but Thatcher was no fool, she must have known that if you ring up a journalistic organisation on the day it loses its franchise, it would inevitably leak out.

By lunchtime the story was already spreading among the staff. The wake had moved on from the vast open-plan atrium of the main TV foyer into the local restaurants and pubs. Jane Ironside-Woods took the press office team to the Camden Brasserie. Others streamed into the Elephant and the Oxford Arms opposite. The mood was already getting angry. Why had Gyngell not bid more? Both Sunrise and Daybreak had bid more than £33 million. Gyngell had bid less than half that: £14 million. His attempts to placate the angry staff – 'The money we put forward was the maximum that could have been afforded' – had fallen on deaf ears. Keighley chatted to the TV-am journalists, pointing out the alternative: to bid £35 million would have meant throwing at least 200 staff out of work, and moving the company into smaller, cheaper premises. Is that what they wanted?

The presenters, too, had their say. Mike Morris, the blokeish, mustachioed star of the main morning show, looked furious as he pushed past journalists. Asked for a comment he muttered: 'I'm gutted.' Ulrika Jonsson, the blonde weather forecaster best known as a girlfriend of Prince Edward, gave a longer speech. 'It's a travesty. The whole affair is dreadful. It's a very, very sad day, but you should not be worrying about me, you should worry about the viewers.'

As she was driven away a reporter shouted hopefully: 'Have you told Prince Edward?'

At the ITC, the press conference over, Russell recorded a series of TV and radio interviews and then disappeared upstairs for a sandwich lunch with senior staff. Waiting for him was an ironic fax from his daughter Livia, working as a researcher at TVS. It said 'Thanks'.

After lunch David Glencross made his excuses and returned to his office. He sat and rang the boss of each losing incumbent in turn. They were not easy calls to make.

'I'm just ringing to express my sympathies. I know how you must feel . . .'

230

He was met with a mixture of anger and bewilderment. The conversations were short but, he reasoned, someone had to do it.

That night ten of the bidders, winners and losers alike, shipped up at the BBC's Television Centre in London's Wood Green for a *Late Show* debate on the franchise awards. The programme's producers had gathered a varied array of pundits, consultants and others to join them. In the hospitality suite before the show the mood was one of tired resilience: commiserations were exchanged between losers. Winners kept their cool. Only Professor Alan Peacock, the belligerent free-marketeer who had originally suggested a competitive tender, was angry. He stuck by his free market beliefs: he felt the emphasis on 'sustainability' and secrecy had completely undermined his original idea. He was particularly upset that TSW, a station that he had advised, had been knocked out for overbidding. As he saw it, it has passed the quality threshold and had bid the most. It should have won.

'I'm furious,' he told everyone in his gruff Scots baritone. 'It's a classic example of why a system like this does not work. I've got a lot to say tonight and I'm going to say it.'

They sat in two sets of tiered rows, seventeen in all, facing the two presenters, Kirsty Wark and *FT*'s Ray Snoddy. Most looked fairly uncomfortable as the introductory credits rolled – they had realised that, with so many guests, they were only likely to get thirty seconds each to say their piece.

The introduction set the tone. 'On the *Late Show* tonight, the great Channel 3 franchise debate. We have assembled some key players. The man who bid £2000 for the franchise reckoned to be worth £232 million a year in advertising revenue!' (Close-up of Central's Leslie Hill, same pinstripe, now in a spotted tie.) 'The man who lost a franchise despite bidding £16 million!' (TSW's Harry Turner, bulldog-morose, in grey double-breasted with red handkerchief exploding out of the top pocket.) 'The man who is contemplating legal action against the ITC!' (Richard Branson, dejected in blue home-knit.) 'And the man who thinks that this was the better way.' (Cento Velanowski, consultant, unrecognisable and inscrutable.)

The question-and-answer format moved desultorily round the interviewees. Hill explained that Central had to pay a lot more than £2000, it also had to pay the 11 per cent levy on its ad revenue as well. Turner said that the system was ludicrous ('Mad King Ludwig of Bavaria would not have invented a more lunatic system.') Yorkshire's Clive Leach insisted that £37 million was not too much to pay for his station's licence. Richard Branson brandished an award for his airline and complained that no one had ever queried Virgin's quality before. Phil Redmond, still sitting in the same Manchester studio from which he had just been interviewed on *Newsnight*, banged on about the lack of innovation being brought into the system.

Eventually Peacock could take it no longer and interrupted to say what a farce the whole process was, and how it was certainly not what he had envisaged when he had suggested competitive tenders in the first place. 'All I have heard tonight has been about the redistribution of television company profits; nothing about the viewers' interests.' It should not have been a question of stopping the Treasury taking money out of the system. His original idea had been to siphon the money off for re-investment in public service broadcasting. But the arguments moved on; everyone had to have their say.

The nadir came as Snoddy directed a question to an independent producer whose involvement in a franchise bid had proved unsuccessful. He looked glassy-eyed and exhausted, his speech slurring as he rambled on, defending the quality of independent production. The other guests grinned mischievously. When the show ended and the lights had dimmed Turner, feeling bruised and spiteful after a long day, turned to the producer. 'You don't bore for Essex, do you?'

A few miles away, sitting at home, Greg Dyke snorted at the TV. At LWT they were still partying; crate after crate of champagne had been brought in to celebrate the station's double victory. Dyke, still euphoric, had been driven home in time to catch the interviews. *What a useless waste of time*, he thought, switching the set off. Seventeen people saying one sentence each, to discuss a complex issue like that, nobody knowing what they are supposed to get out of it. It's the worst way to make a programme. That, he told himself smugly, is not the LWT way of doing things.

A madman drove his pick-up through the window of a cafe in Kileen, Texas, before shooting twenty-two people dead, wounding twenty others and apparently committing suicide. Even that could not keep the ITC's decisions off most front pages the next day. 'Legal threats follow biggest ITV shake-up' (*The Times*). 'Big names lose TV bids' (The *Guardian*). 'ITV auction costs four broadcasters their licences' (The *Daily Telegraph*). 'Auction shakes up ITV system' (The *Financial Times*). The *Sun* found its own angle, majoring on the story that Thames might now sell its popular soap series *The Bill* to Sky. Inside it carried a feature on Michael Green: Twenty Things You Never Knew About ITV's Mr Big. (Number 8. A former girlfriend said: 'At parties Michael was the one upstairs under a pile of coats with a girl.') Green's daughter gleefully pinned it up in his home.

Most of the papers focused on the anger of Bruce Gyngell and the anguish of Richard Dunn. Gyngell's fraught face dominated many front pages. The overnight verdict was that the ITC had done the best job possible with a ropy system, safeguarding quality and turning the tables on Margaret Thatcher's original plan to sell everything off to the highest bidder. 'It has led the bull of market forces out of the china shop of British television licensing without too many breakages,' concluded a leader in *The Times*. 'The Government should never ask such a task of it again.' But in truth there was a variety of interpretations: some argued that Thames was being punished for *Death On The Rock*; others that TV-am's demise was part of the broadcasting establishment's revenge. Like the legislation itself, you could see in it what you wished.

All noted that while the changes were not sweeping, they would make an impact. The replacement of Thames and TVS by two contractors – Carlton and Meridian – relying on outside production for entertainment and drama put radically different organisational structures at the core of commercial broadcasting. The effect on jobs was already obvious. Around 4000, or a quarter of the jobs in ITV, had been lost during 1988–91. With stations like Carlton planning to operate staffs of less than 400, compared to Thames' 1300, another 3000 were likely to leave the network before the new stations started in 1993. The only consolation was the likely boom in independent production. Much of that, however, would be concentrated in London and the south-east.

It was not destined to be Tom Guttridge's best week. The day after his £35 million bid to unseat LWT failed, Guttridge figured in a Nigel Dempster story in the *Daily Mail*: 'Anneka "facing marriage crisis" '. TV presenter Anneka Rice, named as a director in the LIB bid, was in Los Angeles with Guttridge promoting his *Challenge Anneka* series. 'Asked to comment on the reports over Anneka's marriage,' stated the *Daily Mail*, Guttridge replied, 'I am only her producer.' By the end of the week 'Anneka's marriage drama' was all over the tabloids. Rice's husband and Guttridge's wife were consulting solicitors. To some, losing a franchise bid and your wife in the same week seemed a pretty extraordinary achievement.

Other stories were also being dug into. The ill feeling within the Daybreak breakfast group was already well-known among journalists. That consortium, however, was now history. Sunrise was more concerned with limiting the damage caused by Gyngell's well-publicised attack on its bid.

It put out a statement saying it would be seeking institutional investors to take up the spare stake in the company. With Gyngell's prediction that it would be 'bankrupt' by 1994 still ringing in the City's ears, it found it hard to attract any. A month later it sold the bulk of it to Carlton.

In Camden that Thursday morning TV-am's David Keighley, was putting the finishing touches to the speech Bruce Gyngell was due to give that lunchtime. Ironically the franchise announcements had come just a day before TV-am's annual broadcast journalist awards. Despite the bombshell, the awards lunch, already organised for Claridge's in London's West End, had to go ahead. It would give Gyngell a chance to answer his critics with a captive audience of staff and press to listen.

Keighley had been at the station till 10 a.m. the day before, answering calls on the franchise loss. By the time he went into Bruce Gyngell's first-floor office to discuss the speech he was running on adenalin. Gyngell agreed he should take the opportunity to explain why TV-am had bid only £14 million, but should avoid criticising the ITC. That would just look like sour grapes. Then he got up and walked over to his overcoat. 'Have a look at this,' he said.

He passed Keighley an envelope. Keighley pulled out the letter. It was from Margaret Thatcher and had been hand-delivered to Gyngell's Chelsea home late the night before. 'What do you think?'

Keighley's eyebrows hit his hairline as he read it. It was a virtual apology for the competitive tender system. He had no doubts. 'You've got to read it out, Bruce.'

'Are you sure?' said Gyngell.

'Yes,' said Keighley. 'Come on, someone like Margaret Thatcher would not write a letter like that without intending it to be made public. She was Prime Minister for eleven years! And think of the staff. We've got a duty to tell them that the woman who instigated this mess now regrets it. They deserve it.'

Gyngell looked undecided and slipped the letter back in his pocket. Later that morning, sitting in the back of Gyngell's BMW on the way to Claridge's, they went through his speech again. 'You've got to mention that letter,' stressed Keighley. Gyngell looked doubtful, but in the end agreed. At times like this, thought Keighley, it is almost impossible to read him.

The lunch took place in the main ground-floor ballroom at Claridge's. The room was packed with tables, each seating between ten and twelve, with a mix of TV-am staff, guests, journalists and a spattering of politicians. The main award was set to go to the *FT*'s Ray Snoddy, for his series of bid revelations throughout the summer. Not everyone was happy about the decision. Many at the losing ITV companies resented the fact that he had predicted their demise before the results were announced. At lunch one day in an Indian restaurant on the Tottenham Court Road he had even been approached by Thames staff. 'You're Ray Snoddy, aren't you? Well, take a look at us. This is what three unemployed Thames people look like.' His welcome when he entered Claridge's for the awards lunch that day was equally unambiguous. 'I don't know how you have got the nerve to show your face here,' said Jane Ironside-Woods, TV-am's senior press officer. Later she said it was a joke. Snoddy had taken it seriously.

After lunch, the awards were given. Then Gyngell, in a dark suit and bright polka-dot tie, got up on to the raised stage to make his speech. It was brief and covered the main points of why TV-am had not bid as much as its two rivals. He started angry but by the end he was close to tears. His voice was cracking, his eyes looked watery. He finished, said thank-you and started down from the stage. The audience burst into applause.

Keighley's first thought was that Gyngell must have been told not to read the letter. It would have been like him to ask another's advice, maybe one of the politicians in the room. They might have said 'don't do it'. As Gyngell came down from the podium, Keighley, sitting at the front, rose and took his arm. 'The letter, Bruce?'

'Oh yes,' said Gyngell. He had been so wrapped up in his speech he had forgotten. He walked slowly back onto the podium. 'There's something else,' he said above the applause. 'I have this letter which I would like to read to you.' He pulled the letter from his inside pocket and started reading. The room was instantly hushed. The word had got round many of the tables already.

He read: 'Dear Bruce. When I see how some of the other licences have been awarded I am *mystified* that you did not receive yours, and heartbroken. You of all people have done so much for the whole of television – there seems to have been no attention to that. I am only too painfully aware that I was responsible for the legislation.'

Gyngell paused theatrically. 'It is signed, Yours, Margaret – Margaret Thatcher.'

Instantly the room erupted. Journalists sprang for the phones in the lobby, others leapt to surround Gyngell, who seemed suddenly rather taken aback by it all. Later, his composure regained, he posed for photographers with the hand-written letter held out in front of him. The look on his face was one of hurt determination.

The letter caused a furore. Questions were asked in the House of Commons only hours after the lunch. 'It is to be welcomed that Mrs Thatcher admits at least some of her mistakes,' said Roy Hattersley, Labour's deputy leader. 'Doubtless we can look forward to many similar letters of apology to the thousands of others whose careers were blighted or curtailed by her policies.' It appeared as third lead news item on the *News At Ten* that night and headed most front pages the next day. There seemed to be no getting away from Bruce Gyngell's tortured features.

Other ITV chiefs piled in with their comments. The former Prime Minister, said Richard Dunn, 'is not as painfully aware as we are at Thames Television' that she was responsible for the legislation. Greg Dyke, the LWT boss, added an I-told-you-so: 'Some of us tried to explain to the Government at the time that the results of the franchise process that they were introducing were irrational — and they were. I don't remember the Government listening too hard then.' (Later he admitted to an interviewer that by then he had already started receiving congratulatory letters from ex-TV-am staff saying 'You got the bastard'.

'But I don't feel that way at all,' he said. 'I long ago overcame any hostility I had towards Bruce and TV-am.')

Most, though, privately savoured the irony of it all: Thatcher's favourite broadcaster run through by her own legislation. What goes around comes around, as the Americans say.

George Russell first heard about the Thatcher letter on Thursday afternoon. He and David Glencross had been invited to the Claridge's lunch but thought it diplomatic to cry off. A staff member burst into his office with a sheet from the Press Association news-wire. 'Have you seen this?' Russell was amazed, not just because of the apology, but also because Gyngell had decided to make it public. Letters from ex-Prime Ministers just do not get read out that often.

There were more surprises to come. The ITC knew every loser was consulting lawyers to see if there were any grounds for taking the franchise decisions to judicial review. The next day Russell started getting the first phone calls from journalists about links between Marley, the tile company he headed, and Disney. Staff at TV-am had tipped off the press that Russell's office had asked for a video of film shot at EuroDisney, the amusement park near Paris that Disney was building, earlier that summer. The implication was obvious: that Marley and Disney's business links made Russell an odd choice to judge the breakfast bids.

Russell was flabbergasted. A team of roofers from Marley *had* worked on four ticket booths at EuroDisney earlier in the year, but the contract was so small as to be insignificant. When the wife of one of the workers had written to him in July asking for a copy of film TV-am had shot at the building site, Russell had duly obliged, asking his secretary at the ITC to contact the breakfast station. David Keighley, who had handled the request, had thought it odd at the time, given that Disney's involvement in the rival breakfast bid was well-known. He had minuted and memoed his conversations on the matter in case it became an issue later. A copy of the film, which had been lined up for a special report the station was planning on the French economy, was duly sent over to Russell's office at the ITC.

The link, however tangential, was enough to set several Sunday papers on the chase. The *Mail on Sunday*, the *Observer* and the *Sunday Times* all put teams on it. The stories came to nothing. Even so, it was a very uncomfortable weekend for Russell.

Judicial review was the only recourse for losers wanting to challenge the ITC's decisions. They would have to prove that either the ITC's procedure or the decision itself had been unfair in some way. If they took it on, it was likely to be an expensive and lengthy process. There were few precedents to offer any hope.

Despite Gyngell's protestations that he would not challenge the ITC's decision, he did run through the possibilities with Anthony Scrivener, TV-am's QC, a week after the results. Scrivener had been interested in the EuroDisney story and in Russell's statements at the Wednesday morning press conference. In a two-hour meeting with Gyngell, Keighley and Paul Vickers, the TV-am company secretary, he ran through the possibilities. Did the fact that Russell had detailed how much better off the Treasury was going to be imply that the Commission had been working to hit a certain target in bid revenue? It was hardly provable. They agreed an application for judicial review would be a waste of money.

Others were less cautious. In particular many of those who had been failed at the quality threshold wanted to know why. To head off what seemed like a mounting wave of possible legal action Russell agreed to meet individual losers and offer some explanations. In the last week of October teams from TVS, TSW, TVNi, Richard Branson's CPV-TV and Phil Redmond's North-West TV filed into the ITC's Knightsbridge headquarters for meetings.

They all took a similar course. Beginning at 5 p.m., the losers were led into the same boardroom where the fateful decisions had been taken. Russell, Glencross and Michael Redley, the ITC's head of licensing for television, sat with their backs to the window. Across the divide sat the aggrieved losers. Russell kicked off with a speech, pointing out that the ITC had no obligation to offer bidders any further information. He outlined the procedure the ITC had gone through, then Glencross and Redley (a former Treasury official who had been responsible for drawing up the complex 'Invitation to Apply') ran through the sub-sections of the Broadcasting Act on which the applications had failed. These were all parts of Section 16 of the Act, which detailed how the ITC should make its decisions, listing the programming requirements and including the stipulation that the service must appear sustainable over the licence period.

The meetings invariably went well until the losers asked why they had failed, rather than just where. Russell then apologised and said his team could give them no more information.

Inevitably many were angry and confused. TVS's Rudolph Agnew was one. Ever since the result had come in, he had blamed himself for not reading the bidding situation correctly. But he also loathed the way a company's future could be decided in secret without a single question being asked of it. He had wanted to file for judicial review immediately, but had been advised that he must sort out the company's finances first. The £30 million new equity he had organised for TVS was contingent on getting the licence back. Without it, TVS was plunged into crisis. His priority had to be to organise new banking facilities.

To Agnew's eyes, Russell looked acutely embarrassed by the whole charade. Others thought likewise, and swiftly told the press that the meetings offered nothing new and were a waste of time. Phil Redmond's team had been infuriated when a tired Russell confused North-West's name with that of CPV-TV, the Branson bid, during their meeting. Branson and Frost had been the last ones to see the Commission before Redmond. It was clear that each loser was just getting the prepared patter.

Only one acted on it. Harry Turner, boss of TSW, the smallest of the losers, convened a board meeting in his lawyer's offices in the City after his ITC meeting. He was adamant: they must take legal action. His board, with little to lose, backed him. In a notice of application dated 7 November, TSW applied for judicial review. The ITC was horrified. Lengthy legal action could tie up the Commission for months. If others got involved, it would also scuttle any plans to get the new network into shape before 1993. First-time winners would have to postpone plans to set up the new companies until the decisions were ratified by the High Court. It could go all the way to the House of Lords, and there was little the ITC could do about it.

It was the minnow's revenge.

14

*'I suppose if I'd written ''FUCK OFF''
inside the sealed bid the ITC would not
have looked at the rest of the
application. I wish I had now . . .'*

Harry Turner

The first time Harry Turner realised that TSW might be facing
defeat came on 10 October, just a week before the fateful fax.
Turner, 'Flash Harry' to the other ITV bosses, was attending the
MIPCOM programme sales conference in Cannes. Always one
to do things in style, he was staying at the ludicrously expensive
Colombe D'Or hotel in St Paul de Vance, a picture-book village
tucked away in the hills behind Cannes. The hotel, a low
building adorned with bougainvillaea and vines set off a village
side street, was one of the most exclusive in the South of France.
Inpressionist paintings hung in the thirty or so bedrooms. A
mosaic by Leger decorated the swimming pool. Such opulence
came from an enlightened pre-war policy of allowing artists to
pay with their work. Now, to get in, you needed money.

Turner, fifty-seven, a medium-height man with a clipped
moustache and pouter pigeon chest, was in his bedroom when
the call came through. It was Jane Thynne, the *Daily Telegraph*'s
media correspondent. She wanted his response to the rumours
that TSW was going to be failed at the quality threshold.

'We reckon the ITC think you have bid too much.'

Turner, whose mischievous sense of humour made him a
popular contact for journalists, was taken aback. 'Who's we?'
he asked.

'Well, that's the talk among journalists.'

Turner said he could not really comment on it, but after the call, he sat there turning it over in his mind. There was only one thing for it; he would check with Ray Snoddy on the *FT*. Eventually he got through. He told Snoddy about the conversation. 'What do you think, Ray?'

'Well,' said Snoddy in his hesitant Ulster brogue, 'it's the general talk among journalists.' Turner went cold. 'But don't worry, Harry. I think you might get away with it because you are small fry, you know, and TVS might have blown it. But we think, you know, what the hell, it is not the end of the world if you slip through.'

Turner was shocked. If anyone had an inside track it was Snoddy. He had predicted TSW's bid spot-on; he also had a feel for what the Independent Television Commission was doing. Yet that summer the flak had been directed at TVS for overbidding, not at TSW. Everyone acknowledged it had bid the most in its region, and Turner was confident it was going to win. Now this. How did the journalists know? Was the ITC softening them up?

Outside his room he could hear rain. A thunderstorm was crawling its way over the hills around St Paul de Vance. Suddenly the power was cut, leaving him sitting there, as dusk fell, brooding. Later, the power restored, he switched on the TV set. A soft porn movie was playing. On the screen a young woman was spreadeagled with a man crouching over her. You could not see their faces. Somebody, thought Turner, is about to get screwed.

Harry Turner was determined to be ITV's last larger-than-life figure. His wining and dining were legendary, his parties famous, his risqué cartoons, often doodled during the most important of meetings, collector's items. It was all part of his own personal battle against the dour number-crunchers who, he believed, had taken the fun out of running an ITV company. *The grey men in suits are taking over*, he would tell his colleagues. Where are the entrepreneurs, the buccaneers who helped establish ITV and brought verve and innovation to the network? Other ITV bosses thought Turner was living in the past and driven by a lust for publicity, but no one disliked him. His station was too small to be a threat and he was always fun to be with. 'Oh, that's Harry for you,' they would murmur good-naturedly at his latest escapade.

The showmanship came with the job. Turner had spent twenty-three years selling airtime first for Westward, the original franchise holder in the south-west, and then TSW. Westward had been founded and led by the charismatic Peter Cadbury, a colourful multimillionaire who thought nothing of piloting his own plane from London to the station's Plymouth studios, or zipping down in his red Ferrari. For Turner, the policeman's son from Chelsea with a few years in newspaper sales behind him, Cadbury was an irresistible figure. When Westward self-destructed in 1980–1, TSW took on Turner as sales director. Four years later he was managing director, and determined to continue the Cadbury tradition.

Westward was one of the ITV success stories of the 1960s and 1970s. Founded in 1961, it built its reputation as a small but profitable region. With a transmission area that stretched from Land's End to Weymouth, taking in Cornwall, Devon and parts of Somerset and Dorset, it had an audience of less than 2 million. But it used that to its advantage, fostering close links to the local community and producing strong regional programming. Even that, though, was not enough to convince the Independent Broadcasting Authority to renew its franchise in 1980. By then the ambitions and behaviour of its founder had made Westward one of the sure-fire certainties to lose.

Its demise filled the business pages for months. Shortly before the franchise round the company had been split by an extraordinary boardroom battle between Cadbury and another director, Lord Harris of Greenwich, a former Home Office broadcasting minister. At the time Cadbury had got himself involved in highly publicised arguments with both the chief executive of Plymouth council and the chief constable of Devon and Cornwall. He had also angered the IBA by using the station's cash to set up a local airline, Air Westward (it lasted less than a year), and by lobbying to expand the company's transmission area into Bristol, which was served by HTV. At a Westward board meeting in 1980, Harris argued that Cadbury was a liability and persuaded the board to vote him out of a job. The only problem was that Cadbury controlled 60 per cent of the shares. He was also popular with the staff. (The entire sales team, under Turner, signed a petition calling on the board to reinstate him.) The company was in turmoil.

Eventually the IBA blocked Cadbury's reinstatement, and, months later, gave the franchise to a rival bidder, TSW, led by Kevin Goldstein-Jackson, a thirty-three-year-old programme-maker. It was a bold move. Goldstein-Jackson had proposed widespread innovations in regional programming, yet, despite being seen at the IBA as yet another eccentric (he had adopted the 'Goldstein' to show solidarity with Israel), he produced a compelling application. He took on most of Westward's staff. When, in 1985, the pressures of running a small company finally proved disagreeable to Goldstein-Jackson, Turner took on the mantle.

By his own admission, he was never a details man. He often quoted his old headmaster at Sloane grammar school in Chelsea. 'You don't have to worry about mathematics, dear boy,' he had said. 'Let other people add up for you. You need to join the Shakespeare Society, learn to write and speak eloquently and that will get you through life.' Turner had followed his dictum. By the time he took over as boss of TSW, he was one of the best speakers and wittiest writers in the network. His humorous articles made regular appearances in the trade press, as did Turner himself, who liked to phone in his own diary stories. Now boss of a publicly listed company, his flair for the apposite quote won him admirers among the national press too.

He fought hard for the causes he believed in, carrying on a running battle with Central's Leslie Hill – one of his dreaded 'grey men' – over the future shape of the ITV network. Hill had lobbied vociferously for a redrawing of the ITV map into fewer, larger regions. This, he argued, made better economic sense for the 1990s. Rubbish, countered Turner, ITV is nothing without its regionalism. TSW, ITV's fourth-smallest station with just over 2 per cent of network advertising revenue and less than 3 per cent of ITV homes, was the voice of a community. To allow it to be gobbled up by a larger entity was ridiculous.

There were well-publicised spats with Alastair Burnet over ITN's independence (Burnet wanted to get rid of ITV ownership, Turner did not), and with his fellow ITV bosses over multiple bidding in the franchise round. 'If anyone here backs a bid against another ITV company I am walking out,' Turner declared at one of the monthly meetings of ITV bosses. The other bosses put it down to bluster on Turner's part and ignored it. (They were right – Turner eventually relented and pushed TSW into taking a small stake in an unsuccessful bid against HTV.)

He never enjoyed council meetings anyway. When he first started going he thought they would be full of the excitement of programme-making. He swiftly discovered he was wrong. 'I discovered lots of worthy men, a preponderance of accountants in suits,' he told colleagues later. 'And I could have been working in cement manufacture or contraceptive design. It had bugger all to do with making programmes.'

He had swiftly dropped ambitions to increase TSW's contribution to the network; it was all carved up between the major ITV companies. Pushing a programme on nationally was like 'trying to squeeze a marshmallow into a kids' moneybox'. He got his fingers burnt with a £500,000 pilot programme called *Where There's A Will*, starring Patrick MacNee. He had thought it a wonderful production. His ITV colleagues were less impressed. It took him two years to persuade them to show it, and then they played it at different times. TSW had to write off the losses. After that, the company concentrated on what it knew best, providing local programming and building community links.

Like nearly all ITV companies it had its production centre in the regions, while its revenue gathering took place in London, where the advertisers and agencies were. Turner described his job as 'bridging the gap', constantly explaining to staff on both sides why they needed each other. They liked him. He surrounded himself with executives who dealt with the details. He did the broad brush work, splitting his week between the two offices. He had a flat in Knightsbridge, a flat in Plymouth and a house in the Home Counties. He never quite dropped the lifestyle of a boom-years ITV sales director – the chauffeur-driven Mercedes, the Concorde trips, the parties, the fat cigars – to the extent that some ITV rivals queried how TSW paid for it all. But Turner was unrepentant; it was all part of the southwest tradition. It did not occur to him that his was the kind of lifestyle that made Margaret Thatcher uneasy about the industry's soft handling of the ITV unions. In fact he believed he was a model for Thatcher's new England: he did not inherit wealth or make it shifting a stake around on the Stock Exchange. He started with nothing and earned it on results.

He was never a free-marketeer, however. He lobbied with the rest of ITV against the more radical elements of the broadcasting legislation. In early 1990 he even arranged a brief meeting with Thatcher herself. It was, he told friends later, a 'bit like meeting Queen Victoria'. The meeting took place at the Carlton Club, Piccadilly haunt of Conservative party power-brokers, at an after-dinner function for Thatcher and her Cabinet. At 11.30 p.m. she had glided in regally, the exhausted members of her Cabinet in tow. Turner, still dinner-jacketed from dinner elsewhere, had been introduced: 'This is Mr Harry Turner, managing director of Television South-West, who wants to have a word with you about the broadcasting White Paper.'

'Oh yes?' said Thatcher, looking at him.

Turner spoke first. 'I'm a bit concerned about some elements of the White Paper, Mrs Thatcher,' he said hesitantly.

He was fixed with an icy stare. 'Not afraid of competition are you, Mr Turner?' she asked sharply. She moved closer and, seemingly inches from his nose, lectured him briskly. British industry needed competition, and advertisers believed that the choice of media they had was artificially restricted. He need have no worries; there were provisions in the Broadcasting Act for protecting quality.

With that, she swept away in a waft of perfume. Turner, ever the raconteur, said later that he thought of making an obscene suggestion to catch her attention, but decided against it. He never got the chance to say anything. It was, he observed, a proper verbal handbagging.

After that, it all fell into place for Turner. Thatcher wanted to remove the last bastion of restrictive practices; the ITV companies had to put their houses in order. That meant they had to 'be sharp, be nimble, be a lean, mean machine'. TSW was a profitable company (£4.7 million pre-tax profits on £44 million turnover in 1990) with no diversification or 'daft borrowing'. To win, it had to propose the best programmes, and bid the most. It could not, he told his board, rely on winning simply because of its past achievements. 'It is too arrogant. We can't lie back and say we are not bothered about competitive bids, that the ITC will give the licence to us because of our track record.' It was never the intention of the Government legislation anyway. It wanted to inject competition into independent television and raise as much money as possible for the public purse from a scarce resource. It followed that TSW had to bid high.

The problem for Turner was the quality of his opposition. By early 1991 he knew he faced two rivals for the south-west licence. In one corner was Telewest, a bid led by an independent producer, Malory Maltby. In the other was Westcountry, a very different outfit pulled together by Stephen Redfarn, the banker who had advised TVS's James Gatward. He had put together some heavyweight financial backers including Associated Newspapers, owner of the *Daily Mail*, and SouthWest Water, the cash-rich local utility. A plump, soft-spoken man, Redfarn had tracked TSW for some time, assiduously attending media conferences but always keeping a low profile. The long-term planning had paid off; as well as the impressive backers, he had also lined up John Banham, director-general of the Confederation of British Industry, as chairman and Frank Copplestone, former managing director of Southern (the franchise holder which TVS displaced) as deputy chairman. The TSW board was all too conscious that the quality of both personnel and money in the Redfarn bid was ominously strong.

As always Turner left a lot of the detailed work to a small caucus of his senior executives. His deputy, Ivor Stolliday, had been poached from the ITV Association four years earlier specifically because of his experience of regulatory bureaucracy. Stolliday, Turner and Sir Brian Bailey, the TSW chairman, oversaw most of the bid work. Many TSW executives were excluded – a decision taken partly in the belief that some might be passing material on to one of their rivals. (This stemmed from a hoax informant who had convinced Turner in March that he had inside information on the supposed traitors. After repeated trips abroad by the company solicitor to meet the informant, and the payment of around £2000, Turner found he had been the victim of a professional conman.)

Like other ITV companies TSW worked hard to model the rival bids, using, among others, the economic consulting group NERA, which had also worked with the ITC on projections for advertising growth in the 1990s. The advice it received was that, whereas Telewest's financial muscle seemed slight, West-country could bid at least £12 million at 1991 prices (£14 million at 1993 prices). To be certain of winning, TSW would have to bid higher.

Turner put off the final decision until the last moment (despite the misgivings of some who said they should give themselves more time to mull over the exact figure). Some executive directors, excluded from the bid team, did not even know what the bid range was. Earlier meetings had concentrated on such matters as how Turner should deliver the application. In a wheelbarrow? The props department had duly bought one. On his horse? That might not present the right image. In the end they decided it had to be with Gus Honeybun, the mascot rabbit which provided the continuity announcements between TSW children's programmes. The station had inherited Gus, like Turner, from Westward. It seemed fitting he should accompany the boss in his finest hour.

The board meeting to decide the final bid was called for the evening of 14 May, eighteen hours before the application had to be handed in. It was held in the offices of TSW's accountant, Ernst & Young, in the City. For over three hours the board debated the bid. By leaving the decision to the last moment, Turner had ensured that the maximum amount of information about their rivals had been gleaned. The involvement of Associated Newspapers and SouthWest Water in the West-country bid was now confirmed. The bid level went higher and higher until eventually the board agreed on £14 million a year at

1991 prices. There were some worried looks but no one dissented.

They were just winding up when someone pointed out that the bid had to be in 1993 prices. 'It's too round a figure anyway,' said Bailey, the TSW chairman. He suggested adding the date: 14/5/91. The rest of the board laughed but agreed. £14,591,000 was scaled up to a bid of £16.12 million in 1993 prices. They walked upstairs to the Ernst & Young dining rooms for dinner. The next day, Turner himself wrote the sum on to gold embossed blue notepaper to be sealed and handed in to the ITC. If there had been any second thoughts, there was never time to voice them.

The sum was huge, Turner acknowledged that. It was far greater than either London Weekend or Granada bid, and greater than any profits the company had previously made. But it was based on radical cost cutting and bullish ad revenue projections. And the one thing Turner felt he knew about was revenue projections. He had done those for thirty years in sales. He knew the realities of the marketplace, and was confident that TSW could not only hold its own against new media like satellite and cable, but edge a bit extra off any ITV newcomers. Colleagues had mentioned the possibility that the bid might be so high that the station was not worth running – the 'winner's curse' as some called it. Rubbish, Turner told them. 'If it's between the winner's curse and the loser's curse, I know which I would choose.'

So when the application went in, he was supremely confident. Even after Snoddy revealed all the bids for the southwest in the *FT*, he was smiling – TSW was going to win by miles. He was more interested in telling the press about his plans to sponsor a bollard in Hyde Park where he went riding every morning. There was no need to draw up any contingency plans for losing. It was cut and dried.

The night at the Colombe D'Or after he had talked to Snoddy was one of his worst. The conversations had given him a bad feeling; it was the first time any of the press had suggested that TSW had overbid. He ran through it all in his mind again:

SouthWest Water, Associated Newspapers, John Banham. These were all big hitters. Yet everyone told him they had bid less than £8 million. They were supposed to go to the maximum they could bid. £12 million, £13 million. *I had to be safe, I had to be safe*, he kept repeating to himself. That is why he had bid so much – to be safe.

The next morning, when the sun came up, he changed his mind. No, he thought, of course we will win. We will blow the rest out of the water. He flew back to London, his confidence restored, and headed down to Plymouth early the next week to await the ITC's decision. The omens were good. He opened the curtains of his flat on Plymouth Hoe at 6 a.m. on 16 October and scanned the horizon. He was on the same latitude from which Sir Francis Drake had looked for the Spanish Armada 400 years before. There were no ships. Good, thought Turner smiling to himself, I can go on playing bowls.

He went to the studio early, had some coffee and chatted to Bailey, his chairman, as they waited for the allotted hour. A production team had set up a camera outside his office so Turner could announce the result to staff over the closed-circuit TV system. He rehearsed the walk from the fax room to his office. Tense but full of confidence he made the final walk at 9.40 a.m. Minutes later out came the fax. Turner felt like he had been run over by a ten-ton truck. TSW had lost, its proposed bid judged unsustainable. Westcountry had bid just £7.8 million and won.

His first reaction was one of outrage. TSW had been betrayed. Its executives had done nothing wrong, neither had its staff. It was a successful company, it was profitable, it had not borrowed money, it had not made any wild diversifications. It had stuck to its core business and done well. What had it done to deserve this?

Few of the staff were expecting the result that early. When Turner's head and shoulders appeared on the office TVs, reading the fax, many assumed it was still a rehearsal, another of Harry's sick jokes. Gradually, as they listened, they realised it was for real. TSW had lost; with it would go most of their jobs. Turner looked devastated.

The rest of the day passed in a blur. Before lunch Turner took a call from the BBC asking him to take part in that night's *Late Show*. He agreed. After lunch he took the call from David Glencross at the ITC.

'What can I say, Harry? I'm sorry, personally, that we shall be losing you. You've been great fun. I shall miss you. Keep writing and doing your . . .'

It was warm but Turner could feel his embarrassment. He cut it short. 'Thanks David, I appreciate that, but you can understand I am feeling a little bit bruised at the moment.'

While other senior executives hid in their offices, Turner and Paul Stewart-Lang, TSW's programme director, went down to the canteen to talk to staff. There was a mood of disbelief. How could they lose for bidding too much? When the bid had leaked out, a number of staff had queried the figure, wondering how the station could operate while paying such a high sum, but the senior executives must know what they are doing, they reasoned. Now they were confused. What was going on?

That evening Turner was driven back to London for his television appearance. He felt like a man walking through a trauma. In the hospitality room at the BBC before the show he perked up. Spotting his old adversary Leslie Hill, he wandered over and offered his congratulations. 'Two thousand pounds, you've done well, Leslie,' he said. 'It will cost you more than that to get the Central board down to London for the celebrations!' Hill smiled, embarrassed. After the show Turner was driven back to his Knightsbridge flat. It was one in the morning and suddenly he felt like an old man. He sat in his bedroom without the energy to undress, deadbeat. Thirty years in the business, he thought. *Fuck it, what a way to end it.*

Over the next few days Turner's expression hardened into steely resolution. He had 300 staff to answer to for his misjudgement, not to mention the company's shareholders. He wanted reasons why TSW had failed. At a meeting with George Russell, David Glencross and Michael Redley in the ITC boardroom on 31 October he pressed for them.

'On what basis, George, do you say we can't sustain this level of bid?'

'I'm not obliged to tell you.'

'Oh come on, give us a clue. I've got three hundred people in Plymouth who need to know.'

'I'm not obliged to tell you.' Russell, it was clear, was under instructions. The ITC team admitted that TSW had 'played by the rules' in making its application, but the decision to block the bid was 'a matter of judgement' for which no further explanation could be given. Turner was livid. It was, he said later, the most pointless meeting he had ever been invited to in his life.

What annoyed him was that not one scrap of evidence had been given to show that his judgement was flawed. The insistence on total secrecy as to how they reached their decisions was, to him, paranoid in the extreme. Surely any decision that meant the life or death of a company should be in the public domain? It was not exactly atom bomb secrets they were dealing in. Who were these decision-makers? Most of the senior ITC staff had never worked in a real business, they were honours-degree economists or such-like whose experience was limited to Government agencies or consultancies. And the Commission members themselves knew nothing about television.

Even George Russell was not an experienced television professional. Yes, he had been a member of the IBA since 1979, he had been deputy chairman of Channel 4 and chairman of ITN, but that did not make him a television professional. A professional, reasoned Turner, was a person who earns their daily bread solely in the exercise of skills in the television industry. He had been doing projections and business plans for thirty years. Who were they to tell him he was wrong? All he was doing was putting in an aggressive, competitive bid. *Wasn't that what the legislation was all about? Wasn't that what the Government wanted?* Why could the ITC not take a risk? They took a risk on Kevin Goldstein-Jackson's original TSW ten years before. What had changed?

TSW filed for judicial review in early November. Six days later Justice Simon Brown kicked it out of the High Court, saying, 'This application was doomed to inevitable failure.' At a board meeting a week later, TSW agreed to lodge an appeal. On 28

November Turner took the case to the Court of Appeal, presided over by the Master of the Rolls, Lord Donaldson. He got a better response. Donaldson said the ITC must give the court some indication of its reasons. Reluctantly, the ITC produced the secret staff assessment paper, coded 179(91), which had concluded that TSW would not be able to maintain the service proposed. The case was adjourned for a week, after which Donaldson gave TSW leave to apply for judicial review, and said he would hear it himself, with two other judges, in the Court of Appeal in January. No one had ever persuaded ITV's regulatory bodies to divulge the reasoning behind any of their franchise round decisions before. Turner had made television history.

Once TSW had been granted its application for judicial review, others leapt on the bandwagon. TVS, which had been locked in crisis talks with its banks following its franchise loss, TVNi, a consortium whose £3.1 million bid against Ulster had been judged too high, and White Rose, a bidder against Yorkshire which claimed the Leeds-based station was paying too much, also applied. For the winners like MAI's Meridian, which was starting up from scratch and had to take over from TVS in 1993, it was a nightmare. It threatened to throw all their plans into chaos.

Meridian's Roger Laughton was sitting in a suite in the Dorchester discussing co-productions with an American producer on 20 December when he heard. His secretary rang. 'The lawyers say you've got to get down to the High Court.' Laughton left immediately. If there was one thing Americans understood, it was when lawyers call, you answer.

At 2.15 p.m. in Court 14 TVS's, TVNi's and White Rose's cases for judicial review were heard. By 4.30 p.m., after a plea that any delay would be disruptive to the companies concerned, they were pushed up to the Court of Appeal where Lord Donaldson and two colleagues agreed to consider them. At 6.10 p.m. they threw all the cases out on the grounds that none of the companies had applied promptly enough. Everyone was bemused. Only days earlier Laughton had been sitting round a table with TVS executives trying to negotiate the purchase of the station's Southampton offices. The court case over, negotiations recommenced.

So by Christmas Harry Turner was facing up to the ITC on his own. No one gave him much of a chance, but television can be a sentimental industry. At least he was going down fighting.

London's main law courts sit just north of the Thames where the Strand meets Fleet Street. The courts' cavernous entrance hall is always busy. Knots of plaintiffs, defendants and assorted hangers-on congregate round the central notice boards. Dark-suited solicitors and barristers chat at the sides. Occasionally the odd journalist wanders through. But on the morning of Monday 20 January the journalists were all heading one way: up the stairs on the far right-hand side of the entrance hall to the Court of Appeal.

The court itself is a small, square, high-roofed room measuring about fifty feet by fifty feet. Tall, wooden bookshelves stuffed with hidebound books reach round three walls; above, long Gothic windows stretch upwards. At one end of the room, facing the public entrance, are the judges' thrones, three high-backed chairs covered in red velvet standing behind ornately carved desks on a raised podium. At the back of the chairs are two red velvet-curtained doorways. In front of the podium are tiers of wooden benches. The only nod to modernity is the sound system: six hanging microphones, dangling down into the court from a web of wires across the beamed ceiling. Even this looks like some antiquated Heath Robinson contraption.

In the centre of the court that morning, chatting to his lawyers while waiting for proceedings to start, stood Harry Turner. He looked sergeant-major neat, as always: blue double-breasted pinstripe, blue polka-dot tie, red silk handkerchief. The camera crews outside had already caught his entrance. Inside, the atmosphere was tense; the viewing benches were already packed and more journalists were turning up by the minute. The start was delayed while security guards unlocked the public gallery to cope with the overflow. No one knew what to expect. There had never really been a case like it.

TSW's application for judicial review rested on three arguments: that the ITC had applied more stringent criteria than it had set out in its original invitation to apply; that TSW had a 'legitimate expectation' that that would not occur; and that the staff paper on which the ITC's decision was based was neither a fair nor accurate assessment of the TSW bid.

The staff paper, drawn together by Sheila Cassells, a financial officer at the ITC, had already raised eyebrows within TSW. It critised the station's choice of an optimistic 5.3 per cent growth figure for industry advertising revenue, comparing it to the 4 per cent average for other bidders. And it suggested that £10 million in bank facilities promised by Barclays might be withdrawn when the bank became more fully aware of the TSW business plan.

The plan concluded: 'TSW's revenue projections are extremely optimistic, particularly in the earlier years, and the proposed cost structure leaves little room for manoeuvre if trading turns out to be worse than expected ... A more plausible revenue growth of 4 per cent a year (i.e. the figure used by the ITC in its own modelling, and the average used by all other applicants for regional Channel 3 licences) would push TSW into persistent and accumulating borrowings. On this basis fixed costs, including the cash bid, would be 91 per cent over the full licence period, and would actually exceed NAR (network advertising revenue) over the first three years. It does not appear that TSW would be able to maintain the service proposed throughout the ten-year period for which the licence would be in force.'

Affidavits from George Russell and Peter Rogers, the ITC deputy chief executive and director of finance, were equally damning. Russell said he was 'astonished' when he analysed the TSW plan. The company appeared to have taken no account of the fact that ITV faced a more testing future, in particular the ending of its monopoly on television advertising revenue once Channel 4 sold its own advertising and Channel 5 was launched. TSW was forecasting average profit margins of 38 per cent over the new licence period, compared to an average 12–15 per cent in the 1980s. 'It is stretching credulity to believe that the same management could suddenly increase TSW's profit margins by such a dramatic figure in what they accept will be a more competitive environment.'

For six days the three bespectacled judges, Lords Donaldson, Nolan and Steyn, sat listening to the arguments from the opposing QCs. Donaldson led the questioning, otherwise he sat attentively, blinking, grunting and chewing his fingers as he listened. Occasionally he and the other judges took notes. More often they nodded sagely as the barristers apologetically peppered their speeches with the arcane jargon of the television industry: 'network discounts' and 'contributions', NARs and PQRs. With names like TSW, ITC, NERA and KMPG floating around as well, it felt at times as if the debate was drowning in a sea of initials.

They returned repeatedly to the revenue growth projections. Russell's and Rogers' affidavits backed up the arguments in the Cassells paper, and contended that criticism of TSW's projections was fair. TSW's argument was that if the ITC had wanted bidders to use a 4 per cent figure for NAR growth, why did it not say so? It set out other 'sensitivity tests' that bidders had to apply to their projections, and TSW had met all those. Gordon Pollock, its QC, stressed the experience of the company's management. Was Harry Turner, he asked, really a 'wild and woolly man plucking figures from the sky'? What was 'rational'? What was 'credible'?

The judges adjourned for nine days to consider their verdict. Turner was confident. Pollock, a tough six-footer with a broken nose, had easily out-argued Patrick Elias, the ITC's QC. And Donaldson had seemed sympathetic to TSW's plight. At one stage he had even described the ITC staff assessment paper on the company's business plan as a 'hatchet job'. Each day as he waited for the result Turner told himself: *we're going to win it*.

On the morning of Wednesday 5 February Turner and his team returned to the court. The judges filed in and took their seats. Photocopies of the judgement were handed out. 'Application is dismissed,' said Donaldson. Turner was stunned again. The QCs leapt up to argue over costs. Donaldson then revealed it had been a split verdict. Nolan and Steyn had gone against TSW while he supported its case. He would have set aside the

ITC decision, he continued, so that the commissioners could take a 'fresh look' at both the TSW and Westcountry bids for the south-west. TSW's complaint that the ITC staff paper was misleading was well-founded, he believed.

However, the majority verdict must apply. 'The judgement of the ITC may be right or wrong,' said Lord Justice Nolan, 'but it is fully explained and, thus explained, it is plainly one which the ITC was entitled to make.' TSW and the ITC had to pay their own costs, and half each of Westcountry's, which was also represented.

There was still hope for Turner. The Appeal Court gave him leave to take his case to the House of Lords. Standing in the Strand outside the Law Courts, still in his double-breasted pinstripe, he was defiant: 'We have been given a window of opportunity and I think we should take it. We are fighting for the life or death of a company here.'

The next day, in Plymouth, the TSW board voted unanimously to pursue it to the bitter end. On 6 February TSW's petition of appeal was presented to the House of Lords. The hearing, in front of five Law Lords, started on 18 February. On the morning of 25 February, three days before Turner's fifty-eighth birthday, it was dismissed.

There was a sting in the tail for Turner. A month later Allen & Overy, solicitors for the ITC, wrote to the House of Lords, asking it to consider varying the Court of Appeal's order on costs – in short, to make TSW pick up the bill for all the legal work it had brought about. TSW already faced costs of more than £500,000. The ITC's request could double that.

On 26 March the same five Law Lords threw the suggestion out. Turner was satisfied. He thought it had been a vindictive move on the part of the ITC. There was nothing left for TSW anyway. There would not be enough independent production business in Plymouth to justify remaining a listed company, especially after it had angered WestCountry, the new ITV licence holder, by dragging it through the courts for four months. A better bet was seeking a partner which wanted a listing and would organise a reverse takeover of the company. If that could not be found, TSW would have to be liquidated.

Turner told colleagues that, in a sense, he was glad it was all over. 'The fun has long gone from this business. The age of the maverick, the hustler, the salesman has gone. Now it's the age of the grey-faced accountants, and I want no part of that.'

He promised he would see it through. 'I will be here in Plymouth on 31 December switching out the lights.' It was not to be. A month after the Law Lords gave their final verdict, Turner, like every other senior executive at TSW, discussed his future with the company's non-executive directors. It was decided that his was not the style best suited to running down a company. He left a month later, taking Gus Honeybun with him.

15

*'Despite having had the privilege
of reading my own obituary,
I do not yet feel dead.'*

David Plowright

Even before Harry Turner left, the franchise round caught another victim in its turbulent wake. On Monday 27 January David Plowright, Granada TV chairman and one of the most respected bosses in the ITV network, was summoned to Granada headquarters in London's Soho for a meeting with Gerry Robinson, the group's recently appointed chief executive. Two hours later he was out of a job. It seemed harsh treatment for a man who had given thirty-five years of his life to the company, and pulled off a coup in the franchise round, winning the north-west licence with a bid of only £9 million. But times were changing.

Plowright, sixty-one, had no idea the axe was coming. He knew things were bad elsewhere; the problems at Granada group, the conglomerate which ran Granada TV, had worsened in 1991. Group profits had collapsed from £121 million in 1990 to £57 million. Heavy losses in computer services and satellite television, plus the ill-judged forays into new business areas such as holidays and electrical retailing, had cost it dear. Even Granada TV profits had plummeted from £37.1 million in 1990 to £22.4 million in 1991, but that was hardly the fault of bad management, more the recession that was ravaging ITV ad revenue.

To recover, the group had sold its bingo business to Bass for £150 million, made a £163 million distress rights issue and slashed its dividend. The price demanded by investors was the head of group chief executive Derek Lewis. Robinson, an Irish-born accountant who had led the successful £163 million buyout and flotation of Compass, Grand Metropolitan's former catering and cleaning division, was brought in to replace him in November.

Other Granada group directors had warned Robinson that the TV subsidiary was a problem. Partly because of its formidable reputation as one of the leading producers of programmes for the ITV network, it had long been seen as untouchable. They argued that Plowright ran it almost as his personal empire, keeping it at arm's length from the rest of the group. Plowright's track record at Granada – with hits as diverse as *Coronation Street*, *World In Action* and *Brideshead Revisited* – and his connections in the worlds of arts and politics enabled him to brush critics aside. His success in bidding low to win Granada TV's licence entrenched that position. Even when Plowright exercised a ten-year-old contractual perk, buying his house in Mottram St Andrew, Cheshire, off Granada for £81,000 (it was worth £450,000), staff stood by him despite the newspaper interest. For a new group chief executive seeking to establish the lines of power, Plowright, who had more enemies than he thought on the Granada group board, was an inevitable target.

Within days of taking over Robinson called Plowright in and gave him a simple choice: if there was going to be a problem they could sort it out now, either by resolving to work together with a sensible dialogue or by calling it a day and allowing Plowright to resign gracefully. Plowright said he saw no problem in working together and invited Robinson up to Manchester to visit the studios. On 12 November Robinson toured the TV headquarters and had dinner with the senior staff. He left feeling uneasy: it appeared to him they had little grasp of the financial realities facing the group or of the fact that they were moving into a vastly different broadcasting environment in the 1990s. The Granada TV staff were equally un-impressed: Robinson showed no inclination to credit their past triumphs or to understand what quality broadcasting was about. He had never run a media company before and, to them, the inexperience showed. They quickly dubbed him 'the caterer'.

Relations between Manchester and London worsened as Robinson tightened the screw. He asked Plowright to produce monthly accounts for advertising revenue, profitability and costs. Such accounting mechanisms were quite normal in other industries but alien to ITV. The move stoked the TV subsidiary's growing resentment at being the only ITV company to be controlled by a larger conglomerate. The accounting department complained it was so busy filling in forms for group headquarters that it did not have time to cost programmes. Robinson then unveiled a new profits target for Granada TV: a doubling to £45 million by the end of 1992. He also ordered the cancelling of speculative investments, notably the company's growing interest in producing feature films. He believed Plowright had agreed to it. Later he found that the film financing never stopped.

He also pressed for more redundancies. Plowright had already cut Granada TV back from 1600 employees in the mid-1980s to less than 1000 in 1991. Robinson wanted more to go. Executives in Manchester believed he wanted to turn the TV subsidiary into a Channel 4-style publisher-broadcaster. Robinson argued that there was little correlation between cost and quality, and that the cuts would not affect programming. Learning fast about the television business, he looked for ideological friends in the debate. At a long meeting with Michael Green in the Carlton offices shortly before his final show-down with Plowright, he found one. Green's views were well-known: that most ITV companies were still hopelessly overstaffed and inefficient, and living in the past. Days later, Plowright got his cards.

Sitting in Robinson's spacious sixth-floor office Plowright had argued long and hard for his job. Robinson's arguments were that he was inconsistent and impossible to work with. But the demands Robinson was making of the TV subsidiary could not be delivered, he countered. The profits targets were impossible. *How could Granada fulfil the programme promises made in its franchise application last year if it kept cutting jobs and production*? Worst of all, though, he felt betrayed. He had only just returned from a business trip to New Orleans. Robinson had lobbied the board to axe him while he was away. Finally Plowright accepted the inevitable and, saying he would think about a consultancy with the company, returned to his office. There he rang Andrew Quinn, Granada TV's managing director and a close friend, asking him: 'Who betrayed me?'

It took a week for the rest of the media to find out. His blunt memo to Granada TV staff the following Monday – 'I regret to have to announce that I have been asked by our parent company to resign as chairman of Granada Television' – made front-page news the next day. Plowright was gagged from speaking to the press until he left a month later, but he had plenty of colleagues to speak up for him. Petitions were hastily drawn up demanding his reinstatement. Letters poured in to the press. Dozens of leading actors, writers and directors voiced their condemnation of Plowright's ousting. With one decision, Robinson had made himself the pariah of Britain's arts establishment. He even received a fax from John Cleese. It said, 'Fuck off out of it, you ignorant, upstart caterer.' (His response was sardonic. He faxed back: 'Reading between the lines, I think I can safely say that I am a bigger fan of your's than you are of mine.')

It was all to no avail. Plowright released a short press statement thanking everyone for their support. 'My first responsibility is to ensure a smooth handover to my colleagues in Granada Television. After that, I will make my contribution to the debate about the future of the British television broadcasting industry in the aftermath of a flawed piece of broadcasting legislation.' Hours later he put out an amended statement. For 'British television broadcasting industry' he substituted 'British television production industry'.

At the end of February the TV subsidiary gave him a glittering send-off. In front of an audience of 1000 on the *Coronation Street* set in Manchester, actress Julie Goodyear leaped from a cake in a £1200 bodysuit to serenade Plowright (somewhat incongruously) with 'Thank Heaven For Little Girls'. Ray Fitzwalter, Granada TV's head of current affairs, told tearful guests that

Plowright was 'a prince among broadcasters'. Fireworks and champagne followed.

Robinson and Granada rode out the storm. George Russell at the ITC demanded to see both Robinson and Granada group chairman Alex Bernstein to explain the decision. They pledged that Plowright's departure would not affect the promises made in Granada's licence application. Others concluded that Plowright's departure marked the end of an era. 'The key shift you have to remember is that the 1990 Broadcasting Act changed the status of ITV companies from producers to broadcasters,' said one former Granada executive. ITV companies no longer have to produce programmes themselves if they can produce them cheaper elsewhere. 'Plowright's exit is all about managing the pace of that change. He is the last of the great producers, but it is a new era now.'

If there were any doubts that the old days were over, they were finally kicked into touch in May. In a deal heavy with ironies, BSkyB and the BBC outbid ITV for the rights to show English soccer's new Premier League, featuring the country's top twenty-two clubs. It caused an outcry as it was revealed that the £300 million five-year deal would lead to viewers having to pay to watch live football on television. Irony number one: the £300 million deal was done with over £20 million of licence-payers' money from the BBC. For that they got the return of recorded highlights in *Match of the Day* on a Saturday night. Irony number two: the TV deal was put together by the Football Association with the help of a consultant. The consultant was David Plowright.

The loss of top-flight League football was a blow to Greg Dyke, who co-ordinated ITV Sport. The LWT boss had made his name four years earlier snatching live football from the BBC for the then astronomical £44 million. This time round, flushed with the success of regaining the London weekend licence, he lost the auction. (Aside from piquing his pride, it also had implications for LWT's bottom line. The ad breaks in the station's live football coverage brought it in more than £200,000 a game. With Dyke likely to become a paper millionaire under his golden handcuff deal if LWT's share price remains buoyant, the loss had a nasty financial edge to it.)

But most important, for ITV as a whole, it signalled that the gloves were off: at last, the new, more competitive broadcasting environment had arrived.

'I can see Mrs Thatcher, in 1988 or thereabouts, turning on Lawson, Hurd, Young etc. and with that steely gaze saying ''Will no one rid me of these turbulent priests of television?'' After an Act, an auction and a fax, bodies were duly delivered.'

Richard Dunn

In the months that followed the franchise round many sensed a new mood of co-operation sweeping broadcasting. It was not just the BBC and BSkyB joining up to bid for football or discussing joint news ventures, it stretched to ITV as well. After the precariousness of many of their franchise gambles, all the ITV bosses appeared determined to make the new structure work, whatever its failings. The links to underpin that co-operation were already in place. Carlton's 20 per cent stake in Central; Central's 20 per cent stake in Meridian; Carlton, LWT and Scottish TV's stakes in Sunrise (renamed Good Morning TV); Carlton and LWT's joint ownership of a local news provider.

It was no coincidence that Michael Green was behind many of the links. He may not have got the London weekday licence cheap – Carlton TV will be paying about three times as much to the Government as Thames did under the old system – but he got it. The Carlton boss's meticulous preparation for the franchise round, which he almost undermined with his own indecision, paid off precisely because he thought about more than just winning; he thought about what would happen after winning. As power polarises in ITV, his control will grow.

Sitting in his stylishly bare monochrome office, with its up-lit modern art and strategically placed plants, he still pores over the share prices every day, reading the runes for the future of his business and looking for opportunities. ITV will remain the most popular and successful television channel in Britain, he predicts. The main competition will not be BSkyB, whose prospects – certainly of denting ITV's ad revenue – are over-rated, according to Green. The competition is the BBC. His biggest fear is that the BBC may still be forced to take advertising. If that happens, he says, television standards will drop rapidly as both networks get caught in a head-on ratings clash. Carlton TV, he adds with a smile, would still be successful because Carlton management are used to being in free market competition.

Rumours abound of a rift between Green and his former co-stakeholders in the Daybreak breakfast consortium. They are rubbish, he asserts. There were never any arguments with Conrad Black, who, after all, holds a small stake in Carlton TV. And he remains on good terms with Bob Phillis, the ITN boss who used to work for him. Black, who went on to float the Telegraph group (rather unsuccessfully) in the summer of 1992, and Phillis both decline to talk about it. Christopher Bland, Green's friend at LWT, dismisses the stories as 'losers' fantasies', pointing out that ITN in particular are notoriously bad losers. Bland had a good franchise round; his recapitalisation of LWT and targetting of TV-am are now seen as master-strokes. Even Sir George Russell, knighted for his efforts, talks admiringly of the strategy.

Bland never lost his humour or his indignation at the inept way Margaret Thatcher's government brought it all about. At an *Economist* lunch after the bids had been made he found himself sitting opposite Sir Jeffrey Sterling, the P&O boss who had advised the Department of Trade on the broadcasting legislation (despite little knowledge of the industry).

'Oh Jeffrey,' said Bland, 'I've just been invited to head a commission to look into the shipping industry.'

Sterling looked up, his fork halfway to his mouth. He frowned. 'But you don't know anything about shipping?'

Bland smiled. 'Oh, I think I know about as much about shipping as you know about broadcasting . . .'

Sterling looked stupefied. Bland paused and let it sink in.

Then he leaned across. 'Don't worry, Jeffrey. It was a joke.'
Sterling was later ennobled to Lord Sterling of Plaistow.

Greg Dyke completed his inexorable rise by becoming head of
the ITV Association. Some wanted him to become central
scheduler, a suggestion he toyed with but then dismissed.
Michael Grade, boss of Channel 4 and the franchise round's
most sought-after executive, was also canvassed for the job.
Tightly bound by £500,000 worth of golden handcuffs to
Channel 4, he had to say no.

Other winners rode their hobby horses again. Leslie Hill, the
Central boss whose £2000 bid earned him an admiring
doublepage spread in the *Daily Mail*, warned that unless the
ban on takeovers was lifted within ITV, and the blocks on
British ownership of European TV stations removed, the
winners would be gobbled up by foreign predators before they
had a chance to expand. He had his eyes on Anglia, said the
pundits.

Yorkshire's Clive Leach, having fought off a late attempt by
the rival White Rose consortium to get YTV shareholders to
block the company's £37.7 million bid, took his chance with
Tyne Tees. He announced an agreed takeover of the
Newcastle-based station in June 1992. City comment was
sceptical. It was noted that both companies needed cost savings
after paying through the nose for their licences. With the
additional tax on 'qualifying revenue', Yorkshire and Tyne Tees
together had to find around £63 million to pay the Government
in 1993. Granada, on the other side of the Pennines, would
have to find around £27 million.

Leach was unperturbed. He vowed he would get his own back
at the end of 1993, the first year of the new licence. He promised
that, before he announced the results at the annual City
presentation, he would remind the audience of their original
scepticism, then prove them wrong. Others maintain he will
eventually be driven into the arms of the old enemy, Granada.
An all-powerful 'station of the north', with enough revenue
and commissioning clout to offset the southern bias of most
independent production, might be an attractive prospect for all
parties.

The traditional strength of the south may be sapped, however, by the large sums the stations there are paying to the government. Meridian, the MAI-controlled company in the south-east, will have to find three times what TVS paid to run the area. It will need all Clive Hollick's flair for shaving costs to the bone to recreate anything like the profits that TVS squandered on MTM, its American investment.

Many of the politicians and advisers who prepared the broadcasting legislation left active political life soon afterwards. By the summer of 1992 Margaret Thatcher and Geoffrey Howe were in the House of Lords; Nigel Lawson had an office at Barclays, and was busy writing his memoirs; Lord Young had returned to the City, chairing Cable & Wireless. Lord Sterling was running P&O, and Brian Griffiths, also ennobled, was working out of Goldman Sachs, the giant American broker. Only Douglas Hurd, foreign secretary, and David Mellor, back as broadcasting minister after a spell at the Treasury, remained. By July Mellor's future was in doubt after an alleged affair with an out-of-work actress hit the headlines.

For many politicians, the whole manner of the ITV licensing round was clearly an embarrassment even before it had been completed. That was little consolation to the losers. Richard Branson, for one, remained angry and perplexed for some weeks after the ITC's decisions were announced. Eventually he decided that legal action was pointless and got on with running his airline. The post-mortems never revealed just where his CPV-TV bids went wrong. By 1992 the ITC was hinting that the BSB experience of both Virgin and John Gau, the CPV-TV chief executive, might have led them to misunderstand the process. This licensing round was very different from how the BSB franchise was awarded. It was an exam paper, not a dissertation. The implication was that somewhere along the line, someone was not listening properly.

Shortly after the franchise decisions were announced Gau went back to running his independent production company and Charles Levison, the Virgin Mr Fix-it who had put together much of the bid work, left Branson's broadcasting subsidiary to run his own media investment consultancy. It was not long before he was involved with Virgin again, however, helping the company win the second national commercial radio franchise in partnership with TV-am. Branson had a further consolation: he went on to sell his music company in early 1992, receiving £320 million for his two-thirds stake. It was the highest cash payment ever paid to an individual in a British corporate deal. Friends expected at least some of it to find its way back to his airline, Virgin Atlantic. As one put it in March: 'He has fallen in love with a very expensive mistress. Let's hope she does not ruin him.'

David Frost was the only bidder to lose four times over – three times with CPV-TV and once with TV-am. Before that, he had won at the previous two franchise rounds. Defeat did not dent his optimism for long, however. He was still seen in the Carlton Tower and Claridge's for breakfast; the box of Romeo y Juliet cigars still sat confidently on the back shelf of his Bentley. By the summer of 1992 he was planning a Channel 5 bid with Jeremy Fox and pointing out to interviewers that winning two franchise rounds out of three was 'better than 50–50'. The Channel 5 bid never happened. He bowed out of his Sunday morning TV-am show in June, finishing off by interviewing the newly ennobled Lady Thatcher. Typically he negotiated a deal to move his show lock, stock and barrel to the BBC, and place repeats of it on BSkyB – the first BBC performer ever to do so.

Bruce Gyngell also rationalised defeat and moved on. He recorded an interview for Radio 4's *On The Ropes* programme, telling the interviewer, John Humphries, that the loss of the franchise was like a death, and he had gone through the phases of mourning: denial, grief and anger, and finally acceptance. For five weeks the grief and anger manifested itself as a racking cough and cold.

'Finally I decided enough was enough. I remember lying in bed one Sunday evening, reading a book, and I thought to myself: it's about time I gave all this up and got on with my life. I woke up the next morning and the cold and cough were gone.'

After that he concentrated on sorting out TV-am's future. Following up negotiations he had started with BSkyB the year before, he merged parts of the company's sales and news teams with the satellite operation. He also prepared bids for the radio licence and, with Frost, the Channel 5 licence, which he eventually pulled out of. Only one subject was taboo: the loss of the breakfast licence. He declined to talk about it again. He only wanted to look forward, he told colleagues.

Others, likewise, got on with their lives. Mike Hollingsworth, Gyngell's old adversary who found himself frozen out of the Daybreak breakfast bid, took a job with the BBC producing a new daytime series featuring Ann Diamond, his wife. Tom Guttridge, participant in the ill-fated LIB bid against LWT, concentrated on building up the development deals Mentorn had won in the licensing round. Palace, Mentorn's partner in the bid, swiftly hit the rocks after the licence announcement, and had to be rescued by Polygram.

Phil Redmond, barely concealing his delight at David Plowright's departure from Granada, practised his ability to get up the broadcasting establishment's nose. In March he squared up to Michael Grade when the Channel 4 chief confessed he had considered axing Redmond's *Brookside* soap after a ratings slump. Grade told journalists Redmond had been diverted by the licensing round and explained how he had sorted it out. 'We keep Phil on a choke-chain and give it a little tug now and again.'

Redmond's reply was caustic: 'Perhaps I too should qualify for a £500,000 golden choke-chain to match his handcuffs. *Brookside* brings in the cash – he only spends it.'

Like Frost and Gyngell, he planned but then pulled out of a Channel 5 bid, citing the prohibitive cost of establishing the service. He would concentrate on his development deals with Yorkshire and the BBC, and lobbying for new regional TV services instead. John Harris, the East Midlands Electricity chairman who almost bid for Central, also stuck to what he knew best: racking up huge profits for the Nottingham-based utility. The same month he pulled out of the bidding he received a 102 per cent pay rise, pushing his salary to £230,969 – nearly as much as a top ITV boss.

At TVS Rudolph Agnew tried to salvage what he could from

the debacle. The sale in January of MTM's half-share of a Hollywood studio complex to Walt Disney for $27 million reduced the company's American debt. So did the sale of the Southampton studios to Meridian for £7.5 million. They did little to perk up the company's share price, however, which languished below 10p. As 1992 progressed, and the end of its broadcasting franchise loomed, more and more of its staff were laid off. The lucky ones, over 120, got jobs with Meridian. The rest were left to scout the situations vacant in the media pages of Britain's national newspapers. By July, a report in *Broadcast*, the trade paper, estimated that there were forty people chasing every vacancy in ITV.

Agnew said he was angry at the manner of it all – especially how the government handled it – but most of all he was angry at himself. 'I question myself time and again: should I have been able to guess that a bid of £41 million would have worked just as well as a bid of £59 million? With hindsight I think that I should.' Any other station might have pulled it off, he concluded. The problem was, as far as the regulators, the media and the rest of the industry were concerned, TVS's credit had run out. Tony Brook, TVS managing director, insisted that the company would survive, carrying on as a production independent in some form. Others were doubtful.

James Gatward, the company's flamboyant founder who now splits his time between houses in Britain and France, was merciless as he harried TVS down. He summed it up for the *Guardian* in June: 'When you stick your head over the parapet as I did you are liable to get knifed in the back. It hurts but that's life. When those who have knifed you totally fuck it up, that makes me angry.'

At TSW they proceeded to run the company down ready for the hand-over to Westcountry. By June the new station, planning a staff of 101, had taken on only four from TSW. Harry Turner, now retired, stayed at home, concentrating on his writing. In early summer, he bumped into George Russell again, the first time the two had met since TSW's legal action against the ITC. Both were attending an official dinner in London.

'Still smoking the cigars, I see, Harry,' Russell had joked.

'Why not?' grinned Turner.

Later, deep in conversation with Leslie Hill, the ITC chairman had felt a hand grasp his elbow. It was Turner, grinning again.

'Gissa franchise, guv?'

Richard Dunn, the Thames boss, brooded on it all longer than most. His friendship with George Russell was over. Russell had said nothing about Thames' contribution to the network in his 16 October press conference, and made no attempt to call him after the decision was announced. That hurt. But Dunn got on with finding a new future for Thames, preparing a bid for Channel 5, and cutting the company down in size.

In February he made his first public statement since that day in October. In a speech to a media conference, he predicted a healthy future for Thames as Britain's biggest production independent. Not only did it have a formidable array of television brands – *The Bill, Minder, Wish You Were Here* – to sell to the highest bidder, it also had 10,000 hours of programme rights, the most valuable commercial television library in Britain. And it had the financial resources to fund programme development, or move back into broadcasting, through a Channel 5 bid, an ITV takeover or its options on two transponders on the Astra satellite used by BSkyB. Thames would do more than survive; it would prosper.

He did not say whether it would hit the £140 million without-licence valuation that Thorn EMI had been promised.

He did, however, read excerpts from a letter he wrote to the *Financial Times* in June 1989. In it he rattled through the arguments against the Thatcher government's proposals for ITV: big money would outbid good quality; a £1.5 billion industry would be 'catastrophically destabilised' for at least two years before and two years after the auction; the auction outcome would be entirely unpredictable; conditions like programme 'quality' would be impossible to define in terms valid for a sale contract or acceptable in a judicial review; and the likelihood of overbidding would impact adversely on the investment needed for quality programmes.

By 1992 he felt vindicated. It was little consolation.

Appendix I

Afterword

What did it all achieve? By 1992 most in the television industry had concluded that the 1991 franchise round was a botch-up of herculean proportions, the last death-twitch of Thatcherism alleviated by some quick thinking on the part of the Independent Television Commission. The Commission's success could be measured in the results: it kept the majority of ITV companies in place, many of whom have a good track record of producing quality programming; and it prevented the Treasury from squeezing so much money out of the network that programming would suffer. Between them, David Mellor and George Russell had rescued British commercial television from the ravages of the free market.

Up to a point. Those who applauded Mellor and Russell also criticised Thatcher for pushing through legislation that failed to meet her own original objectives: that ITV should be prepared for the competitive environment ahead, that there should be a reduction in regulation and that a clear and objective licensing system should be introduced. Not for the want of trying, Thatcher might argue. The ITC's insistence on secrecy and the late introduction of old-style subjective judgements – the Beechers Brook of quality threshold – fudged some of that. They were not her initiatives. Unconvinced by the argument that the market would protect quality and worried about the consequences, her own politicians conspired to turn the original legislation on its head. It was all caught on the cusp of her slide from power. What emerged was worse than a muddle; it was probably an opportunity missed.

Of course, a lot did stem from the inconsistencies of Thatcher's own ideas. She advocated the free market, but at the same time wanted to restrict what could be shown. She wanted less regulation, but somehow spawned more regulatory bodies covering broadcasting than ever before. Characteristically, she did not listen when she was told that her aims could be achieved more efficiently and painlessly by other methods. Equally characteristically, the politicians around her – many of whom later disowned the legislation – made little attempt to deflect her more destructive energies. They talked about 'level playing fields', but failed to offer a strategy any more sophisticated than that applied to council services. None of them watched television, anyway. Then, as the Prime Minister's attention was deflected elsewhere, it all shifted again.

So the industry was left with an auction that was not an auction, and an 'exam paper', as George Russell liked to see it, that in the end probably favoured the incumbents. As David Plowright said when he saw the 100-page 'invitation to apply': 'They have revealed the bible of how to sit the exam and, as far as I can see, you need to be someone well-versed in the current system to answer the questions.' All the incumbents needed to do was hold their nerve, assess the opposition and choose the right tactics.

Which in many cases was a lot to ask. Could Thames have won? Yes, if it had wanted to make the cuts suggested to it by its advisers. Likewise TV-am. But who wants to spend years building up a business only to tear it apart because of an artificially created licence round? TVS and TSW too could claim they were only following the logical thrust of the legislation: bid high to buy a scarce resource. What they missed was that the political climate had changed. The playing field may have remained level but the game had subtly changed from baseball to cricket. They just had not read the signs correctly.

It could not have happened in any other industry. The peculiar mix of public service broadcasting and public company profits turned ITV into a Jekyll and Hyde outfit in the 1980s, a push-me-pull-you of conflicting values that produced £300,000-a-year executives embracing Mammon and the quality-before-ratings ethic as easy bedfellows. Thatcher pushed one way, the ITC eventually pulled back. It could only temporarily resolve the conflict in a typically British compromise – George Russell's victory for 'quality' (for which read 'common sense'), the shift back towards 'consensus' thinking after the radicalism of the Thatcher years. It is typically British because it attempted to retain the best of the past, while trying to win more time to stave off the future. For the free marketeers, it is yet another example of 'the regulators being captured by the regulated'. Yet it is difficult to see what else the ITC could have done.

In the end nearly all the television executives involved – even some that were not, like those paid to stay at Channel 4 – got a lot more money (golden handcuffs, win bonuses, share options). £3 million to lock in key staff at Central, £3 million to lock in key staff at Yorkshire, £3 million to lock in key staff at Granada, up to £43 million to lock in key staff at LWT. ITV started life with the live transmission of an inaugural banquet in 1955, and some executives appear to have been scoffing at the table ever since. But the 1991 licensing system encouraged it and anyway the rewards were spread around. Many of the politicians and advisers who drew up the original legislation got ennobled. So everyone is happy, except the losers and those on the ITV job scramble. It is hard not to conclude that the whole affair could have been better managed.

The fudging leaves a dangerous legacy. To prepare ITV for a more competitive environment, many now acknowledge that the regional map should have been torn up. Instead sixteen licences are left when four or five would have been a more sensible number, strong enough to withstand the extra competition at home and from abroad. The average ITV company simply does not have the size to compete internationally with modern media giants like Time Warner, Sony CBS and Bertelsmann, huge operations that threaten to swallow up everything in their paths. Now ITV is likely to waste four or five years looking inwards, sorting out the precarious instability left by the franchise round as low bidders and high bidders fight over network contributions. Only the polarisation of power will alleviate it. Takeovers or mergers are inevitable. In many cases, the 1990 Broadcasting Act will forbid it, but much of the Act is already redundant and will inevitably be rewritten. Such polarisation need not affect the regional services, which are protected by the terms of the individual licences. Some in the industry believe the process could even continue to its logical conclusion – until, by the next century, just one company is left. That would certainly make scheduling easier.

For the biggest problem ITV faces is still organising a competitive network out of a federation of companies. In the bad old days they did it by force: the big companies commissioned each other and forced the schedule on their smaller colleagues. This worked fine until the Government cried foul. The legislation's stipulation that the companies appoint an independent scheduler who will commission and schedule for the network, free of the special interests of individual companies, appears wishful thinking. It may become easier as more ITV companies forsake production and turn themselves into 'publisher-broadcasters', but it is still a hopelessly complex operation which may look increasingly anachronistic as the new competition finds its feet.

The better way? By the end of his tenure as Independent Broadcasting Authority chairman Lord Thomson was arguing vociferously for the abolition of any franchise or licence round. Just open ITV up for takeover; that would introduce the necessary competitive instincts and prevent a lot of talent getting tied up in a wasteful and morale-sapping process. At the same time Professor Alan Peacock, progenitor of the original competitive tender idea, was complaining that he had never been fully briefed about the possibilities offered by new technology: especially the advances of digital compression, which would allow a number of channels to be broadcast terrestrially on a wavelength where previously just one had been carried. That would break the 'cosy duopoly' of ITV and BBC, and give advertisers the competition in the ad market they had been lobbying for.

Neither men were listened to. The upshot was a licensing round that led to thousands being made redundant by the ITV companies, before there was enough competition – either from other broadcasters or a larger independent production sector – to offer alternative employment. Worse still, it may have left the ITC in a position where it feels it has to hold back new technology to protect ITV companies who have just bid millions to gain valuable licences.

And what of the programmes? Most acknowledge that the sheer variety of programmes made by ITV will inevitably diminish. More competitive scheduling will push current affairs out of prime-time and discourage risk-taking. There will be more popular, middlebrow drama, much of it derivative. By 1992 the success of *Inspector Morse* had already spawned endless different detective series on both ITV and BBC. Likewise any hit show, like any hit film, will pull a host of similar vehicles behind it. As in America, the big successes will run for longer. In the past, the political necessity of giving all the big ITV companies a turn at making the big shows often knocked some ratings winners off the schedule before the end of their natural life. The network cannot afford to do that any more. There will also be greater pressure on costs; in short, many series will run longer and look cheaper.

The American experience also suggests that the drive for ratings will discourage innovation. Some of British television's most cherished successes, such as *Monty Python*, have emerged from unpromising starts. Such fresh thinking may have to be confined to the BBC, if its public service brief is maintained. Some in the ITC believe that the regulators may be able to insist on a proper variety of programming on ITV even as the 1990s progress. However, as competition increases, ITV will inevitably want more, not less, freedom. Those programmes that do not attract the audiences that advertisers want will inevitably be marginalised.

All agree that the Government will have a chance to redeem itself when it settles the future of the BBC on the renewal of its charter in 1996. It appears inconceivable, so soon after the licensing round, that it will allow BBC TV to take advertising. One option is a strengthening of the corporation's public service commitments. So as ITV becomes more populist, the slack can be taken up by the BBC. But, as had been argued before, that leaves the corporation ever more vulnerable to political pressure. It also, of course, presupposes that the Government does have a strategy for broadcasting. Given the power of the medium – some are even now describing it as part of the 'social cement' that holds Britain together – it should have.

Appendix II

Extracts from an interview with Sir George Russell and David Glencross, June 1992

ANDREW DAVIDSON: When you arrived at the IBA in January 1989, did you have a clear idea of the changes Mrs Thatcher wanted to see in the broadcasting industry?

SIR GEORGE RUSSELL: No, nothing other than what I had seen in the White Paper.

AD: When, at a press conference later in 1989, you suggested you would resign if the franchise round became a simple highest-bid-wins auction, was that an off-the-cuff response to a question, or had you thought about it before?

GR: It was off-the-cuff to a question, but I had long been of that view. You see I was one of the those here all those years ago that helped draw up the remit for Channel 4, part of the group that appointed Dell, Isaacs and Attenborough to the station, and later I was deputy chairman of it; I also battled for ITN, and was chairman of that, so my commitment to quality broadcasting and my views on it were well known. It was not a rehearsed comment, if that's what you mean, but it was one I had thought very carefully about before I made it at that press conference . . . We have lots of things to do in life and to spend your time undermining something you believe in is not my idea of too smart a way of life.

AD: Was there ever any danger of the Government introducing a highest-bids-win auction?

GR: That's what the White Paper said. There was only a very fragmented kind of quality hurdle. Douglas Hurd announced that he had asked us to build a hurdle; I took that and raised it a little by calling it Becher's Brook, which was deliberate phraseology just to indicate it was not going to be the easiest fence to leap . . . Exceptional circumstances evolved around the same time as the quality threshold became a major fact. It was Hurd who first introduced the words . . . It was on the agenda here and elsewhere. I've very rarely gone through a period where a very large number of people, and I couldn't name them all, picked up a sort of wave and pushed it forward. One day you'd see the Campaign for Quality Television had come out on the subject and a minister was confirming something to them, then someone else would pick up a bit and carry it forward slightly.

AD: Did you have any idea as to what the arguments were that were going on within the Cabinet Committee? It is believed that the Treasury was one of the strongest advocates of a highest-bid-wins auction, against Home Office opposition.

GR: I think you are right, the Treasury was a strong advocate. I have no idea if they fought with the Home Office because I wasn't involved with any of that. Surprising as it may be, although we were linked by paper work, we were fairly distant as an organisation.

AD: Was there a distinct change in tone when David Mellor came in?

GR: No, Tim Renton had already done a tremendous amount of work as the Broadcasting Minister because he really went out and understood many bits that were not generally understood. One example was that he picked up the tremendous impact of separating Channel 4 from the revenues of the small ITV companies. I don't think anyone at that time anticipated the damaging impact of that loss, because the small companies were paying very little for the programmes but getting a reasonable sum in for selling the advertising. This is the kind of detailed work that he deserves a lot of the credit for. David Mellor was a very good advocate, and to see him go through the House the way he did on his own without support picking up the whole brief, day in, day out was a remarkable performance – and the final stand that he took on exceptional circumstances was one which, in my opinion, he took very much on his own at that time.

AD: By that, you mean it was not the sort of proposal that Mrs Thatcher or others on the Cabinet Committee welcomed?

GR: I think those that were there for the pure auction certainly didn't welcome it.

AD: And you think at the end there were still Cabinet ministers who wanted a pure auction?

GR: I think there were many long after the end who still believed in the utter simplicity of a straight auction. Because, whatever way you want to talk about it, what came out was a complex system that we managed.

AD: How good do you think the ITV lobby was over the broadcasting legislation?

GR: I think the IBA lobby was superb.

AD: And the ITV companies?

GR: I think they were in a terribly difficult defensive situation. What started off as the Peacock Committee inquiry into the funding of the BBC swung round to the ITV system and it is very difficult to argue your corner when you are as much on the defensive as they were placed by this.

AD: Was there a reluctance on the part of the Government to listen to the ITV bosses?

GR: No, as far as I know they had all sorts of access to various people.

AD: Was it politically sensible of the ITV companies to elect Richard Dunn as chairman of the ITVA just months after the controversy over *Death On The Rock*?

GR: It is the first time anyone had mentioned that to me . . . Do you think *Death On The Rock* had that big an impact?

AD: It seems to have caused a degree of antipathy.

GR: I think the whole thing started many years earlier. Not antipathy towards ITV, but antipathy towards the selection process for the 16 franchises. That started I think last time round. George Thomson made his statement which, let's say, confirmed prejudices, with the result that, although he put forward a very logical solution which fitted in many respects the Government's market pattern, it wasn't accepted. So we rolled inexorably forward towards the situation of the franchise round again.

AD: Do you think it was not accepted because *he* made it rather than someone else?

GR: No, he is very highly respected and his proposals were made long before *Death On The Rock*. They weren't trimmed down just because *Death On The Rock* flared up. Logically you say if you have sixteen companies that are doing a reasonably good job, you award them their franchise, decide what money you, the Government, want for the rights to do this, then allow them to be taken over. Everything is rolled over every so often, and the change comes from takeover, rather than a sudden-death franchise round. I have a great deal of sympathy to that because I have always believed that if a company is good enough it doesn't get taken over and if it's not very good it can be. This was a good way of affecting change if you wanted a few new players in the industry, both small and big.

DAVID GLENCROSS: It was interesting that the ITV companies in the 1980s certainly lobbied the Government about what they regarded as the unsatisfactory nature of the 1980 contract round, and it was partly their dissatisfaction which came out when Margaret Thatcher asked Lady Plowden 'What about Southern?', though I wasn't there. That led the Government to look very hard at the whole system and indeed treat any proposals, long before *Death On The Rock*, with a great deal of suspicion. But the companies to some degree were the architects of their own discomfiture this time round.

AD: Did you go into the licence process with the mechanism that you wanted?

GR: I know it is very hard to separate this, but I will try. The methodology of trying to see who is good, bad, indifferent; the financial analysis, no public meetings, no beauty parades, the formal requests for further information in writing and getting a considered reply back – this is a process I would stand by totally, because I happen to think that it is a very good way of assessing what people are offering, what the flannelling is, whether the money is there, whether you can balance out one against the other, and as you know under challenge it stood. All of that I can stand by. The question of the bid method itself is a very difficult one because what I did expect to happen when this was finally settled was that we would get people putting in topping up bids. I will explain what I mean by that: remember we had two parts of the tender, one of which was that we had to put a sort of rent down. We took a view that if we put a reasonable size rent down, people would then just take that and top up above it. What we didn't expect was that in many cases the rent would be the smaller part of it.

AD: Was that mechanism what you wanted or were you just trying to make the best of what the Government offered you?

GR: The Government did not lay down the mechanism or the methodology, we did, and we thought that we did many things that had not been done before, such as putting the whole invitation to apply out in draft form three months in advance, so that all those who didn't understand it, or thought we had made a cod of bits of it, would tell us and we would amend it.

AD: Was there a precedent for this? Were you looking at what was done in any other country?

GR: We worked it out as best we could, to try and not do the things that we felt, in terms of process, were weak last time round.

AD: What happened after the bids came in? Were you the only person to see inside the sealed envelopes?

GR: No, four of us – myself, the deputy chairman, David Glencross and Ken Blyth, ITC company secretary. We opened them all, signed all of them, and locked them away again in the secretary's safe. Only he and David had keys to it all through the process.

AD: So the teams that were looking at the applications did not know how much had been bid?

GR: The applications were looked at in phases: this is important. Firstly, the four people mentioned were not part of any of the working parties looking at the applications. We kept ourselves separate and worked individually. The quality teams, of which key members were part, had no idea of the money in the envelope, or of Section C – the business plan – until the quality work was concluded. After the quality decisions were taken then we all worked on Section C, though they still didn't know what was in the envelope. It was only in the last days that we actually presented them with the envelopes. And you must remember they are different to Section C.

AD: Did you have in your mind, or on paper, the likely bids for each station?

GR: Remember I told you that we saw the cash bids as a topping up concept. We told applicants for the five smallest areas that the first part of the tender was set at zero, tell us how much you will bid on top. We didn't expect too much to come in from those . . . Putting those aside, for the other nine areas, the first part of the tender was likely to be more than half the total. Otherwise it would not be topping up, it would be doubling.

AD: Do you believe your discussions were absolutely watertight throughout the summer?

GR: I must admit there some extraordinarily good guesses as to what was in the bids. Some were far enough away to indicate they were nothing more than guesses, to me anyway. I was satisfied there was nothing leaked.

DG: The thing is one remembers the guesses that were good and forgets the ones that were not good.

AD: How difficult was it to decide if an application failed at the quality threshold for programming?

GR: The initial thing was to assess what had been formally asked for in the Broadcasting Bill in terms of breadth and diversity.

DG: These are categories which are set out in the Bill. A successful application had to satisfy the Commission in these categories. So a sort of checklist is already there in the legislation.

GR: If you look at the staff assessment paper on TSW, you can see the methodology that we went through on each of the things that were written in the Bill. We talked each of these through. It is also wise for you to remember, because I kept telling people at the time, that it was genuinely 15 or 16 different races, the threshold for each and the size of Becher's Brook for each being different. We were expecting different things of each of them. For example, if you were to take the licence in the far north of Scotland, they had to show quite a lot of form as to how to cope with Gaelic broadcasting. So much more of their threshold was in that area, than let's say Westcountry's or TSW's, because they did not have to contribute on that. So it is how people approached some things that were special to each area. Again, had Border, which is a good company, faced a challenger that was demonstrating a very major network input, we might have been impressed, but it would not have convinced us that they knew what they were doing, because you can't run a Border and have the money to make lots of network programmes. Each one is assessed differently.

DG: The point about the quality threshold, laid down in section 16 of the Broadcasting Act, is that the Commission is not asked to say if X's programmes are better than Y's. What it was asked was: are X's proposals and Y's proposals, assessed separately, of a sufficient quality to pass through the quality threshold?

AD: The threshold being the existing service?

DG: Not entirely, because the threshold had to be based on what was in the legislation. The requirements are set out in some detail.

GR: It was basically a modification of the existing service.

DG: But clearly related to the existing service.

GR: I had said publicly that we would start by asking 'are you up to the standard of the incumbent?' but that had to be modified because bits of what the incumbents offer were no longer needed under the Broadcasting Act, or extra bits were – remember, all sorts of things were added. We used that as a yardstick.

AD: When it came to making the final decisions, did they have to be unanimous?

GR: It didn't have to be but it was.

DG: That didn't mean to say that there was not a great deal of discussion, there was of course, but there was never a vote as such.

AD: What were the most contentious areas that discussion focused on?

GR: The really contentious ones turned out to be those where we were worried the bidders could not sustain a decent quality financially, in particular – among the incumbents – TSW and TVS. Those were two of the big ones in terms of desperately heavy work, double and triple checking.

DG: To have two companies who we were quite content with on the programming quality threshold, that we have known for years, and end up having to say no, that was very tough.

AD: What about exceptional circumstances. I have been told that you had taken advice that you could not actually use exceptional circumstances, as it would be legally very difficult to defend. Is that true?

GR: No. In the cases where more than one got through the quality threshold, we examined whether there was an exceptional-circumstances case . . . We went through and assessed each one of them. At a later date we re-examined two of them, asking again were there exceptional circumstances and if there were, were they of the kind that we believed we could sustain against any challenge.

AD: Those two being Thames and TV-am?

GR: Yes.

AD: And what did your lawyers say? That however good their programme performance, you cannot give them exceptional circumstances?

GR: They did not say that. The first thing was, we were not allowed to say which was the best of the three bids in both areas. That was not the job we were allowed to do. We had to decide whether they passed on quality, and then we had to ask, and this was a phrase that David Mellor used, the one bit of guidance we had: 'are these people's proposals of exceptionally high quality and are they also of exceptionally higher quality than their rivals?' The decision was over on quality, we just had to look at this thing in total isolation, and the view that we took at that time was they were not exceptionally better, because you could not say to yourself: had they been exceptionally better for the last twenty-five years? . . . You had to look at what they were offering now. That was the first dilemma. One of them, for instance, had a 75 per cent market share, which is outstanding, but if that was the judgement call for exceptional circumstances, nobody could have bid with any hope of winning.

AD: Is it true that the discussion over Thames was the longest and hardest?

DG: On exceptional circumstances, yes, I think that is true. But at no stage were we advised by our lawyers not to invoke exceptional circumstances whether in favour of Thames or anybody else.

AD: When you decided not to award exceptional circumstances to Thames and TV-am, what were your feelings? Presumably you knew that refusing exceptional circumstances to a company the size of Thames, with its programming history, would raise more than an eyebrow?

GR: You have got to remember that in the case of certain of us, some of our best friends were at Thames. I had worked with Richard Dunn right through the whole broadcasting bill. I knew him and others quite well. Likewise I worked very closely with Bruce Gyngell.

DG: And TVS's Tony Brook used to be the IBA's director of finance. So you talk about raising eyebrows, but I think whatever decisions we had taken would have raised eyebrows somewhere.

GR: If you look at it carefully, the thing we were determined to stand on was to use the Bill to avoid money flowing out and ruining the ITV system. We would stand as best we could for whatever we thought quality meant, and at the end of the day that's the judgement call that was placed on us. It meant one of the toughest times any of us would ever go through, in this respect it was much tougher than the previous occasion.

AD: Why? Because you are more accountable now?

GR: I don't think it was the accountability. That didn't worry us. I suppose the last time it was more in the IBA's gift – gift is the wrong word, but you know what I mean – it was the IBA's right to take decisions that did not ruin the system.

DG: The big difference was that in 1980 the Authority was choosing what it thought was the best company to do the job in any particular area. This time that wasn't the task that was set, it was to see who passed the quality threshold as defined and then give it to the highest bidder, unless there were exceptional circumstances. So you had this combination of certainly very complex judgement calls, but judgement calls that didn't say, do you think X is better than Y, but simply have X and Y passed a particular standard, and then you had to decide whether to invoke exceptional circumstances, and all against an expectation that under normal circumstances the highest bidder would win because in a crude way that is what the Act said. But in detail that is what the Act didn't say . . .

GR: We had the job to make sure that anyone who won was good enough . . . But thereafter, even if we were perturbed by certain shapes emerging, we could not necessarily do anything about it.

AD: Did you get more applications than you expected?

GR: We were expecting about thirty-six.

AD: Who were the surprises?

DG: I think we got more applications in Wales and the West than we thought, and more in north of Scotland and Northern Ireland than we expected.

GR: There was also the triple bid, and certainly the surprise for me was that there was no challenge to Central. Scottish I was less surprised by.

AD: Anything else?

GR: Obviously the really big surprise, which I have stated publicly, was the size of the TSW bid.

AD: Do you understand with hindsight why some bids went higher than the ITC expected?

GR: Yes, I have worked for quite a few companies in my time, here and overseas, and no matter what I have been given and merchant banks have been given, I don't know anybody that has been trained to value their own company and place a single figure on it once in a lifetime. It is an incredible task to ask of a board. When you make a takeover bid you win or you lose, but it's not yourself that is going down. I think the sheer pressure of not losing drove the bids. It's as simple as that.

GR: One has many difficult things to do in life, this was just a very difficult commercial decision. It's easy in theory if you talk about a greenfield bid. If you get it wrong you have lost the initial money you have put up, but you have not lost thirty-five years of your life. It is not difficult if you are a challenger. But it is very difficult if you have got a major responsibility to shareholders and up to 2500 staff.

AD: When the announcements were made on 16 October, were you expecting the media scrum? At times you looked a bit shaken by it.

GR: I wasn't shaken by the media thing, I was surprised to see people climbing over each other to get in. I didn't expect that . . . What was obvious to me then was that it was the climax of nearly three years' work, because October was when I was first asked to take on the job. It was three years of inexorable growth in pressure, and it had to be finished to give the system a chance to get away three months early, to give everyone three months more time to get on air this year.

AD: A few weeks later you held meetings with certain losers. Afterwards they were angry you could not give them reasons for losing. Why hold the meetings if you could not tell them why they had lost?

GR: We did tell them. Just because you can't tell them all the things they want to know, doesn't mean you are not informing them of certain other things. All they got on 16 October was a simple faxed letter saying you failed quality or in some cases failed on finance. In the meetings later we were able to say, you failed quality under section 2a, but passed under c,d,e,f or whatever. We formally told them the bits they had failed under. That was not what they all wanted but that was what we were prepared to give, because that was what we felt was proper under the Act.

AD: And were you surprised when the judicial review went through?

GR: No, they usually do. We have got another one, a much smaller one, already on the way for months on satellite charges. We were not surprised it went through; we were sorry it went so far.

AD: In the Fleming lecture you gave earlier this year, you mentioned the restrictions on takeovers within and outside ITV might be a problem for the future. Do you see those restrictions changing? Is it something the ITC will be lobbying David Mellor on?

GR: I think we have got a lot of work to do. If you remember, there was a lot of speculation about how you could not buy a thing in Germany, but you could in France, you could do this and not that, but when you get down to it there was an awful lot of assertion and not much fact. Now we are through this period there is a lot of work we want to do ourselves to get our ideas clear. The moratorium on takeovers buys time; whether the Government accept they should extend it a little is something the new Minister will be working on, I am sure. All I was trying to do in my speech was to signal the sort of things that people should be watching out for, and see whether there are solutions. If you dig very carefully at the facts you can usually get the solutions. If you work on the assertions, you quite often solve the wrong problem.

AD: Do you think the ITV companies will be swamped by foreign takeovers?

GR: I don't think so.

AD: Were you surprised at how few foreign companies bid in the competitive tender last year?

DG: A bit, yes. There were some minority shareholders, but I suspect they found the whole process a bit too complicated.

AD: There was certainly a lot more paperwork this time round.

GR: But there were a lot less people coming in, and no public meetings. I never believed that was a good way to consult. We have regional officers who spent nearly two years meeting local leaders, local women's guilds, talking to them about the type of questions we were asking through this time. And when it came to the crunch we had viewer consultative committees in the areas getting information back. That was better than having what looked like a big triple football game with three sets of supporters trying to out-do each other. It may have been great fun but it was not very relevant.

AD: Did that mean the incumbents had an advantage on this occasion, in that they had more time to communicate with the community?

GR: The answer is the incumbents always had an advantage if they had done their job well . . . and to be quite honest, if they are well loved by everybody it is a bit rough if they get chucked out.

AD: Is it fair to say that the incumbents turned what looked like a very unpromising piece of legislation into something that was actually skewed a bit in their favour?

DG: Not at all. Four incumbents lost which is a far higher proportion than in any other previous round. The Commission did not set out to make four lose, but the results actually were more dramatic than they were in the previous rounds. In that sense I don't think they did skew it in their favour.

GR: The legislation gave everyone a better chance to produce something better for the next ten years. It was still a tough bit of legislation, that is for sure.

A Brief History of ITV

1951
Committee of enquiry under Lord Beveridge established 'to consider the constitution, control, finance and other aspects of the sound and television broadcasting services of the UK'. No recommendation for commercial TV.

1952
New Conservative Government, elected 1951, introduces White Paper which proposes 'some element of competition'.

1953
Second White Paper, policy for structure of new TV service: private enterprise under public control.

1954
Act provides for independent TV to be set up under Independent Television Association (ITA).

1955
ITV begins on 22 September 1955 with the live transmission of inaugural banquet from Guildhall in the City of London. First TV ad: 'tingling fresh' Gibbs SR toothpaste. Programmes provided by the first two contractors: Associated Rediffusion and Associated Broadcasting Company. Full ITV coverage not complete for seven years when the last of the regional companies, Wales West and North, go on air. Network companies – the four contractors for London, the Midlands and the North of England – have responsibility for providing network programming. ITN set up,

the first news organisation to present news pictorially with actuality coverage. Until then, BBC news had been read by unseen newsreaders over caption cards.

1957
ITV schools service starts.

1961
Imposition of Television Advertisement Duty.

1962
Report of the Pilkington Committee 'to consider the future of broadcasting services in the UK' recommends that the ITA should take over the direct planning of programmes and sales of airtime, leaving the ITV companies merely to produce programmes. This is rejected, although a later White Paper proposes strengthening the role of the ITA to supervise programme scheduling, ensuring high standards and control over advertising.

1963
New Act gets Royal Assent. ITA assumes responsibility for timing, amounts, distribution and standards of advertising. Provision made for Exchequer levy of 'additional payments' from the companies, based on net advertising revenue in excess of £1.5m, to replace Television Advertisement Duty. Act also covers limit on games show prizes, provision of news, and newspaper shareholdings in ITV companies. ITA re-awards the ITV contracts: despite 22 applications, no changes are made, existing contractors are reappointed from 1964 to 1967.

1964
Act to consolidate Television Act 1954 and Television Act 1963, BBC2 launched. TAD replaced by Exchequer Levy.

1965
Ban on TV ads for cigarettes and hand-rolling tobacco announced.

1967
First regular colour television service launched.

1968
New ITV contracts awarded for 1968–74. New franchise area for Yorkshire, dropping of split weekday/weekend franchises except

for London. New contractors: Thames (the result of an enforced merger between Rediffusion and ABC TV), LWT, Harlech (later HTV) and Yorkshire.

1969
Colour extended to BBC1 and ITV. Labour relations become strained.

1972
Act enabling the provision of local commercial radio reaches Statute Book. ITA renamed Independent Broadcasting Authority (IBA).

1973
IBA announces Teletext, utilising unused lines of 625 UHF. Act to consolidate Television Act 1964 and Sound Broadcasting Act 1972: IBA Act 1973.

1974
Ministry of Posts and Telecommunications wound up, and responsibility for broadcasting passed to the Home Office. IBA Act 1974 changes the basis for additional payments (the Exchequer Levy collected by the IBA for the Treasury) from one on ad revenue to one on profits derived from business of providing programmes. The Crawford Committee report recommends a separate service for Welsh language programmes for Wales. Annan Committee on future of broadcasting set up.

1977
Annan Committee reports: objectives are to preserve broadcasting as a public service accountable to the public, through Parliament; to devise a new structure to enable broadcasting to expand and evolve over the next 15 years, achieving full diversity of services; and keep broadcasters free from political pressure and control. Recommends setting up Local Broadcasting Authority to control local radio and Open Broadcasting Authority to run fourth TV channel. Rejected.

1978
White Paper on Annan recommendations not legislated before Labour loses 1979 election. Life of IBA extended to July 1981 in IBA Act 1978.

1979

Queen's Speech: Conservative Government announces fourth TV channel under IBA. Engineering work empowered in IBA Act 1979. Labour relations reach crisis with longest strike in broadcasting history. 11-week stoppage from 10 August to 19 October drains £100 million from the network in revenue.

1980

IBA announces details of new ITV contracts to run from 1982 to 1989, including the possibility of a breakfast TV franchise. By 9 May, 43 applications for 16 franchises. Contracts ended on 28 December. Southern and Westward not renewed. Associated required to restructure itself and base itself in the Midlands. IBA persuaded of viability of breakfast franchise by TV-am.

1981

Broadcasting Complaints Commission set up.

1982

Cabinet office report urges early start on Direct Broadcast by Satellite (DBS) services distributed by cable. Two DBS services allocated to BBC with objective of having service in operation by 1986. Joint company of BT, British Aerospace and Marconi formed to provide the services. Channel 4 launched on 2 November. SC4 launched in Wales on 1 November.

1983

BBC launches Breakfast Time on BBC1 on 17 January. TV-am launches on 1 February. Government White Paper on cable TV published.

1984

Sky Channel, the first satellite TV programme channel in the UK, starts on 16 January owned by Rupert Murdoch. Legislation for cable TV reaches statute book in July: Cable and Broadcasting Act 1984. BBC initiates Club of 21 consortium for DBS: it comprises the BBC, the ITV companies and Consolidated Satellite Broadcasting, Granada TV Rental, Pearson, Thorn EMI and Virgin.

1985

Club of 21 tells Government that it won't proceed because the requirement to buy costly British equipment makes it too much of a risk.

1986

Oracle teletext service launched. Finance Act 1986 changes Exchequer levy: introduction of 25% levy on overseas programme sales, balanced by reduction of the levy on the contractors' domestic profits. Peacock Report rejects idea of putting advertising on the BBC but suggests tender of ITV franchises. Yorkshire TV begins experimental all-night programming with music videos from Music Box. DBS contract awarded to British Satellite Broadcasting, a consortium of Granada, Anglia, Virgin, Amstrad and Pearson.

1987

Amendment to Broadcasting Act 1981 changes maximum period of contracts between IBA and ITV companies from 12 to 15 years. Broadcasting Act 1987: contracts now expire 31 December 1992, giving more time to Government for consideration of the franchise system. Election returns Conservative government with broadcasting reform promised in manifesto. It proposes new Broadcasting Bill to 'enable broadcasters to take full advantage of the opportunities presented by technical advances and to broaden the choice of viewing and listening', to create 'stronger and more effective arrangements' to reflect the public concern over the display of sex and violence on television, and to remove the exemption broadcasters had under the Obscene Publications Act 1959.

1988

House of Commons Select Committee recommends establishment of Commercial Television Authority to act as sole regulatory body for all commercial TV, including cable and satellite. Broadcasting White Paper published which proposes the replacement of the IBA with a different body operating with a 'lighter touch' and the award of ITV franchises by competitive tender.

1989

Broadcasters lobby Government to tone down radical aspects of White Paper. Quality safeguards finally introduced in prospective legislation to prevent franchises simply being sold to the highest bidder.

1990

Broadcasting Act includes competitive tender proposal but also stipulates quality threshold for bids and obligation to provide certain programming strands.

1991

Invitations to apply for ITV licences published by newly formed Independent Television Commission. On 16 May, 40 bids are received for 16 licences. After five months of deliberation new licences awarded. Incumbents Thames, TVS, TSW and TV-am lose. Carlton, Meridian, Westcountry and Sunrise are the new winners. TSW, told it had overbid by the ITC, applies for judicial review but is refused. It appeals.

1992

TSW's appeal is eventually heard by the Master of the Rolls, and two other judges. TSW loses verdict by 2–1. It takes case to House of Lords but loses again.

Independent Television Companies 1955–1993

On-air	Off-air	Company	Franchise
22.09.55	29.07.68	Associated Rediffusion	London weekday
24.09.55	28.07.68	Associated TV (ATV)	London weekend
17.02.56	31.12.81	Associated TV (ATV)	Midlands weekday
18.02.56	28.07.68	ABC TV	Midlands weekend
03.05.56	—	Granada TV	North England weekday
05.05.56	28.07.68	ABC TV	North England weekend
31.08.57	—	Scottish TV	Central Scotland
14.01.58	03.03.68	TWW	Wales/West England
30.08.58	31.12.81	Southern TV	South England
15.01.59	—	Tyne Tees TV	North-East England
27.10.59	—	Anglia TV	East England
31.10.59	—	Ulster TV	Northern Ireland
29.04.61	11.08.81	Westward TV	Southwest England
01.09.61	—	Border TV	The Borders
30.09.61	—	Grampian TV	North Scotland
01.09.62	—	Channel TV	Channel Islands
19.09.62	26.01.64	Wales (West and North)	West/North Wales
04.03.68	—	HTV	Wales/West England
30.07.68	31.12.92	Thames TV	London weekday
29.07.68	—	Yorkshire TV	Yorkshire
02.08.68	—	London Weekend TV	London weekend
12.08.81	31.12.92	TSW	South West England
01.01.82	31.12.92	TVS	South/S-East England
01.01.82	—	Central Independent TV	East/West Midlands
01.02.83	31.12.92	TV-am	Breakfast
01.01.93	—	Carlton TV	London weekday
01.01.93	—	GMTV (Sunrise)	Breakfast
01.01.93	—	Meridian TV	South/S-East England
01.01.93	—	Westcountry TV	South West England

The 1991 Bidders

(winners in bold)

Licence	Company	Major Backers	Bid	PQR[1]	QT[2]
Breakfast	**Sunrise**	(LWT, STV, Disney GMEN)	£34.61m	15%	Passed
	Daybreak	(Carlton, ITN, NBC, Telegraph, Taylor Woodrow)	£33.26m		Passed
	TV-am		£14.13m		Passed
Borders	**Border TV**		£52,000	0%	Passed
Channel Islands	**Channel TV**		£1,000	0%	Passed
	C13		£102,000		Failed
Central Scotland	**Scottish TV**		£2,000	2%	Passed
East	**Anglia TV**		£17.8m	7%	Passed
	Three East	(EMAP, CLT)	£14.08m		Passed
	CPV-TV	(Virgin, David Frost Charterhouse)	£10.13m		Failed
London weekday	**Carlton TV**	(Carlton, Telegraph, RCS)	£43.17m	11%	Passed
	Thames TV		£32.79m		Passed
	CPV-TV	(as above)	£45.32m		Failed
London weekend	**LWT**		£7.58m	11%	Passed
	LIB	(Mentorn, Palace, Polygram, Working Title)	£35.41m		Failed
Midlands	**Central TV**		£2,000	11%	Passed
Northern Ireland	**Ulster TV**		£1.03m	0%	Passed
	Lagan TV	(Andrews Holdings, Hastings Hotels, BJ Eastwood, Fraser Homes)	£2.71m		Failed
	TVNi	(Thomson Newspapers, 3i, WG Baird)	£3.1m		Failed
North East	**Tyne Tees TV**		£15.06m	2%	Passed
	North East TV	(Granada, Border, Newcastle Chronicle)	£5.01m		Passed

[1] Percentage of 'qualifying' revenue to be paid

[2] Quality threshold

The 1991 Bidders

(winners in bold)

Licence	Company	Major Backers	Bid	PQR	QT
North of Scotland	**Grampian TV**		£0.72m	0%	Passed
	North of Scotland TV		£2.71m		Failed
	C3 Caledonia		£1.13m		Failed
North West	**Granada TV**		£9m	11%	Passed
	North West TV	(Mersey TV, 3i, Yorkshire TV, Tyne Tees TV)	£35.3m		Failed
South and South East	**Meridian**	(MAI, Central TV, SelecTV)	£36.52m	11%	Passed
	Carlton TV	(as above)	£18.08m		Passed
	TVS		£59.76m		Failed
	CPV-TV	(as above)	£22.11m		Failed
South West	**Westcountry TV**	(Associated Newspapers, South West Water, Brittany Ferries)	£7.82m	0%	Passed
	TSW		£16.12m		Failed
	Telewest	(Malory Maltby)	£7.27m		Failed
Wales and the West	**HTV**		£20.53m	2%	Passed
	C3W	(Flextech, United Artists, RTE)	£17.76m		Passed
	Merlin	(Associated Newspapers, Chrysalis, Trillion)	£19.37m		Passed
	C3 Wales & West	(TSW)	£18.29m		Failed
Yorkshire	**Yorkshire TV**		£37.7m	7%	Passed
	White Rose TV	(Chrysalis, Joseph Woodhead, Barnsley Chronicle)	£17.4m		Passed
	Viking TV	(TVF, Barr & Wallace, Arnold Trust)	£30.12m		Failed

Index

300